ITALIAN JOURNEYS

BY

W. D. HOWELLS

ITALIAN JOURNEYS

BY

W. D. HOWELLS

WITH ILLUSTRATIONS
BY JOSEPH PENNELL

THE MARLBORO PRESS
MARLBORO, VERMONT
1988

First published in 1867.

The present reprint of ITALIAN JOURNEYS follows
the revised edition, augmented by the addition
of a final chapter on "Ducal Mantua," and with
illustrations by Joseph Pennell, published in 1901.

T M P

Manufactured in the United States of America

Library of Congress Catalog Card Number 87-62519

ISBN 0-910395-35-7

A CONFIDENCE

WHEN the publishers suggested the notion of revising this book, and taming its wild youthfulness here and there, making it a little more just, if not a little wiser, and possibly shedding upon the belated text some light from the events occurring since it was written well-nigh forty years ago, I promptly refused. I also promptly refused to write any sort of introduction for this new edition; and as I presently did revise the book, I am not now surprised to find myself addressing these prefatory lines to an imaginable reader.

They are mainly to tell him of my odd experience in going over my work, which at times moved me to doubt not only of the perfection of my taste, the accuracy of my knowledge, and the infallibility of my judgment, but the sincerity of my feelings and the veracity of my statements. From time to time it seemed to me that I was aware of posing, of straining, even, in some of my attitudes, and I had a sense of having put on more airs than I could handsomely carry, and of having at other times assumed an omniscience for which I can now find no reasonable grounds. There were moments when I thought I had indulged unseemly spites and resentments towards nationalities that had never injured me, and yet blacker moments when I fancied I had pretended to feel these, but when in fact I was at heart most amiably affected toward all alien peoples.

So exacting is one at sixty-four, that I fell upon these faults and pruned them away with a free hand; and though I cannot hope to have removed them all, I can now honestly commend the book as much worthier credence than it was before. As for bringing it up to-date, there I own that even my age has been powerless. My Italy was the Italy of the time when the Austrians seemed permanent in Lombardy and Venetia, and when the French garrison was apparently established indefinitely at Rome;

when Napoleon III. was emperor, and Pio Nono was pope, and the first Victor Emanuel was king, and Garibaldi was liberator, and Francis Joseph was kaiser. Of these the last alone remains to attest the past, and it seems to me that as far as my poor word can go, it ought to be left to corroborate the reality of his witness, with no hint of change in conditions which are already sufficiently incredible.

W. D. HOWELLS

August 28, 1901.

CONTENTS

LIST OF ILLUSTRATIONS

ITALIAN JOURNEYS

THE ROAD TO ROME

I. LEAVING VENICE

WE did not know, when we started from home in Venice, on the 8th of November, 1864, that we had taken the longest road to Rome. We thought that of all the proverbial paths to the Eternal City that leading to Padua, and thence through Ferrara and Bologna to Florence, and so down the seashore from Leghorn to Civita Vecchia, was the best, the briefest, and the cheapest. Who could have dreamed that this path, so wisely and carefully chosen, would lead us to Genoa, conduct us on shipboard, toss us four dizzy days and nights, and set us down, void, battered, and bewildered, in Naples? Luckily,

"The moving accident is not my trade,"

for there are events of this journey (now happily at an end) which, if I recounted them with unsparing sincerity, would forever deter the reader from taking any road to Rome.

Though, indeed, what is Rome, after all, when you come to it?

II. FROM PADUA TO FERRARA

AS far as Ferrara there was no sign of deviation from the
direct line in our road, and the company was well enough.
We had a Swiss family in the car with us to Padua, and they told
us how they were going home to their mountains from Russia,
where they had spent nineteen years of their lives. They were
mother and father and only daughter; and the last, without ever
having seen her ancestral country, was so Swiss in her yet childish
beauty, that she filled the morning twilight with vague images of
glacial height, blue lake, snug chalet, and whatever else of
picturesque there is in paint and print about Switzerland. Of
course, as the light grew brighter these images melted away, and
left only a little frost upon the window-pane.

The mother was restively anxious at nearing her country, and
told us everything of its loveliness and happiness. Nineteen years
of absence had not robbed it of the poorest charm, and I hope that
seeing it again took nothing from it. We said how glad we should

be if we were as near America as she was to Switzerland. "America!" she screamed; "you come from America! Dear God, the world is wide—the world is wide!" The thought was so paralyzing that it silenced the fat little lady for a moment, and gave her husband time to express his sympathy with us in our war, which he understood perfectly well. He trusted that the revolution to perpetuate slavery must fail, and he hoped that the war would soon end, for it made cotton very dear.

Europe is material: I doubt if, after Victor Hugo and Garibaldi, there were many upon that continent whose enthusiasm for American unity (which is European freedom) was not somewhat chilled by the expensiveness of cotton. The fabrics were all doubled in price, and every man in Europe paid tribute in hard money to the devotion with which we prosecuted the war, and, incidentally, interrupted the cultivation of cotton.

We shook hands with our friends, and dismounted at Padua, where we were to take the diligence for the Po. In the diligence their loss was more than made good by the company of the only honest man in Italy. Of course this honest man had been a great sufferer from his own countrymen, and I wish that all English and American tourists, who think themselves the sole victims of publican rapacity and deceit in Italy, could have heard our honest man's talk. The truth is, these ingenious people prey upon their own kind with an avidity quite as keen as that with which they devour strangers; and I am half persuaded that a ready-witted foreigner fares better among them than a traveler of their own nation. Italians will always pretend, on any occasion, that you have been plundered much worse than they; but the reverse often happens. They give little in fees; but their landlord, their porter, their driver, and their boatman pillage them with the same impunity that they rob an Inglese. As for this honest man in the diligence, he had suffered such enormities at the hands of the Paduans, from which we had just escaped, and at the hands of the Ferrarese, into which we were rushing (at the rate of five miles scant an hour), that I was almost minded to stop between the nests of those brigands and pass the rest of my days at Rovigo, where the honest man lived. His talk was amusingly instructive, and went to illustrate the strong municipal spirit which still dominates all Italy, and which is more inimical to an effectual unity among Italians than Pope or Kaiser has ever been. Our honest man of Rovigo was a *foreigner* at Padua, twenty-five miles north, and a foreigner at Ferrara, twenty-five miles south; and throughout Italy the native of one city is an alien in another, and is as lawful prey as a Russian or an American with people who consider every stranger as sent them by the bounty of Providence to be eaten alive. Heaven knows what our honest man had paid at his hotel in Padua, but in Ferrara the other week he had been made to give five francs apiece for two small roast chickens, besides a fee to the waiter; and he pathetically warned us to beware how we dealt with Italians. Indeed, I never met a man so thoroughly persuaded of the rascality of his nation and of his own exceptional virtue. He took snuff with his whole person; and he volunteered, at sight of a flock of geese, a recipe which I give the reader: stuff a goose with sausage; let it hang in the weather during the winter; and in the spring cut it up and stew it, and you have an excellent and delicate soup.

But after all, our friend's talk, though constant, became dispiriting, and we were willing when he left us. His integrity had, indeed, been so oppressive that I was glad to be swindled in the charge for our dinner at the Iron Crown, in Rovigo, and rode more cheerfully on to Ferrara.

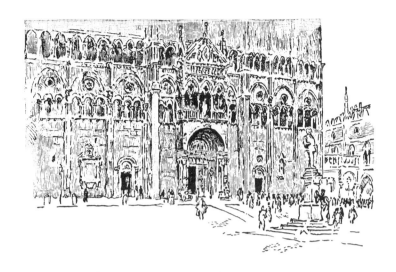

III. THE PICTURESQUE, THE IMPROBABLE, AND THE
PATHETIC IN FERRARA

I

IT was one of the fatalities of travel, rather than any real interest in the poet, which led me to visit the prison of Tasso on the night of our arrival, which was mild and moonlit. The *portier* at the Stella d'Oro suggested the sentimental homage to sorrows which it is sometimes difficult to respect, and I went and paid this homage in the coal-cellar in which was never imprisoned the poet whose works I had not read.

The famous hospital of St. Anna, where Tasso was confined for seven years, is still an asylum for the infirm and sick, but is no longer used as a mad-house. It stands on one of the long, silent Ferrarese streets, not far from the Ducal Castle, and it is said that from the window of his cell the unhappy poet could behold Leonora in her tower. It may be so; certainly those who can believe in the genuineness of the cell will have no trouble in believing that the vision of Tasso could pierce through several brick walls and a Doric portico, and at last comprehend the lady in her casement in the castle. We entered a modern gateway and passed into a hall of the elder edifice, where a slim young soldier sat reading a romance of Dumas. This was the keeper of Tasso's prison; and knowing me, by the instinct which teaches an Italian custodian to distinguish his prey, for a seeker after the True and Beautiful, he relinquished his romance, lighted a waxen taper, unbolted a heavy door with a dramatic clang, and preceded me to the cell of Tasso. We descended a little stairway, and found ourselves in a sufficiently spacious court, which was still ampler in the poet's time, and was then a garden planted with trees and flowers. On a low doorway to the right was inscribed the legend "PRIGIONE DI TASSO," and passing through this doorway into a kind of reception-cell, we entered the poet's dungeon. It is an oblong room, with a low wagon-roof ceiling, under which it is barely possible to stand upright. A single narrow window admits the light, and the stone casing of this window has a hollow in a certain place, which might well have been worn there by the friction of the hand that for seven years passed the prisoner his food through the small opening. The young custodian pointed to this memento of suffering, without effusion, and he drew my attention to other remarkable things in the cell, without troubling himself to palliate their improbability in the least. They were his stock in trade; you paid your money, and took your choice of believing in them or not. On the other hand, my *portier,* an ex-*valet de place,* pumped a softly murmuring stream of enthusiasm, and expressed the freshest delight in the inspection of each object of interest.

One still faintly discerns among the vast number of names with which the walls of the ante-cell are be-written, that of Lamartine. The name of Byron, which was once deeply graven in the stucco, had been scooped away by the Grand Duke of Tuscany (so the custodian said), and there is only part of a capital B now visible. But the cell itself is still fragrant of associations with the noble bard, who, according to the story related to Valery, caused himself to be locked up in it, and there, with his head fallen upon his breast, and frequently smiting his brow, spent two hours in pacing the floor with great strides. It is a touching picture; but its pathos becomes somewhat embarrassing when you enter the cell, and see the impossibility of taking more than three generous paces without turning. When Byron issued forth, after this exercise, he said (still according to Valery) to the custodian: "I thank thee, good man! The thoughts of Tasso are now all in my mind and heart." "A short time after his departure from Ferrara," adds the Frenchman, maliciously, "he composed his 'Lament of Tasso,' a mediocre result from such an inspiration." No doubt all this is colored, for the same author adds another tint to heighten the absurdity of the spectacle: he declares that Byron spent part of his time in the cell in writing upon the ceiling Lamartine's verses on Tasso, which he misspelled. The present visitor has no means of judging of the truth concerning this, for the lines of the poet have been so smoked by the candles of the successive pilgrims in their efforts to get light on them, that they are now utterly illegible. But if it is uncertain what were Byron's emotions on visiting the prison of Tasso, there is no doubt about Lady Morgan's: she "experienced a suffocating emotion; her heart failed her on entering that cell; and she satisfied a melancholy curiosity at the cost of a most painful sensation."

I find this amusing fact stated in a translation of her ladyship's own language, in a clever guide-book called "Il Servitore di Piazza," which I bought at Ferrara, and from which, I confess, I have learnt all I know to confirm me in my doubt of Tasso's prison. The Count Avventi, who writes this book, prefaces it by saying that he is a *valet de place* who knows how to read and write, and he employs these unusual gifts with singular candor and clearness. No one, he says, before the nineteenth centrury, ever dreamed of calling the cellar in question Tasso's prison, and it was never before that time made the shrine of sentimental pilgrimage, though it has since been visited by every traveler who has passed through Ferrara. It was used during the poet's time to hold charcoal and lime; and not long ago died an old servant of the hospital, who remembered its use for that purpose. It is damp, close, and dark, and Count Avventi thinks it hardly possible that a delicate courtier could have lived seven years in a place unwholesome enough to kill a stout laborer in two months; while it seems to him not probable that Tasso should have received there the visits of princes and other distinguished persons whom Duke Alfonso allowed to see him, or that a prisoner who was often permitted to ride about the city in a carriage should have been thrust back into such a cavern on his return to the hospital. "After this," says our *valet de place* who knows how to read and write, "visit the prison of Tasso, certain that *in the hospital of St. Anna* that great man was confined for many years;" and, with this chilly warning, leaves his reader to his emotions.

I am afraid that if as frank caution were uttered in regard to other memorable places, the objects of interest in Italy would dwindle sadly in number, and the *valets de place*, whether they know how to read and write or not, would be starved to death. Even the learning of Italy is poetic; and an Italian would rather enjoy a fiction than know a fact—in which preference I am not ready to pronounce him unwise. But this characteristic of his embroiders the stranger's progress throughout the whole land with fanciful improbabilities; so that if one use his eyes half as much as his wonder, he must see how much better it would have been to visit, in fancy, scenes that have an interest so largely imaginary. The utmost he can make out of the most famous place is, that it is possibly what it is said to be, and is more probably as near that as anything local enterprise could furnish. He visits the very cell in which Tasso was confined, and has the satisfaction of knowing that it was the charcoal-cellar of the hospital in which the poet dwelt. And the *genius loci*—where is that? Away in the American woods, very likely, whispering some dreamy, credulous youth,—telling him charming fables of its *locus*, and proposing to itself to abandon him as soon as he sets foot upon its native ground. You see, though I cared little about Tasso, and nothing about his prison, I was heavily disappointed in not being able to believe in it, and felt somehow that I had been awakened from a cherished dream.

II

But I have no right to cast the unbroken shadow of my skepticism upon the reader, and so I tell him a story about Ferrara which I actually believe. He must know that in Ferrara the streets are marvelously long and straight. On the corners formed by the crossing of two of the longest and straightest of these streets stand four palaces, in only one of which we have a present interest. This palace my guide took me to see, after our visit to Tasso's prison, and, standing in its shadow, he related to me the occurrence which has given it a sad celebrity. It was, in the time of the gifted toxicologist, the residence of Lucrezia Borgia, who used to make poisonous little suppers there, and ask the best families of Italy to partake of them. It happened on one occasion that Lucrezia Borgia was thrust out of a ball-room at Venice as a disreputable character, and treated with peculiar indignity. She determined to make the Venetians repent their unwonted accession of virtue, and she therefore allowed the occurrence to be forgotten till the proper moment of her revenge arrived, when she gave a supper, and invited to her board eighteen young and handsome Venetian nobles. Upon the preparation of this repast she bestowed all the resources of her exquisite knowledge; and the result was the Venetians were so felicitously poisoned that they had just time to listen to a speech from the charming and ingenious lady of the house before expiring. In this address she reminded her guests of the occurrence in the Venetian ball-room, and perhaps exulted a little tediously in her present vengeance. She was surprised and pained when one of the guests interrupted her, and, justifying the treatment she had received at Venice, declared himself her natural son. The lady instantly recognized him, and in the sudden revulsion of maternal feeling, begged him to take an antidote. This he not only refused to do, but continued his dying reproaches, till his mother, losing her self-command, drew her poniard and plunged it into his heart.

The blood of her son fell upon the table-cloth, and this being hung out of the window to dry, the wall received a stain, which neither the sun nor rain of centuries sufficed to efface, and which was only removed with the masonry, when it became necessary to restore the wall under that window, a few months before the time of my visit to Ferrara. Accordingly, the blood-stain has now disappeared; but the conscientious artist who painted the new wall has faithfully restored the tragic spot, by bestowing upon the stucco a bloody dash of Venetian red.

III

It would be pleasant and merciful, I think, if old towns, after having served a certain number of centuries for the use and pride of men, could be released to a gentle, unmolested decay. I, for my part, would like to have the ducal cities of North Italy, such as Mantua, Modena, Parma, and Ferrara, locked up quietly within their walls, and left to crumble and totter and fall, without any harder presence to vex them in their decrepitude than that of some gray custodian, who should come to the gate with clanking keys, and admit the wandering stranger, if he gave signs of a reverent sympathy, to look for a little while upon the reserved and dignified desolation. It is a shame to tempt these sad old cities into unnatural activity, when they long ago made their peace with the world, and would fain be mixing their weary brick and mortar with the earth's unbuilded dust; and it is hard for the emotional traveler to restrain his sense of outrage at finding them inhabited, and their rest broken by sounds of toil, traffic, and idleness; at seeing places that would gladly have done with history still doomed to be parts of political systems, to read the newspapers, and to expose railway guides and caricatures of the Pope and Napoleon in their shop windows.

Of course, Ferrara was not incorporated into a living nation against her will, and I therefore marveled the more that she had become a portion of the present kingdom of Italy. The poor little State had its day long before ours; it had been a republic, and then subject to lords; and then, its lords becoming dukes, it had led a life of gayety and glory till its fall, and given the world such names and memories as had fairly won it the right to rest forever from making history. Its individual existence ended with that of Alfonso II., in 1597, when the Pope declared it reverted to the Holy See; and I always fancied that it must have received with a spectral, yet courtly kind of surprise, those rights of man which bloody handed France distributed to the Italian cities in 1796; that it must have experienced a ghostly bewilderment in its rapid transformation, thereafter, under Napoleon, into part of the Cispadan Republic, the Cisalpine Republic, the Italian Republic, and the Kingdom of Italy, and that it must have sunk back again under the rule of the Popes with gratitude and relief at last—as phantoms are reputed to be glad when released from haunting the world where they once dwelt. I speak of all this, not so much from actual knowledge of facts as from personal feeling; for it seems to me that if I were a city of the past, and must be inhabited at all, I should choose just such priestly domination, assured that though it consumed my substance, yet it would be well for my fame and final repose. I should like to feel that my old churches were safe from demolition; that my old convents and monasteries should always shelter the pious indolence of friars and nuns. It would be pleasant to have studious monks exploring quaint corners of my unphilosophized annals, and gentle, snuff-taking abbés writing up episodes in the history of my noble families, and dedicating them to the present heirs of past renown; while the thinker and the reviewer should never penetrate my archives. Being myself done with war, I should be glad to have my people exempt, as they are under the Pope, from military service; and I should hope that if the Legates taxed them, the taxes paid would be as so many masses said to get my soul out of the purgatory of perished capitals. Finally, I should trust that in the sanctified keeping of the Legates my mortal part would rest as sweetly as bones laid in hallowed

earth brought from Jerusalem; and that under their serene protection I should be forever secure from being in any way exhumed
and utilized by the ruthless hand of Progress.

However, as I said, this is a mere personal preference, and other
old cities might feel differently. Indeed, though disposed to
condole with Ferrara upon the fact of her having become part of
modern Italy, I could not deny, on better acquaintance with her,
that she was still almost entirely of the past. She has certainly
missed that ideal perfection of non-existence under the Popes
which I have just depicted, but she is practically almost as
profoundly at rest under the King of Italy. One may walk long
through the longitude and rectitude of many of her streets without
the encounter of a single face: the place, as a whole, is by no
means as lively as Pompeii, where there are always strangers;
perhaps the only cities in the world worthy to compete with
Ferrara in point of agreeable solitude are Mantua and Herculaneum. It is the newer part of the town—the modern quarter built
before Boston was settled or Ohio was known—which is the
loneliest; and whatever motion and cheerfulness are still felt in
Ferrara linger fondly about the ancient holds of life—about the
street before the castle of the Dukes, and in the elder and narrower
streets branching away from the piazza of the Duomo, where, on
market days, there is a kind of dreamy tumult. In the Ghetto we
were almost crowded, and people wanted to sell us things, with
an enterprise that contrasted strangely with shopkeeping apathy
elsewhere. Indeed, surprise at the presence of strangers spending
two days in Ferrera when they could have got away sooner, was
the only emotion which the whole population agreed in
expressing with any degree of energy, but into this they seemed
to throw their whole vitality. The Italians are everywhere an
artless race, so far as concerns the gratification of their curiosity,
from which no consideration of decency deters them. Here in
Ferrara they turned about and followed us with their eyes, came
to windows to see us, lay in wait for us at street corners, and
openly and audibly debated whether we were English or German.

This interest rose almost into a frenzy of craving to know more of us all, when on the third day the whole city assembled before our hotel, and witnessed, with a sort of desperate cry, the departure of the heavy-laden omnibus which bore us and our luggage from their midst.

IV

I DOUBT if, after St. Mark's in Venice, the Duomo at Parma, and the Four Fabrics at Pisa, there is a church more worthy to be seen for its quaint, rich architecture, than the cathedral at Ferrara. It is of that beloved Gothic of which eye or soul cannot weary, and we continually wandered back to it from other more properly interesting objects. It is horribly restored indoors, and its baroque splendors soon drove us forth, after we had looked at the Last Judgment by Bastianino. The style of this painting is muscular and Michelangelic, and the artist's notion of putting his friends in heaven and his foes in hell is by no means novel; but he has achieved fame for his picture by the original thought of making it his revenge for a disappointment in love. The unhappy lady who refused his love is represented in the depths, in the attitude of supplicating the pity and interest of another maiden in Paradise who accepted Bastianino, and who consequently has no mercy on her that snubbed him. But I counted of far more value than this fresco the sincere old sculptures on the façade of the cathedral, in which the same subject is treated, beginning from the moment the archangel's trump has sounded. The people getting suddenly out of their graves at the summons are all admirable; but the best among them is the excellent man with one leg over the side of his coffin, and tugging with both hands to pull himself up, while the coffin-lid tumbles off behind. One sees instantly that the conscience of this early riser is clean, for he makes no miserable attempt to turn over for a nap of a few thousand years more, with the pretense that it was not the trump of doom, but some other and unimportant noise he had heard. The final reward of the blessed is expressed by the repose of one small figure in the lap of a colossal effigy, which I understand to mean rest in Abraham's bosom; but the artist has bestowed far more interest and feeling upon the fate of the damned, who are all boiling in rows of immense pots. It is doubtful (considering the droll aspect of heavenly bliss as figured in the one small saint and the large patriarch) whether the artist intended the condition of his sinners to be so horribly comic as it is; but the effect is just as great, for all that, and the slowest conscience might well take alarm from the spectacle of fate so grotesque and ludicrous; for, wittingly or unwittingly, the artist here punishes, as Dante knew best how to do, the folly of sinners as well as their wickedness. Boiling is bad enough; but to be boiled in an undeniable dinner-pot, like a leg of mutton, is to suffer shame as well as agony.

We turned from these horrors, and walked down by the side of the Duomo toward the Ghetto, which is not so foul as one could wish a Ghetto to be. The Jews were admitted to Ferrara in 1275, and, throughout the government of the Dukes, were free to live where they chose in the city; but the Pope's Legate assigned them afterward a separate quarter, which was closed with gates. Large numbers of Spanish Jews fled hither during the persecutions, and there are four synagogues for the four languages,—Spanish, German, French, and Italian. Avventi mentions, among other interesting facts concerning the Ferrarese Jews, that one of the Rabbins, Isaaco degli Abranelli, a man of excellent learning in the Scriptures, claimed to be descended from David. His children still abide in Ferrara; and it may have been one of his kingly line that kept the tempting antiquarian's shop on the corner from which you turn up toward the Library. I should think such a man would find a sort of melancholy solace in such a place: filled with broken and fragmentary glories of every kind, it would serve him for that chamber of desolation, set apart in the houses of the Oriental Hebrews as a place to bewail themselves in; and, indeed, this idea may go far to explain the universal Israelitish fondness for dealing in relics and ruins.

V

THE Ghetto was in itself indifferent to us; it was merely our way
to the Library, whither the great memory of Ariosto invited us to
see his famous relics treasured there.

We found that the dead *literati* of Ferrara had the place wholly
to themselves; not a living soul disputed the solitude of the halls
with the custodians, and the bust of Ariosto looked down from his
monument upon rows of empty tables, idle chairs, and dusty
inkstands.

The poet, who was painted by Titian, has a tomb of abandoned
ugliness, and sleeps under three epitaphs; while cherubs frescoed
on the wall behind affect to disclose the mausoleum, by lifting a
frescoed curtain, but deceive no one who cares to consider how
impossible it would be for them to perform this service and caper
so ignobly as they do at the same time. In fact, this tomb of
Ariosto shocks with its hideousness and levity. It stood formerly in
the Church of San Benedetto, where it was erected shortly after
the poet's death, and it was brought to the Library by the French,
when they turned the church into a barrack for their troops. The
poet's dust, therefore, rests here, where the worm, working
silently through the vellum volumes on the shelves, feeds upon the
immortality of many other poets. In the adjoining hall are the
famed and precious manuscripts of Ariosto and of Tasso. A
special application must be made to the librarian, in order to see
the fragment of the "Furioso" in Ariosto's hand, and the manuscript copy of the "Gerusalemma," with the corrections by Tasso.
There are some pages of Ariosto's Satires, framed and glazed for
the satisfaction of the less curious; as well as a letter of Tasso's,
written from the Hospital of St. Anna, which the poet sends to a
friend, with twelve shirts, and in which he begs that his friend will
have the shirts mended, and cautions him "not to let them be
mixed with others." But when the slow custodian had at last
unlocked that more costly fragment of the "Furioso," and placed
it in my hands, the other manuscripts had no value for me. It

seems to me that the one privilege which travel has reserved to itself is that of making each traveler, in presence of its treasures, forget whatever other travelers have said or written about them. I had read so much of Ariosto's industry, and of the proof of it in this manuscript, that I doubted if I should at last marvel at it. But the wonder remains with the relic, and I paid it my homage devoutly and humbly, and was disconcerted afterward to read again in my Valery how sensibly all others had felt the preciousness of that famous page, which, filled with half a score of previous failures, contains in a little open space near the margin, the poet's final triumph in a clearly written stanza. Scarcely less touching and interesting than Ariosto's painful work on these yellow leaves is the grand and simple tribute which another Italian poet was allowed to inscribe on one of them: "Vittorio Alfieri beheld and venerated;" and I think, counting over the many memorable things I saw on the road to Rome and the way home again, this manuscript was the noblest thing and best worthy to be remembered.

When at last I turned from it, however, I saw that the custodian had another relic of Messer Lodovico, which he was not ashamed to match with the manuscript in my interest. This was the bone of one of the poet's fingers, which the pious care of Ferrara had picked up from his dust (when it was removed from the church to the Library), and neatly bottled and labeled. They keep a great deal of sanctity in bottles with the bones of saints in Italy; but I found very little savor of poesy hanging about this literary relic.

As if the melancholy fragment of mortality had marshaled us the way, we went from the Library to the house of Ariosto, which stands at the end of a long, long street, not far from the railway station. There was not a Christian soul, not a boy, not a cat nor a dog to be seen in all that long street, at high noon, as we looked down its narrowing perspective, and if the poet and his friends had ever a mind for a posthumous meeting in his little reddish brick house, there is nothing to prevent their assembly, in broad daylight, from any part of the neighborhood. There was no presence, however, more spiritual than a comely country girl to respond to our summons at the door, and nothing but a tub of corn-meal disputed our passage inside. When I found the house inhabited by living people, I began to be sorry that it was not as empty as the Library and the street. Indeed, it is much better with Petrarch's house at Arquà, where the grandeur of the past is never molested by the small household joys and troubles of the present. That house is vacant, and no eyes less tender and fond than the poet's visitors may look down from its windows over the slope of vines and olives which it crowns; and it seemed hard, here in Ferrara, where the houses are so many and the people are so few, that Ariosto's house could not be left to him. *Parva sed apta mihi*, he has contentedly written upon the front; but I doubt if he finds it large enough for another family, though his modern housekeeper reserves him certain rooms for visitors. To gain these, you go up to the second story—there are but two floors—and cross to the rear of the building, where Ariosto's chamber opens out on an anteroom, and looks down upon a pinched and faded bit of garden.[1] In this chamber they say the poet died. It is oblong, and not large. I should think the windows and roof were of the poet's time, and that everything else had been restored; I am quite sure the chairs and inkstand were kindly-meant inventions; for the poet's burly great armchair and graceful inkstand are both preserved in the Library. But the house is otherwise decent and probable; and I do not question but it was in the hall where we encountered the meal-tub that the poet kept a copy of his "Furioso," subject to the corrections and advice of his visitors.

The ancestral house of the Ariosti has been within a few years

---

[1] In this garden the poet spent much of his time—chiefly in plucking up and transplanting the unlucky shrubbery, which was never suffered to grow three months in the same place,—such was the poet's rage for revision. It was probably never a very large or splendid garden, for the reason that Ariosto gave when reproached that he who knew so well how to describe magnificent palaces should have built such a poor little house: "It was easier to make verses than houses, and the fine palaces in his poem cost him no money."

restored out of all memory and semblance of itself; and my wish to see the place in which the poet was born and spent his childhood resulted, after infinite search, in finding a building faced newly with stucco and newly French-windowed.

Our *portier* said it was the work of the late English vice-consul, who had bought the house. When I complained of the sacrilege, he said: "Yes, it is true. But then, you know, the Ariosti were not one of the noble families of Ferrara."

VI

THE castle of the Dukes of Ferrara, about which cluster so many sad and splendid memories, stands in the heart of the city. I think that the moonlight which, on the night of our arrival, showed me its massive walls rising from the shadowy moat that surrounds them, and its four great towers, heavily buttressed, and expanding at the top into bulging cornices of cavernous brickwork, could have fallen on nothing else in all Italy so picturesque, and so full of the proper dread charm of feudal times, as this pile of gloomy and majestic strength. The daylight took nothing of this charm from it; for the castle stands isolated in the midst of the city, as its founder meant that it should,[1] and modern civilization has not crossed the castle moat to undignify its exterior with any visible touch of the present. To be sure, when you enter it, the magnificent

---

[1] The castle of Ferrara was begun in 1385 by Nicolò d'Este to defend himself against the repetition of the scenes of tumult, in which his princely rights were invaded. One of his tax-gatherers, Tommaso da Tortona, had, a short time before, made himself so obnoxious to the people by his insolence and severity, that they rose against him and demanded his life. He took refuge in the palace of his master, which was immediately assailed. The prince's own life was threatened, and he was forced to surrender the fugitive to the people, who tore Tortona limb from limb, and then, after parading the city with the mutilated remains, quietly returned to their allegiance. Nicolò, therefore, caused this castle to be built, which he strengthened with massive walls and towers commanding the whole city, and rendered inaccessible by surrounding it with a deep and wide canal from the river Reno.

life is gone out of the old edifice; it is no stately halberdier who stands on guard at the gate of the drawbridge, but a stumpy Italian soldier in baggy trousers. The castle is full of public offices, and one sees in its courts and on its stairways, not brilliant men-at-arms, nor gay squires and pages, but whistling messengers going from one office to another with docketed papers, and slipshod serving-men carrying the clerks their coffee in very dirty little pots. Dreary-looking suitors, slowly grinding through the mills of law, or passing the routine of the offices, are the guests encountered in the corridors; and all that bright-colored throng of the old days, ladies and lords, is passed from the scene. The melodrama is over, and now we have a play of real life, founded on fact and inculcating a moral.

Of course the custodians were slow to admit any change of this kind. If you could have believed them,—and the poor people told as many lies as they could to make you,—you would believe that nothing had ever happened of a commonplace nature in this castle. The taking-off of Hugo and Parisina they think the great merit of the castle; and one of them, seeing us, made haste to light his taper and conduct us down to the dungeons where those unhappy lovers were imprisoned. It is the misfortune of memorable dungeons to acquire, when put upon show, just the reverse of those properties which should raise horror and distress in the mind of the beholder. It was impossible to deny that the cells of Parisina and of Hugo were both singularly warm, dry, and comfortable; and we, who had never been imprisoned in them, found it hard to command, for our sensation, the terror and agony of the miserable ones who suffered there. We, happy and secure in these dungeons, could not think of the guilty pair bowing themselves to the headsman's stroke in the gloomy chamber under the Hall of Aurora; nor of the Marquis, in his night-long walk, breaking at last into frantic remorse and tears to know that his will had been accomplished. Nay, there upon its very scene, the whole tragedy faded from us; and, seeing our wonder so cold, the custodian tried to kindle it by saying that in the time of the event these cells were much dreadfuller than now, which was no doubt true. The floors of the dungeons are both below the level of the moat, and the narrow windows, or rather crevices to admit the light, were cut in the prodigiously thick wall just above the water, and were defended with four successive iron gratings. The dungeons are some distance apart: that of Hugo was separated from the outer wall of the castle by a narrow passageway, while Parisina's window opened directly upon the moat.

When we ascended again to the court of the castle, the custodian, abetted by his wife, would have interested us in two memorable wells there, between which, he said, Hugo was beheaded; and unabashed by the small success of this fable, he pointed out two windows in converging angles overhead, from one of which the Marquis, looking into the other, discovered the guilt of the lovers. The windows are now walled up, but are neatly represented to the credulous eye by a fresco of lattices.

Valery mentions another claim upon the interest of the tourist which this castle may make, in the fact that it once sheltered John Calvin, who was protected by the Marchioness Renée, wife of Hercules II.; and my "Servitore di Piazza" (the one who knows how to read and write) gives the following account of the matter, in speaking of the domestic chapel which Renée had built in the castle: "This lady was learned in belles-lettres and in the schismatic doctrines which at that time were insinuating themselves throughout France and Germany, and with which Calvin, Luther, and other proselytes agitated the people and threatened war to the Catholic religion. Nationally fond of innovation, and averse to the court of Rome on account of the dissensions between her father and Pope Julius II., Renée began to receive the teachings of Calvin, with whom she maintained a correspondence. Indeed, Calvin himself, under the name of Huppeville, visited her in Ferrara, in 1536, and ended by corrupting her mind and seducing her into his own errors, which produced discord between her and her religious husband, and resulted in his placing her in temporary seclusion, in order to attempt her conversion. Hence, the chapel is faced with marble, paneled in relief, and studied to avoid giving place to saints or images, which were disapproved by the almost Anabaptist doctrines of Calvin, then fatally imbibed by the princess."

We would willingly, as Protestants, have visited this wicked chapel; but we were prevented from seeing it, as well as the famous frescoes of Dosso Dossi in the Hall of Aurora, by the fact that the prefect was giving a little dinner (*pranzetto*) in that part of the castle. We were not so greatly disappointed in reality as we made believe; but our *servitore di piazza* (the unlettered one) was almost moved to *lesa maestà* with vexation. He had been full of scorching patriotism the whole morning; but now electing the unhappy and apologetic custodian representative of Piedmontese tyranny, he bitterly assailed the government of the king. In the times of His Holiness the Legates had made it their pleasure and duty to show the whole castle to strangers. But now strangers must be sent away without seeing its chief beauties, because, forsooth, the prefect was giving a little dinner. Presence of the Devil!

VII

IN our visits to the different churches in Ferrara we noticed devotion in classes of people who are devout nowhere else in Italy. Not only came solid-looking business men to say their prayers, but gay young dandies, who knelt and repeated their orisons and then rose and went seriously out. In Venice they would have posted themselves against a pillar, sucked the heads of their sticks, and made eyes at the young ladies kneeling near them. This degree of religion was all the more remarkable in Ferrara, because that city had been so many years under the Pope.

Valery speaks of the delightful society which he met in the gray old town; and it is said that Ferrara has an unusual share of culture in her wealthy class, which is large. With such memories of learning and literary splendor as belong to her, it would be strange if she did not in some form keep alive the sacred flame. But, though there may be refinement and erudition in Ferrara, she has given no great name to modern Italian literature. Her men of letters seem to be of that race of grubs singularly abundant in Italy,—men who dig out of archives and libraries some topic of special and momentary interest and print it, unstudied and unphilosophized. Their books are material, not literature, and it is marvelous how many of them are published. A writer on any given subject can heap together from them a mass of fact and anecdote invaluable in its way; but it is a mass without life or light, and must be vivified by him who uses it before it can serve the world, which does not care for its dead local value.

What numbers of people used to write verses in Ferrara! By operation of the principle which causes things concerning whatever subject you happen to be interested in to turn up in every direction, I found a volume of these dead-and-gone immortals at a book-stall, one day, in Venice. It is a curiously uncomfortable volume of the year 1703, printed all in italics. I suppose there are two hundred odd rhymers selected from in that book,—and how droll the most of them are, with their unmistakable traces of descent from Ariosto, Tasso, and Guarini! What acres of enameled meadow there are in those pages! Brooks enough to turn all the mills in the world go purling through them. I should say some thousands of nymphs are constantly engaged in weaving garlands there, and the swains keep such a piping on those familiar notes,— *Amore, dolore, crudele,* and *miele.* Poor little poets! they knew no other tunes!

VIII

I THINK some of the pleasantest people in Italy are the army gentlemen. There is the race's gentleness in their ways, in spite of their ferocious trade, and met in travel they are ready to render any little kindness.

The other year at Reggio (which is not far from Modena) we stopped to dine at a restaurant where the whole garrison had its coat off and was playing billiards, with the exception of one or two officers, who were dining. These rose and bowed as we entered their room, and when the waiter pretended that such and such dishes were out (in Italy the waiter, for some mysterious reason, always pretends that the best dishes are out), they bullied him for the honor of Italy, and made him bring them to us. We were in deep despair at finding no French bread, and the waiter swore with pathos that there was none; but as soon as his back was turned, a tightly laced little captain rose and began to forage for the bread. He opened every drawer and cupboard in the room, and finding none, invaded another room, captured several loaves from the plates laid there, and brought them back in triumph, presenting them to us amid the applause of his comrades. The dismay of the waiter, on his return, was ineffable.

Three officers, who dined with us at the *table d'hôte* of the Stella d'Oro in Ferrara (and excellent dinners were those we ate there), were visibly anxious to address us, and began not uncivilly, but still in order that we should hear, to speculate on our nationality among themselves. It appeared that we were Germans; for one of these officers, who had formerly been in the Austrian service at Vienna, recognized the word *bitter* in our remarks on the *beccafichi*. As I did not care to put these fine fellows to the trouble of hating us for others' faults, I made bold to say that we were not Germans, and to add that *bitter* was also an English word. Ah! yes, to be sure, one of them admitted; when he was with the Sardinian army in the Crimea, he had frequently heard the word used by the English soldiers. He nodded confirmation of what he said to his comrades, and then was good enough to display what English he knew. It was barely sufficient to impress his comrades; but it led the way to a good deal of talk in Italian.

"I suppose you gentlemen are all Piedmontese?" I said.

"Not at all," said our Crimean. "I am from Como; this gentleman, il signor Conte (il signor Conte bowed), is of Piacenza; and our friend across the table is Genoese. The army is doing a great deal to unify Italy. We are all Italians now, and you see we speak Italian, and not our dialects, together."

My cheap remark that it was a fine thing to see them all united under one flag, after so many ages of mutual hate and bloodshed, turned the talk upon the origin of the Italian flag; and that led our Crimean to ask what was the origin of the English colors.

"I scarcely know," I said. "We are Americans."

Our friends at once grew more cordial. "Oh, Americani!" They had great pleasure of it. Did we think Signor Leencolen would be reëlected?

I supposed that he had been elected that day, I said.

Ah! this was the election day, then. *Cospetto!*

At this the Genoese frowned superior intelligence, and the Crimean, gazing admiringly upon him, said he had been nine months at Nuova York, and that he had a brother living there. The poor Crimean boastfully added that he himself had a cousin in America, and that the Americans generally spoke Spanish. The count from Piacenza wore an air of pathetic discomfiture, and tried to invent a transatlantic relative, as I think, but failed.

I am persuaded that none of these warriors really had kinsmen in America, but that they all pretended to have them, out of politeness to us, and that they believed each other. It was very kind of them, and we were so grateful that we put no embarrassing questions. Indeed, the conversation presently took another course, and grew to include the whole table.

There was an extremely pretty Italian present with her newly wedded husband, who turned out to be a retired officer. He fraternized at once with our soldiers, and when we left the table they all rose and made military obeisances. Having asked leave to light their cigars, they were smoking—the sweet young bride blowing a fairy cloud from her rosy lips with the rest. "Why," I once heard an Italian lady ask, "should men pretend to deny us the privilege of smoking? It is so pleasant and innocent." It is but just to the Italians to say that they do not always deny it; and there is, without doubt, a certain grace and charm in a pretty *fumatrice*. I suppose it is a habit not so pleasing in an ugly or middle-aged woman.

IV. THROUGH BOLOGNA TO GENOA

I

W E had intended to stay only one day at Ferrara, but just at that time the storms predicted on the Adriatic and Mediterranean coasts, by Mathieu de la Drôme, had been raging all over Italy, and the railway communications were broken in every direction. The magnificent work through and under the Apennines, between Bologna and Florence, had been washed away by the mountain torrents in a dozen places, and the roads over the plains of the Romagna had been sapped by the flood, and rendered useless, where not actually laid under water.

On the day of our intended departure we left the hotel, with other travelers, gayly incredulous of the landlord's fear that no train would start for Bologna. At the station we found a crowd of people waiting and hoping, but there was a sickly cast of doubt in some faces, and the labeled employés of the railway wore looks of ominous importance. Of course the crowd did not lose its temper. It sought information of the officials running to and fro with telegrams, in a spirit of national sweetness, and consoled itself with saying, as Italy has said under all circumstances of difficulty for centuries: *Ci vuol pazienza!* At last a blank silence fell upon it, as the *Capo-Stazione* advanced toward a well-dressed man in the crowd, and spoke to him quietly. The well-dressed man lifted his forefinger and waved it back and forth before his face:—

The Well-dressed Man.—Dunque, non si parte più? (No departures, then?)

The Capo-Stazione (waving *his* forefinger in like manner.)—Non si parte più. (Like a mournful echo.)

We knew quite as well from this pantomime of negation as from the dialogue our sad fate, and submitted to it. Some adventurous spirit demanded whether any trains would go on the morrow. The Capo-Stazione, with an air of one who would not presume to fathom the designs of Providence, responded: "Who knows? To-day, certainly not. To-morrow, perhaps. But"—and vanished.

This break in the line was only a few miles in extent, and trains could have approached both to and from Bologna, so that a little enterprise on the part of the company could have passed travelers from one side to the other with very small trouble or delay. But the railway company was as much daunted by the inundation as a peasant going to market, and for two months after the accident no trains carried passengers from one city to the other. No doubt, however, the line was under process of very solid repair meanwhile.

For the present the only means of getting to Bologna was by carriage on the old highway, and accordingly we took passage thither in the omnibus of the Stella d'Oro.

There was little of interest in the country over which we rode. It is perfectly flat, and I suppose the reader knows what quantities of hemp and flax are raised there. The land seems poorer than in Lombardy, and the farmhouses and peasants' cottages are small and mean, though the peasants themselves, when we met them, looked well fed, and were certainly well clad. The landscape lay soaking in a dreary drizzle the whole way, and the town of Cento, when we reached it, seemed miserably conscious of being too wet and dirty to go indoors, and was loitering about in the rain. Our arrival gave the poor little place a sensation, for I think such a thing as an omnibus had not been seen there since the railway of Bologna and Ferrara was built. We went into the principal caffè to lunch,—a caffè much too large for Cento, with immense red-leather cushioned sofas, and a cold, forlorn air of half-starved gentility, a clean, high-roofed caffè and a breezy,—and thither the youthful nobility and gentry of the place followed us, and ordered a cup of coffee, that they might sit down and give us the pleasure of their distinguished company. They put on their very finest manners, and took their most captivating attitudes for the ladies' sake; and the gentlemen of our party fancied that it was for them these young men began to discuss the Roman question. How loud they were, and how earnest! And how often they consulted the ancient newspapers of the caffè!

The great painter Guercino was born at Cento, and they have a noble and beautiful statue of him in the piazza, which the town caused to be erected from contributions by all the citizens. Formerly his house was kept for a show to the public; it was full of the pictures of the painter and many mementos of him; but recently the paintings have been taken to the gallery, and the house is now closed. The gallery is, consequently, one of the richest second-rate galleries in Italy, and one may spend much longer time in it than we gave, with great profit. There are some most interesting heads of Christ, painted, as Guercino always painted the Saviour, with a great degree of humanity in the face. It is an excellent countenance, and full of sweet dignity, but quite different from the conventional face of Christ.

II

AT night we were again in Bologna, of which we had not seen the gloomy arcades for two years. It must be a dreary town at all times: in a rain it is horrible; and I think the whole race of arcaded cities, Treviso, Padua, and Bologna, are dull, blind, and comfortless. The effect of the buildings vaulted above the sidewalks is that of a continuous cellar-way; your view of the street is constantly interrupted by the heavy brick pillars that support the arches; and the arcades are not even picturesque. Liking to leave Bologna as quickly as possible, and learning that there was no hope of crossing the Apennines to Florence, we made haste to take the first train for Genoa, meaning to proceed thence directly to Naples by steamer.

In our car there were none but Italians, and the exchange of "La Perseveranza" of Milan for "Il Popolo" of Turin with one of them quickly opened the way for conversation and acquaintance. My new-made friend turned out to be a Milanese. He was a physician, and had served as a surgeon in the late war of Italian independence; but was now placed in a hospital in Milan. There was a gentle little blonde with him, and at Piacenza, where we stopped for lunch, "You see," said he, indicating the lady, "we are newly married,"—which was, indeed, plain enough to any one who looked at their joyous faces, and observed how great disposition that little blonde had to nestle on the young man's broad shoulder. "I have a week's leave from my place," he went on, "and this is our wedding journey. We were to have gone to Florence, but it seems we are fated not to see that famous city."

He spoke of it as immensely far off, and greatly amused us Americans, who had outgrown distances.

"So we are going to Genoa instead, for two or three days."
"Oh, have you ever been at Genoa?" the bride broke in. "What magnificent palaces! And then the bay, and the villas in the environs! There is the Villa Pallavicini, with beautiful gardens, where an artificial shower breaks out from the bushes, and sprinkles the people who pass. Such fun!" and she continued to describe vividly a city of which she had only heard from her husband; and it was easy to see that she walked in paradise wherever he led her.

They say that Italian husbands and wives do not long remain fond of each other, but it was impossible in the presence of these happy people not to believe in the eternity of their love. Their bliss infected everybody in the car, and in spite of the weariness of our journey, and the vexation of the misadventures which had succeeded one another unsparingly ever since we left home, we found ourselves far on the way to Genoa before we thought to grumble at the distance. There was with us, besides the bridal party, a lady traveling from Bologna to Turin, who had learned English in London, and spoke it much better than most Londoners. It is surprising how thoroughly Italians master a language so alien to their own as ours, and how frequently you find them acquainted with English.

As we drew near Genoa, the moon came out on purpose to show us the superb city, and we strove eagerly for a first glimpse of the proud capital where Columbus was born. To tell the truth, the glimpse was but slight and false, for railways always enter cities by some mean level, from which any picturesque view is impossible.

Near the station in Genoa, however, is the weak and ugly monument which the municipality has lately raised to Columbus. The moon made the best of this, which stands in a wide open space, and contrived, with an Italian skill in the arrangement of light, to produce an effect of undeniable splendor. On the morrow, we found out by the careless candor of the daylight what a uselessly big head Columbus had, and how the sculptor had not very happily thought proper to represent him with his sea-legs on.

V. UP AND DOWN GENOA

A FORMER consul at ——, whom I know, has told me a good many stories about the pieces of popular mind which he received at different times from the traveling public, in reproof of his difficulty of discovery; and I think it must be one of the most jealously guarded rights of American citizens in foreign lands to declare the national representative hard to find, if there is no other complaint to lodge against him. It seems to be, in peculiar degree, a quality of consulship at ——, to be found remote and inaccessible. My friend says that even at New York, before setting out for his post, when inquiring into the history of his predecessors, he heard that they were one and all hard to find; and he relates that on the steamer, going over, there was a low fellow who set the table in a roar by a vulgar anecdote to this effect:—

"There was once a consul at ——, who indicated his office hours by the legend on his door, 'In from ten to one.' An old ship-captain, who kept coming for about a week without finding the consul, at last furiously wrote, in the terms of a wager, under this legend, 'Ten to one you're out!' "

My friend also states that one day a vistor of his remarked: "I am rather surprised to find you in. As a general rule, I never do find consuls in." Habitually, his fellow-countrymen entertained him with accounts of their misadventures in reaching him. It was useless to represent to them that his house was in the most convenient locality in ——, where, indeed, no stranger can walk twenty rods from his hotel without losing himself; that their guide was an ass, or their courier a rogue. They listened to him politely, but they never pardoned him in the least; and neither will I forgive the consul at Genoa. I had no earthly consular business with him, but a private favor to ask. It was Sunday, and I could not reasonably expect to find him at his office, or anybody to tell me where he lived; but I have seldom had so keen a sense of personal wrong and national neglect as in my search for that consul's house.

In Italy there is no species of fact with which any human being you meet will not pretend to have perfect acquaintance, and, of course, the driver whose fiacre we took professed himself a complete guide to the consul's whereabouts, and took us successively to the residences of the consuls of all the South American republics. It occurred to me that it might be well to inquire of these officials where their colleague was to be found; but it is true that not one consul of them was at home! Their doors were opened by vacant old women, in whom a vague intelligence feebly guttered, like the wick of an expiring candle, and who, after feigning to throw floods of light on the object of my search, successively flickered out, and left me in total darkness.

Till that day I never knew what lofty flights stairs were capable of. As out-of-doors, in Genoa, it is either all up or down hill, so indoors it is either all up or down stairs. Ascending and descending, in one palace after another, those infinite marble steps, it became a question, not solved to this hour, whether it was worse to ascend or descend,—each ordeal in its turn seemed so much more terrible than the other.

At last I resolved to come to an understanding with the driver, and I spent what little breath I had left—it was dry and hot as the simoom—in blowing up that infamous man. "You are a great driver," I said, "not to know your own city. What are you good for if you can't take a foreigner to his consul's?" "Signore," answered the driver patiently, "you would have to get a book in two volumes by heart, in order to be able to find everybody in Genoa. This city is a labyrinth."

Truly, it had so proved, and I could scarcely believe in my good luck when I actually found my friend, and set out with him on a ramble through its toils.

A very great number of the streets in Genoa are footways merely, and these are as narrow, as dark, as full of jutting chimney-places, balconies, and opened window-shutters, and as picturesque as the little alleys in Venice. They wander at will around the bases of the gloomy old stone palaces, and seem to have a vagabond fondness for creeping down to the port, and losing themselves there in a certain cavernous arcade which curves round the water with the flection of the shore, and makes itself a twilight at noonday. Under it are clangorous shops of ironsmiths, and sizzling shops of marine cooks, and, looking down its dim perspective, one beholds chiefly sea-legs coming and going, more or less affected by strong waters; and as the faces to which these sea-legs belong draw near, one discerns sailors from all parts of the world,—tawny men from Sicily and Norway, as diverse in their tawniness as olive and train-oil; sharp faces from Nantucket and from the Piræus, likewise mightily different in their sharpness; blond Germans and blond Englishmen; and now and then a colored brother also in the seafaring line, with sea-legs, also, more or less affected by strong waters like the rest.

What curious people are these seafarers! They coast the whole world, and know nothing of it, being more ignorant and helpless than children on shore. I spoke with the Yankee mate of a ship one day at Venice and asked him how he liked the city.

Well, he had not been ashore yet.

He was told he had better go ashore; that the Piazza San Marco was worth seeing.

Well, he knew it; he had seen pictures of it; but he guessed he wouldn't go ashore.

Why not, now he was here?

Well, he laid out to go ashore the next time he came to Venice.

He lay three weeks at Venice with his ship, after a voyage of two months, and he sailed away without ever setting his foot on that enchanted ground.

I should have liked to stop some of those seafarers and ask them what they thought of Genoa.

It must have been in the little streets—impassable for horses— that the people sat and talked, as Heine fabled, in their doorways, and touched knees with the people sitting and talking on the thresholds of the opposite side. But we saw no gossipers there on our Sunday in Genoa; and I think the domestic race of Heine's day no longer lives in Genoa; for everybody we saw on the streets was gayly dressed in the idea of the last fashions, and was to be met chiefly in the public promenades. The fashions were French; but here still lingers the lovely phantom of the old national costume of Genoa, and snow-white veils fluttered from many a dark head, and caressed many an olive cheek. It is the kindest and charitablest of attirements, this white veil, and, while decking beauty to the most perilous effect, befriends and modifies age and ugliness.

The pleasure with which I look at the splendor of an Italian crowd in winter is always touched with melancholy. I know that, at the time of its noonday promenade, it has nothing but a cup of coffee in its stomach; that it has emerged from a house as cold and dim as a cellar; and that it will presently go home to dine on rice and boiled beef. I know that chilblains secretly gnaw the hands inside of its kid gloves, and I see in the rawness of its faces the anguish of winter-long suffering from cold. But I also look at many in this crowd with the eye of the economist, and wonder how people practicing even so great self-denial can contrive to make so much display on their little means,—how those clerks of public offices, who have rarely an income of five hundred dollars a year, can dress with such peerless gorgeousness. I suppose the national instinct teaches them ways and means unknown to us. The passion for dress is universal: the men are as fond of it as the women; and, happily, clothes are comparatively cheap. We walked with the brilliant Genoese crowd upon the hill where the public promenade overlooks a landscape of city and country, houses and gardens, vines and olives, which it makes the heart ache to behold, it is so faultlessly beautiful. Behind us the fountain was—

"Shaking its loosened silver in the sun;"

the birds were singing; and there were innumerable pretty girls going by, about whom one might have made romances if one had not known better. Our friend pointed out to us the "pink jail" in which Dickens lived while at Genoa; and showed us on the brow of a distant upland the villa, called Il Paradiso, which Byron had occupied. I dare say this Genoese joke is already in print: that the Devil reëntered Paradise when Byron took this villa. Though in loveliest Italy, one is half persuaded that the Devil had never left Paradise.

After lingering a little longer on that delicious height, we turned and went down for a stroll through the city.

My note-book says that Genoa is the most magnificent city I ever saw, and I hold by my note-book, though I hardly know how to prove it. Venice is, and remains, the most beautiful city in the world; but her ancient rival impresses you with greater splendor. I suppose that the exclusively Renaissance architecture, which Ruskin declares the architecture of pride, lends itself powerfully to this effect in Genoa. It is here in its best mood, and there is little grotesque rococo to be seen, though the palaces are, as usual, loaded with ornament. The Via Nuova is the chief thoroughfare of the city, and the crowd pours through this avenue between long lines of palaces. Height on height rise the stately, sculptured façades, colonnaded, statued, pierced by mighty doorways and lofty windows; and the palaces seem to gain a kind of aristocratic *hauteur* from the fact that there are for the most part no sidewalks, and that the carriages, rolling insolently through the crowd, threaten constantly to grind the pedestrian up against their carven marbles, and immolate him to their stony pride. There is something gracious and gentle in the grandeur of Venice, and much that the heart loves to cling to; but in Genoa no sense of kindliness is touched by the magnificence of the city.

It was an unspeakable relief, after such a street, to come, on a sudden, upon the Duomo, one of the few Gothic buildings in Genoa, and rest our jaded eyes on that architecture which Heaven seems truly to have put into the thoughts of man together with the Christian faith. O beloved beauty of aspiring arches, of slender and clustered columns, of flowering capitals and window-traceries, of many-carven breadths and heights, wherein all Nature breathes and blossoms again! There is neither Greek perfection, nor winning Byzantine languor, nor insolent Renaissance opulence, which may compare with this loveliness of yours! Alas that the interior of this Gothic temple of Genoa should abound in the abomination of rococo restoration! They say that the dust of St. John the Baptist lies there within a costly shrine; and I wonder that it can sleep in peace amid all that heathenish show of bad taste. But the poor saints have to suffer a great deal in Italy.

Outside, in the piazza before the church, there was an idle, cruel crowd, amusing itself with the efforts of a blind old man to find the entrance. He had a number of books which he desperately laid down while he ran his helpless hands over the clustered columns, and which he then desperately caught up again, in fear of losing them. At other times he paused, and wildly clasped his hands upon his eyes, or wildly threw up his arms; and then began to run to and fro again uneasily, while the crowd laughed and jeered. He seemed the type of a blind soul that gropes darkly about through life, to find the doorway of some divine truth or beauty,—touched by the heavenly harmonies from within, and miserably failing, amid the scornful cries and bitter glee of those who have no will but to mock aspiration.

The girl turning somersaults in another place had far more popular sympathy than the blind man at the temple door, but she was hardly a more cheerful spectacle. For all her festive spangles and fairy-like brevity of skirts, she had quite a work-a-day look upon her honest, blood-red face, as if this were business though it looked like sport, and her part of the diversion were as practical as that of the famous captain of the waiters, who gave the act of peeling a sack of potatoes a playful effect by standing on his head. The poor damsel was going over and over, to the sound of most dismal drumming and braying in front of the immense old palace of the Genoese Doges,—a classic building, stilted on a rustic base, and quite worthy of Palladio, if anybody thinks that is praise.

There was little left of our day when we had dined; but having seen the outside of Genoa, and not hoping to see the inside, we found even this little heavy on her hands, and were glad as the hour drew near when we were to take the steamer for Naples.

It had been one of the noisiest days spent during several years in clamorous Italy, whose voiceful uproar strikes to the summits of her guardian Alps, and greets the coming stranger, and whose loud Addio would stun him at parting, if he had not meanwhile become habituated to the operatic pitch of her every-day tones. In Genoa, the hotels, taking counsel of the vagabond streets, stand about the cavernous arcade already mentioned, and all the noise of the shipping reaches their guests. We rose early that Sunday morning to the sound of a fleet unloading cargoes of wrought-iron, and of the hard swearing of all nations of seafaring men. The whole day long the tumult followed us, and seemed to culminate at last in the screams of a parrot, who thought it fine to cry *"Piove! piove! piove!"*—"It rains! it rains! it rains!"—and had, no doubt, a secret interest in some umbrella-shop. This unprincipled bird dwelt somewhere in the neighborhood of the street where you see the awful tablet in the wall devoting to infamy the citizens of the old republic that were false to their country. The sight of that pitiless stone recalls with a thrill the picturesque, unhappy past, with all the wandering, half-benighted efforts of the people to rend their liberty from now a foreign and now a native lord. At best, they only knew how to avenge their wrongs; but now, let us hope, they have learnt, with all Italy, to prevent them. The will was never wanting of old to the Ligurian race, and in this time they have done their full share to establish Italian freedom.

I do not know why it should have been so surprising to hear the boatman who rowed us to the steamer's anchorage speak English; but, after his harsh Genoese profanity in getting his boat into open water, it was the last thing we expected from him. It had somehow the effect of a furious beast addressing you in your native tongue, and telling you it was "Wary poordy wedder;" and it made us cling to his good-nature with the trembling solicitude of Little Red-Riding-Hood when she begins to have the first faint suspicions of her grandmother. However, our boatman was no wild beast, but took our six cents of *buonamano* with the servility of a Christian man, when he had put our luggage in the cabin of the steamer. I wonder how he should have known us for Americans? He did so know us, and said he had been at New York in better days, when he voyaged upon higher seas than those he now navigated.

On board, we watched with compassion an old gentleman in the cabin making a hearty meal of sardines and fruit-pie, and I asked him if he had ever been at sea. No, he said. I could have wept over that innocent old gentleman's childlike confidence of appetite, and guileless trust of the deep.

We went on deck, where one of the gentle beings of our party declared that she would remain as long as Genoa was in sight; and, to tell the truth, the scene was worthy of the promised devotion. There, in a half-circle before us, blazed the lights of the quay; above these twinkled the lamps of the steep streets and climbing palaces; over and behind all hung the darkness on the heights,—a sable cloud dotted with ruddy points of flame burning in the windows of invisible houses.

"Merrily did we drop"

down the bay, and presently caught the heavy swell of the open sea. The other gentle being of our party then clutched my shoulder with a dreadful shudder, and after gasping, "O Mr. Scribbler, why *will* the ship roll so?" was meekly hurried below by her sister, who did not return for a last glimpse of Genoa the Proud.

In a moment heaven's sweet pity flapped away as with the sea-gull's wings, and I too felt that there was no help for it, and that I must go and lie down in the cabin. With anguished eyes I beheld upon the shelf opposite mine the innocent old gentleman who had lately supped so confidently on sardines and fruit-pie. He lay upon his back groaning softly to himself.

The Marlboro Press is an independent publisher of serious literature: works of fiction, of intellectual history and philosophic travel, biography, chronicles, essays—a good many of them in translation.

If you have found this book of particular interest you may wish to know what others have appeared on our list and are forthcoming. We will be happy to send you a catalogue, and to answer any queries you may have.

Name

Street or box number

City

State   Zip

T M p

THE MARLBORO PRESS

P.O. BOX 157

MARLBORO, VERMONT 05344

VI. BY SEA FROM GENOA TO NAPLES

I

O UR captain would in any company have won notice for his
gentle and high-bred way; in his place at the head of the
table, he seemed to me one of the finest gentlemen I had ever seen.
He had spent his whole life at sea, and had voyaged in all parts of
the world except Japan, where he meant some day, he said, to go.
He had been first a cabin-boy on a little Genoese schooner, and he
had gradually risen to the first place on a sailing-vessel, and now he
had been selected to fill a commander's post on this line of steamers.
He had sailed a good deal in American waters, but chiefly on the
Pacific coast, trading from the Spanish republican ports to those of
California. He had been in that State during its effervescent days,
when everything foul floated to the top, and I am afraid he formed
there but a bad opinion of our people, though he was far too
courteous to say outright anything of this sort.

He had very fine, shrewd blue eyes, a lean, weather-beaten,

kindly face, and a cautious way of saying things. I hardly expected him to turn out so red-hot a Democrat as he did on better acquaintance, but being a warm friend of man myself, I was not sorry. Garibaldi was the beginning and ending of his political faith, as he is with every enthusiastic Italian. The honest soul's conception of all concrete evil was brought forth in two words, of odd enough application. In Europe, and Italy more particularly, true men have suffered chiefly from this form of evil, and the captain could evidently conceive of no other cause of suffering anywhere. We were talking of the American war, and when the captain had asked the usual question, *"Quando finirà mai questa guerra?"* and I responded as usual, *"Ah, ci vuol pazienza!"* the captain gave a heavy sigh, and, turning his head pensively aside, plucked his grapes from the cluster a moment in silence.

Then he said: "You Americans are in the habit of attributing this war to slavery. The cause is not sufficient."

I ventured to demur and explain. "No," said the captain, "the cause is not sufficient. We Italians know the only cause which could produce a war like this."

I was naturally anxious to be instructed in the Italian theory, hoping it might be profounder than the English notion that we were fighting about tariffs.

The captain frowned, looked at me carefully, and then said:—

"In this world there is but one cause of mischief,—the Jesuits."

II

THE first night out, from Genoa to Leghorn, was bad enough, but that which succeeded our departure from the latter port was by far the worst of the three we spent in our voyage to Naples. How we envied the happy people who went ashore at Leghorn! I think we even envied the bones of the Venetians, Pisans, and Genoese who met and slew each other in the long-forgotten sea-fights, and sank too deeply through the waves to be stirred by their restless tumult. Every one has heard tell of how cross and treacherous a sea the Mediterranean is in winter, and my own belief is that he who has merely been seasick on the Atlantic should give the Mediterranean a trial before professing to have suffered everything of which human nature is capable. Our steamer was clean enough and stanch enough, but she was not large—no bigger, I thought, than a gondola, that night as the waves tossed her to and fro, till unwinged things took flight all through her cabins and over her decks. My berth was placed transversely instead of lengthwise with the boat,—an ingenious arrangement to heighten seasick horrors, and dash the blood of the sufferer from brain to boots with exaggerated violence at each roll of the boat; and I begged the steward to let me sleep upon one of the lockers in the cabin. I found many of my agonized species already laid out there; and there was something eldritch and unearthly in the whole business, and I think a kind of delirium must have resulted from the seasickness. Otherwise, I shall not know how to account for having attributed a kind of consciousness to the guide-book of a young American who had come aboard at Leghorn. He turned out afterward to be the sweetest soul in the world, and I am sorry now that I regarded with amusement his failure to smoke off his sickness. He was reading his guide-book with great diligence and unconcern, when suddenly I marked him lay it softly, softly down, with that excessive deliberation men use at such times, and vanish with great dignity from the scene. Thus abandoned to its own devices, the guide-book began its night-long riots, setting out upon a tour of the cabin with the first lurch of the boat that threw it from the table upon the floor. I heard it career at once wildly to the cabin door, and knock to get out; and failing in this, return more deliberately to the stern of the boat, interrogating the tables and chairs, which had got their sea-legs on, and asking them how they found themselves. Arrived again at the point of starting, it seemed to pause a moment, and then I saw it setting forth on a voyage of pleasure in the low company of a French hat, which, being itself a French book, I suppose it liked. In these travels they both ran under the feet of one of the stewards and were replaced by an

immense *tour de force* on the table, from which the book eloped
again,—this time in company with an overcoat; but it seemed the
coat was too miserable to go far: it stretched itself at full length on
the floor, and suffered the book to dance over it, back and forth,
I know not how many times. At last, as the actions of the book
were becoming unendurable, and the general seasickness was
waxing into a frenzy, a heavy roll, that made the whole ship shriek
and tremble, threw us all from our lockers; and gathering myself
up, bruised and sore in every fibre, I lay down again and became
sensible of a blissful, blissful lull; the machinery had stopped, and
with the mute hope that we were all going to the bottom, I fell
tranquilly asleep.

III

It appeared that the storm had really been dangerous. Instead
of being only six hours from Naples, as we ought to be at this
time, we were got no further than Porto Longone, in the Isle of
Elba. We woke in a quiet, sheltered little bay, whence we could
only behold, not feel, the storm left far out upon the open sea.
From this we turned our heavy eyes gladly to the shore, where
a white little town was settled, like a flight of gulls upon the
beach, at the feet of green and pleasant hills, whose gentle lines
rhymed softly away against the sky. At the end of either arm of
the embracing land in which we lay, stood gray, placid old
forts, with peaceful sentries pacing their bastions, and weary
ships creeping round their feet, under guns looking out so kindly
and harmlessly, that I think General —— himself would not
have hesitated (except, perhaps, from a profound sentiment of
regret for offering the violence) to attack them. Our port was
full of frightened shipping—steamers, brigs, and schooners—of
all sizes and nations; and since it was our misfortune that
Napoleon spent his exile in Elba at Porto Ferrato instead of
Porto Longone, we amused ourselves with looking at the vessels
and the white town and the soft hills, instead of hunting up dead
lion's tracks.

Our fellow passengers began to develop themselves: the regiment of soldiers whom we were transporting picturesquely breakfasted forward, and the second-cabin people came aft to our deck, while the English engineer (there are English engineers on all the Mediterranean steamers) planted a camp-stool in a sunny spot, and sat down to read the "Birmingham Express."

Our friends of the second cabin were chiefly officers with their wives and families, and they talked for the most part of their suffering during the night. They spoke such exquisite Italian that I thought them Tuscans, but they told me they were of Sicily, where their beautiful speech first had life. Let us hear what they talked of in their divine language, and with that ineffable *tonic* accent which no foreigner perfectly acquires, and let us for once translate the profanities Pagan and Christian, which adorn common parlance in Italy:—

"Ah, my God! how much I suffered!" says a sweet little woman with gentle brown eyes, red, red lips, and blameless Greek lines of face. "I broke two basins!"

"There are ten broken in all, by Diana!" says this lady's sister.

"Presence of the Devil!" says her husband; and

"Body of Bacchus!" her young brother, puffing his cigar.

"And you, sir," said the lady, turning to a handsome young fellow in civil dress, near her, "how did you pass this horrible night?"

"Oh!" says the young man, twirling his heavy blond mustache, "mighty well, mighty well!"

"Oh, mercy of God! You were not sick?"

"I, signora, am never seasick. I am of the navy."

At which they all cry oh, and ah, and declare they are glad of it, though why they should have been I don't know to this day.

"I have often wished," added the young man meditatively, and in a serious tone, as if he had indeed given the subject much thought, "that it might please God to let me be seasick once, if only that I might know how it feels. But no!" He turned the conversation, as if his disappointment were too sore to dwell upon; and hearing our English, he made out to let us know that he had been at New York, and could spik our language, which he proceeded to do, to the great pride of his countrymen.

IV

WE set out from Porto Longone that night at eight o'clock, and next evening, driving through much-abated storm southward into calm waters and clear skies, reached Naples. At noon, Monte Circeo, where Circe led her disreputable life, was a majestic rock against blue heaven and broken clouds; after nightfall, and under the risen moon, Vesuvius crept softly up from the sea, and stood a graceful steep, with wreaths of lightest cloud upon its crest, and the city lamps circling far round its bay.

VII. CERTAIN THINGS IN NAPLES

I

PERHAPS some reader of mine who visited Naples under the old disorder of things, when the Bourbon and the Camorra reigned, will like to hear that the pitched battle which travelers formerly fought, in landing from their steamer, is now gone out of fashion. Less truculent boatmen I never saw than those who rowed us ashore at Naples; they were so quiet and peaceful that they harmonized perfectly with that tranquil scene of drowsy-twinkling city lights, slumbrous mountains, and calm sea, as they dipped softly toward us in the glare of the steamer's lamps. The mystery of this placidity had been already solved by our captain, whom I had asked what price I should bargain to pay from the steamer to the shore. "There is a tariff," said he, "and the boatmen keep to it. The Neapolitans are good people (*buona gente*), and only needed justice to make them obedient to the laws." I must say that I found this to be true. The fares of all public conveyances are now fixed, and the attempts which drivers occasionally make to cheat you seem to be rather the involuntary impulses of old habit than deliberate intentions to do you wrong. You pay what is due, and as your man merely rumbles internally when you turn away, you must be a very timid *signorin*, indeed, if you buy his content with anything more. I fancy that all these things are now much better managed in Italy than in America, only we grumble at them there and stand them in silence at home. Every one can recall frightful instances of plunder, in which he was the victim, at New York—in which the robbery had none of the neatness of an operation, as it often has in Italy, but was a brutal mutilation. And then as regards civility from the same kind of people in the two countries, there is no comparison that holds in favor of us. All questions are readily and politely answered in Italian travel, and the servants of companies are required to be courteous to the public, whereas one is only too glad to receive a silent snub from such people at home.

II

THE first sun that rose after our arrival in Naples was mild and warm as a May sun, though we were quite in the heart of November. We early strolled out under it into the crowded ways of the city, and drew near as we might to that restless, thronging, gossiping southern life, in contrast with which all northern existence seems only a sort of hibernation. The long Toledo, on which the magnificence of modern Naples is threaded, is the most brilliant and joyous street in the world; but I think there is less of the quaintness of Italian civilization to be seen in its vivacious crowds than anywhere else in Italy. One easily understands how, with its superb length and straightness, and its fine, respectable, commonplace-looking houses, it should be the pride of a people fond of show; but after Venice and Genoa it has no picturesque charm; nay, even busy Milan seems less modern and more picturesque. The lines of the lofty palaces on the Toledo are seldom broken by the façade of a church or other public edifice; and when this does happen, the building is sure to be coldly classic or frantically baroque.

You weary of the Toledo's perfect repair, of its monotonous iron balconies, its monotonous lofty windows; and it would be insufferable if you could not turn out from it at intervals into one of those wondrous little streets which branch up on one hand and down on the other, rising and falling with flights of steps between the high, many-balconied walls. They ring all day with the motleyest life of fishermen, fruit-venders, chestnut-roasters, and idlers of every age and sex; and there is nothing so full of local color, unless it be the little up-and-down-hill streets in Genoa. Like those, the by-streets of Naples are meant only for foot-passengers, and a carriage never enters them; but sometimes, you may see a mule climbing the long stairways, moving solemnly under a stack of straw, or tinkling gayly downstairs, bestridden by a swarthy, handsome peasant—all glittering teeth and eyes and flaming Phrygian cap. The rider exchanges lively salutations and sarcasms with the bystanders in his way, and perhaps brushes against the bagpipers who bray constantly in those hilly defiles. They are in Neapolitan costume, these *pifferari*, and have their legs incomprehensibly tied up in the stockings and garters affected by the peasantry of the provinces, and wear brave red sashes about their waists. They are simple, harmless looking people, and would no doubt rob and kill in the most amiable manner, if brigandage came into fashion in their neighborhood.

Sometimes the student of men may witness a Neapolitan quarrel in these streets, and may pick up useful ideas of invective from the remarks of the fat old women who always take part in the contests. But, though we were ten days in Naples, I only saw one quarrel, and I could have heard much finer violence of language among the gondoliers at any ferry in Venice than I heard in this altercation.

The Neapolitans are, of course, furious in traffic. They sell a great deal, and very boisterously, the fruit of the cactus, which is about as large as an egg, and which they peel to a very bloody pulp, and lay out, a sanguinary presence, on boards for purchase. It is not good to the uncultivated taste; but the stranger may stop and drink, with relish and refreshment, the orangeade and lemonade mixed with snow and sold at the little booths on the street- corners. These stands look much like the shrines of the Madonna in other Italian cities, and a friend of ours was led, before looking carefully into their office, to argue immense Neapolitan piety from the frequency of their ecclesiastical architecture. They are, indeed, the shrines of a god much worshiped during the long Neapolitan summers; and it was the profound theory of the Bourbon kings of Naples, that, if they kept their subjects well supplied with snow to cool their drink, there was no fear of revolution. It shows how little liable statesmen are to err, that, after all, the Neapolitans rose, drove out the Bourbons, and welcomed Garibaldi.

The only part of the picturesque life of the side streets which seems ever to issue from them into the Toledo is the goatherd with his flock of milch-goats, which mingle with the passers in the avenues as familiarly as with those of the alley, and thrust aside silk-hidden hoops, and brush against dandies' legs in their course, but keep on perfect terms with everybody. The goatherd leads the eldest of the flock, and the rest follow in docile order, and stop as he stops to ask at the doors if milk is wanted. When he happens to have an order, one of the goats is haled, much against her will, into the entry of a house, and there milked, while the others wait outside alone, nibbling and smelling thoughtfully about the masonry. It is noticeable that none of the good-natured passers seem to think these goats a great nuisance in the crowded street; but all make way for them as if they were there by perfect right, and were no inconvenience.

On the Toledo, people keep upon the narrow sidewalks, or strike out into the carriageway, with an indifference to hoofs and wheels which one, after long residence in tranquil Venice, cannot acquire, in view of the furious Neapolitan driving. That old comprehensive gig of Naples, with which many pens and pencils have familiarized the reader, is nearly as hard to find there now as the *lazzaroni*, who have gone out altogether. You may still see it in the remoter quarters of the city, with its complement of twelve passengers to one horse, distributed, two on each thill, four on the top seats, one at each side, and two behind; but in the Toledo it has given place to much finer vehicles. Slight buggies, which take you anywhere for half a franc, are the favorite means of public conveyance, and the private turn-outs are of every description and degree. Indeed, all the Neapolitans take to carriages, and the Strand in London at six o'clock in the evening is not a greater jam of wheels than the Toledo in the afternoon. Shopping feels the expansive influence of the out-of-doors life, and ladies do most of it as they sit in their open carriages at the shop-doors, ministered to by the neat-handed shopmen. They are very languid ladies, as they recline upon their carriage cushions; they are all black-eyed, and of an olive pallor, and have gloomy rings about their fine eyes, like the dark-faced dandies who bow to them. This Neapolitan look is very curious, and I have not seen it elsewhere in Italy; it is a look of peculiar pensiveness, and comes, no doubt, from the peculiarly heavy growth of lashes which fringes the lower eyelid. Then there is the weariness in it of all peoples whose summers are fierce and long.

As the Italians usually dress beyond their means, the dandies of Naples are very gorgeous. If it is now, say, four o'clock in the afternoon, they are all coming down the Toledo with the streams of carriages bound for the long drive around the bay. But our foot-passers go to walk in the beautiful Villa Reale, between this course and the sea. The Villa is a slender strip of Paradise, a mile long; it is rapture to walk in it, and it comes, in description, to be a garden-grove, with feathery palms, Greekish temples, musical fountains, white statues of the gods, and groups of fair girls in spring silks. If I remember aright, the sun is always setting on the bay, and you cannot tell whether this sunset is cooled by the water or the water is warmed by the golden light upon it, and upon the city, and upon all the soft mountain-heights around.

III

WALKING westward through the whole length of the Villa Reale, and keeping with the crescent shore of the bay, you come, after a while, to the Grot of Posilippo, which is not a grotto but a tunnel cut for a carriageway under the hill. It serves, however, the purpose of a grotto, if a grotto has any, and is of great length and dimness and is all a-twinkle night and day with numberless lamps. Overlooking the street which passes into it is the tomb of Virgil, and it is this you have come to see. To reach it, you knock first at the door of a blacksmith, who calls a species of custodian, and, when this latter has opened a gate in a wall, you follow him upstairs into a market-garden.

In one corner, and standing in a leafy and grassy shelter somewhat away from the vegetables, is the poet's tomb, which has a kind of claim to genuiness by virtue of its improbable appearance. It looks more like a bake-oven than even the Pompeian tombs; the masonry is antique, and is at least in skillful imitation of the fine Roman work. The interior is a small chamber with vaulted or wagon-roof ceiling, under which a man may stand upright, and at the end next the street is a little stone, commemorating the place as Virgil's tomb, which was placed there by the Queen of France in 1840, and said by the custodian to be an exact copy of the original, whatever the original may have been. This guide could tell us nothing more about it, and was too stupidly honest to pretend to know more. The laurel planted by Petrarch at the door of the tomb, and renewed in later times by Casimir Delavigne, has been succeeded by a third laurel. The present twig was so slender, and looked so friendless and unprotected, that even enthusiasm for the memory of two poets could not be brought to rob it of one of its few leaves; and we contented ourselves with plucking some of the grass and weeds that grew abundantly on the roof of the tomb.

There was a dusty quiet within the tomb, and a grassy quiet without, that pleased exceedingly; but though the memories of the place were so high and epic, it only suggested bucolic associations, and, sunken into that nook of hillside verdure, made me think of a spring-house on some far-away Ohio farm; a thought that, perhaps, would not have offended the poet, who loved and sang of humble country things, and, drawing wearily to his rest here, no doubt turned and remembered tenderly the rustic days before the excellent veterans of Augustus came to exile him from his father's farm at Mantua, and banish him to mere glory. But I believe most travelers have much nobler sensations in Virgil's tomb, and there is a great deal of testimony borne to their lofty sentiments on every scribbleable inch of its walls. Valery reminded me that Boccaccio, standing near it of old, first felt his fate decided for literature. Did he come there, I wonder, with poor Fiammetta, and enter the tomb with her tender hand in his, before ever he thought of that cruel absence she tells of? "O donne pietose!" I hope so, and that this pilgrimage, half of love and half of letters, took place, "nel tempo nel quale la rivestita terra più che tutto l'altro anno si mostra bella."

If you ascend from the tomb and turn Naplesward from the crest of the hill, you have the loveliest view in the world of the sea and of the crescent beach, mightily jeweled at its further horn with the black Castel dell'Ovo. Fishermen's children are playing all along the foamy border of the sea, and boats are darting out into the surf. The present humble muse is not above saying also that the linen which the laundresses hang to dry upon lines along the beach takes the sun like a dazzling flight of white birds, and gives a breezy life to the scene which it could not spare.

IV

THERE was a little church on our way back from Posilippo, into which we lounged a moment, pausing at the altar of some very successful saint near the door. Here there were great numbers of the usual offerings from the sick whom the saint had eased of their various ills,—waxen legs and arms from people who had been in peril of losing their limbs, as well as eyes, noses, fingers, and feet, and the crutches of those cured of lameness; but we were most amused with the waxen effigies of several entire babies hung up about the altar, which the poor souls who had been near losing the originals had brought there in gratitude to the saint.

Generally, however, the churches of Naples are not very interesting, and one who came away without seeing them would have little to regret. The pictures are seldom good, and though there are magnificent chapels in St. Januarius, and fine Gothic tombs at Santa Chiara, the architecture is usually rococo. I fancy that Naples has felt the damage of Spanish taste in such things as well as Spanish tyranny in others. At any rate, all Italian writers are agreed in attributing the depravation of Naples to the long Spanish dominion. It is well known how the Spanish rule their provinces, and their gloomy despotism was probably never more cruelly felt than in Italy, where the people were least able to bear it. I had a heartfelt exultation in walking through the quarter of the city where the tumults of Nassaniello had raged, and, if only for a few days, struck mortal terror to the brutal pride of the viceroy; but I think I had a better sense of the immense retribution which has overtaken all memory of Spanish rule in Naples as we passed through the palace of Capo di Monte. This was the most splendid seat of the Spanish Bourbon, whose family, inheriting its power from the violence of other times, held it with violence in these; and in one of the chief saloons of the palace, which is now Victor Emanuel's, were pictures representing scenes of the revolution of 1860, while the statuette of a Garibaldino, in his red shirt and all his heroic rudeness, was defiantly conspicuous on one of the tables.

V

THERE was nothing else that pleased me as well in the palace, or in the grounds about it. These are laid out in pleasant successions of grove, tangled wilderness, and pasture-land, and were thronged, the Saturday afternoon of our visit, with all ranks of people, who strolled through the beautiful walks and enjoyed themselves in the peculiarly peaceful Italian way. Valery says that the Villa Reale in the Bourbon time was closed, except for a single day in the year, to all but the nobles; and that on this occasion it was filled with pretty peasant women, who made it a condition of their marriage bargains that their husbands should bring them to the Villa Reale on St. Mary's Day. It is now free to all on every day of the year, and the grounds of the Palace Capo di Monte are opened every Saturday. I liked the pleasant way in which sylvan Nature and Art had made friends in these beautiful grounds, in which Nature had consented to overlook the vanity of the long aisles of lime, cut and trimmed in formal and fantastic shapes, according to the taste of the times of bagwigs and patches. On every side wild birds fluttered through these absurd trees, and in the thickets lurked innumerable pheasants, which occasionally issued forth and stalked in stately, fearless groups over the sunset-crimsoned lawns. There was a brown gamekeeper for nearly every head of game, wearing a pheasant's wing in his hat and carrying a short, heavy sword; and our driver told us, with an awful solemnity in his bated breath, that no one might kill this game but the king, under penalty of the galleys.

VI

THE Italians are simple and natural folks, pleased through all their show of conventionality with little things, and as easy and unconscious as children in their ways. There happened to be a new caffè opened in Naples while we were there, and we had the pleasure of seeing all ranks of people affected by its magnificence. Artless throngs blocked the sidewalk day and night before its windows, gazing upon its mirrors, fountains, and frescoes, and regarding the persons over their coffee within as beings lifted by sudden magic out of the common orbit of life and set dazzling in a higher sphere. All the waiters were uniformed and brass-buttoned to blinding effect, and the head waiter was a majestic creature in a long blue coat reaching to his feet, and armed with a mighty silver-headed staff. This gorgeous apparition did nothing but walk up and down, and occasionally advance toward the door, as if to disperse the crowds. At such times, however, before executing his purpose, he would glance round on the splendors they were admiring, and, as if smitten with a sense of the enormous cruelty he had meditated in thinking to deprive them of the sight, would falter and turn away, leaving his intent unfulfilled.

VIII. A DAY IN POMPEII

I

ON the second morning after our arrival in Naples, we took the seven o'clock train, which leaves the Nineteenth Century for the first cycle of the Christian Era, and, skirting the waters of the Neapolitan bay almost the whole length of our journey, reached the railroad station of Pompeii in an hour. As we rode along by that bluest sea, we saw the fishing-boats go out, and the foamy waves (which it would be violence to call breakers) come in; we saw the mountains slope their tawny and golden manes caressingly downward to the waters, where the islands were dozing yet; and landward, on the left, we saw Vesuvius, with his brown mantle of ashes drawn close about his throat, reclining on the plain, and smoking a bland and thoughtful morning pipe, of which the silver fumes curled lightly, lightly upward in the sunrise.

We dismounted at the station, walked a few rods eastward through a little cotton-field, and found ourselves at the door of the

Hotel Diomed, where we took breakfast for a nunmber of sesterces which I am sure it would have made an ancient Pompeian stir in his urn to think of paying. But in Italy one learns the chief Italian virtue, patience, and we paid our account with the utmost good-nature. There was compensation in store for us, and the guide whom we found at the gate leading up the little hill to Pompeii inclined the disturbed balance in favor of our happiness. He was a Roman, spoke Italian that Beatrice might have addressed to Dante, and was numbered Twenty-six. I suppose it is known that the present Italian government forbids people to be pillaged in any way on its premises, and that the property of the state is no longer the traffic of custodians and their pitiless race. At Pompeii each person pays two francs for admission, and is rigorously forbidden by recurrent sign-boards to offer money to the guides. Ventisei (as we shall call him) himself pointed out one of these notices in English, and did his duty faithfully without asking or receiving fees in money. He was a soldier, like all the other guides, and was a most intelligent, obliging fellow, with a self-respect and dignity worthy of one of our own volunteer soldiers.

Ventisei took us up the winding slope, and led us out of this living world through the Sea-gate of Pompeii back into the dead past—the past which, with all its sensuous beauty and grace, and all its intellectual power, one is not sorry to have dead, and, for the most part, buried. Our feet had hardly trodden the lava flagging of the narrow streets when we came in sight of the laborers who were exhuming the inanimate city. They were few in number, not perhaps a score, and they worked tediously, with baskets to carry away the earth from the excavation, boys and girls carrying the baskets, and several athletic old women plying picks, while an overseer sat in a chair near by, and smoked, and directed their exertions.

They dig down about eight or ten feet, uncovering the walls and pillars of the houses, and the mason, who is at hand, places little iron rivets in the stucco to prevent its fall where it is weak, while an artist attends to wash and clean the frescoes as fast as they are exposed. The soil through which the excavation first passes is not of great depth; the ashes which fell damp with scalding rain, in the second eruption, are perhaps five feet thick; the rest is of that porous stone which descended in small fragments during the first eruption. A depth of at least two feet in this stone is always left untouched by the laborers till the day comes when the chief superintendent of the work comes out from Naples to see the last layers removed; and it is then that the beautiful mosaic pavements of the houses are uncovered, and the interesting and valuable objects are nearly always found.

The wonder was, seeing how slowly the work proceeded, not that two thirds of Pompeii were yet buried, but that one third had been exhumed. We left these hopeless toilers, and went downtown into the Forum, stepping aside on the way to look into one of the Pompeian Courts of Common Pleas.

II

POMPEII is so full of marvel and surprise, in fact, that it would be unreasonable to express disappointment with Pompeii in fiction. And yet I cannot help it. An exuberant carelessness of phrase in most writers and talkers who describe it had led me to expect much more than it was possible to find there. In my Pompeii I confess that the houses had no roofs—in fact, the rafters which sustained the tiles being burnt, how could the roofs help falling in? But otherwise my Pompeii was a very complete affair: the walls all rose to their full height; doorways and arches were perfect; the columns were all unbroken and upright; putting roofs on my Pompeii, you might have lived in it very comfortably. The real Pompeii is different. It is seldom that any wall is unbroken; most columns are fragmentary; and though the ground-plans are very distinct, very few rooms in the city are perfect in form, and the whole is much more ruinous than I thought.

But this ruin once granted, and the idle disappointment at its greatness overcome, there is endless material for study, instruction, and delight. It is the revelation of another life, and the utterance of the past is here more perfect than anywhere else in the world. I think that the true friend of Pompeii should make it a matter of conscience, on entering the enchanted city, to cast out of his knowledge all the rubbish that has fallen into it from novels and travels, and to keep merely the facts of the town's luxurious life and agonizing death, with such incidents of the eruption as he can remember from the description of Pliny. There are the spells to which the sorcery yields, and with these in your thought you can rehabilitate the city until Ventisei seems to be a *valet de place* of the first century, and yourselves a set of blond barbarians to whom he is showing off the splendors of one of the most brilliant towns of the empire of Titus. Those silent furrows in the pavement become vocal with the joyous rattle of chariot-wheels on a sudden, and you prudently step up on the narrow sidewalks and rub along by the little shops of wine, and grain, and oil, with which the thrifty voluptuaries of Pompeii flanked their street-doors. The counters of the shops run across their fronts, and are pierced with round holes on the top, through which you see dark depths of oil in the jars below, and not sullen lumps of ashes; those stately *amphoræ* behind are full of wine, and in the corners are bags of wheat.

"This house, with a shop on either side, whose is it, XXVI.?"

"It is the house of the great Sallust, my masters. Would you like his autograph? I know one of his slaves who would sell it."

You are a good deal stared at, naturally, as you pass by, for people in Pompeii have not much to do, and, besides, a Briton is not an every-day sight there, as he will be one of these centuries. The skins of wild beasts are little worn in Pompeii, and those bold-eyed Roman women think it rather odd that we should like to powder our shaggy heads with brick-dust. However, these are matters of taste. We, for our part, cannot repress a feeling of disgust at the loungers in the street, who, XXVI. tells us, are all going to soak themselves half the day in the baths yonder; for, if there is in Pompeii one thing more offensive than another to our savage sense of propriety, it is the personal cleanliness of the inhabitants. We little know what a change for the better will be wrought in these people with the lapse of time, and that they will yet come to wash themselves but once a year, as we do.

(The reader may go on doing this sort of thing at some length for himself; and may imagine, if he pleases, a boastful conversation among the Pompeians at the baths, in which the barbarians hear how Agricola has broken the backbone of a rebellion in Britain; and in which all the speakers begin their observations with "Ho! my Lepidus!" and "Ha! my Diomed!" In the mean time we return to the present day, and step down the Street of Plenty along with Ventisei.)

III

IT is proper, after seeing the sites of some of the principal temples in Pompeii (such as those of Jupiter and Venus), to cross the fields that cover a great breadth of the buried city, and look into the amphitheatre, where, as everybody knows, the lions had no stomach for Glaucus on the morning of the fatal eruption. The fields are now planted with cotton, and of course we thought those commonplaces about the wonder the Pompeians would feel could they come back to see that New World plant growing above their buried homes. We might have told them, the day of our visit, that this cruel plant, so long watered with the tears of slaves, and fed with the blood of men, was now an exile from its native fields, where war was ploughing with sword and shot the guilty land, and rooting up the subtlest fibres of the oppression in which cotton had grown king.

But the only Pompeian presences which haunted our passage of the cotton-field were certain small

"Phantoms of delight,"

with soft black eyes and graceful wiles, who ran before us and plucked the bolls of the cotton and sold them to us. Embassies bearing red and white grapes were also sent out of the cottages to our excellencies; and there was some doubt of the currency of the coin which we gave those poor children in return.

There are now but few peasants living on the land over the head of Pompeii, and the government allows no sales of real estate to be made except to itself. The people who still dwell here can hardly be said to own their possessions, for they are merely allowed to cultivate the soil. A guard stationed night and day prevents them from making excavations, and they are severely restricted from entering the excavated quarters of the city alone.

The cotton whitens over two thirds of Pompeii yet interred: happy the generation that lives to learn the wondrous secrets of that sepulchre! For, when you have once been at Pompeii, this phantasm of the past takes deeper hold on your imagination than any living city, and becomes and is the metropolis of your dreamland forever. O marvelous city! who shall reveal the cunning of your spell? Something not death, something not life— something that is the one when you turn to determine its essence as the other! What is it comes to me at this distance of that which I saw in Pompeii? The narrow and curving, but not crooked streets, with the blazing sun of that Neapolitan November falling into them, or clouding their wheel-worn lava with the black, black shadows of the many-tinted walls; the houses, and the gay columns of white, yellow, and red; the delicate pavements of mosaic; the skeltons of dusty cisterns and dead fountains; inanimate garden spaces with pygmy statues suited to their littleness; suites of fairy bed-chambers, painted with exquisite frescoes; dining-halls with joyous scenes of hunt and banquet on their walls; the ruinous sites of temples; the melancholy emptiness of booths and shops and jolly drinking-houses; the lonesome tragic theatre, with a modern Pompeian drawing water from a well there; the baths with their roofs perfect yet, and the stucco bas-reliefs all but unharmed; around the whole, the city wall crowned with slender poplars; outside the gates, the long avenue of tombs, and the Appian Way stretching on to Stabiæ; and, in the distance, Vesuvius, brown and bare, with his fiery breath scarce visible against the cloudless heaven;—these are the things that float before my fancy as I turn back to look at myself walking those enchanted streets, and to wonder if I could ever have been so blest.

The amphitheatre, to which we came now, after our stroll across the cotton-fields, was small, like the vastest things in Pompeii, and had nothing of the stately magnificence of the Arena at Verona, nor anything of the Roman Coliseum's melancholy and ruinous grandeur. But its littleness made it all the more comfortable and social, and, seated upon its benches under a cool awning, one could have almost chatted across the arena with one's friends; could have witnessed the spectacle on the sands without losing a movement of the quick gladiators, or an agony of the victim given to the beasts—which must have been very delightful to a Pompeian of companionable habits. It is quite impossible, however, that the bouts described by Bulwer as taking place all at the same time on the arena should really have done so: the combatants would have rolled and tumbled and trampled over each other an hundred times in the narrow space.

Of all the voices with which it once rang the poor little amphitheatre has kept only an echo. But this echo is one of the most perfect ever heard; prompt, clear, startling, it blew back the light chaff we threw to it with amazing vehemence, and almost made us doubt if it were not a direct human utterance. Yet how was Ventisei to know our names? And there was no one else to call them but ourselves. Our *"dolce duca"* gathered a nosegay from the crumbling ledges, and sat down in the cool of the once-cruel cells beneath, and put it prettily together for the ladies. When we had wearied ourselves with the echo he arose and led us back to Pompeii.

IV

THE plans of nearly all the houses in the city are alike: the entrance-room next the door; the parlor or drawing-room next that; then the *impluvium*, or unroofed space in the middle of the house, where the rains were caught and drained into the cistern, and where the household used to come to wash itself, primitively, as at a pump; the little garden, with its painted columns, behind the *impluvium*, and, at last, the dining-room. There are minute bed-chambers on either side, and, as I said, a shop at one side in front, for the sale of the master's grain, wine, and oil. The pavements of all the houses are of mosaic, which, in the better sort, is very delicate and beautiful, and is found sometimes perfectly uninjured. Of course there were many picturesque and fanciful designs, of which the best have been removed to the Museum in Naples; but several good ones are still left, and (like that of the Wild Boar) give names to the houses in which they are found.

But, after all, the great wonder, the glory, of these Pompeian houses is in their frescoes. If I tried to give an idea of the luxury of color in Pompeii, the most gorgeous adjectives would be as poorly able to reproduce a vivid and glowing sense of those hues as the photography which now copies the drawing of the decorations; so I do not try.

I know it is a cheap and feeble thought, and yet, let the reader please to consider: A workman nearly two thousand years ago laying upon the walls those soft lines that went to make up fauns and satyrs, nymphs and naiads, heroes and gods and goddesses; and getting weary and lying down to sleep, and dreaming of an eruption of the mountain; of the city buried under a fiery hail, and slumbering in its bed of ashes seventeen centuries; then of its being slowly exhumed, and, after another lapse of years, of some one coming to gather the shadow of that dreamer's work upon a plate of glass, that he might infinitely reproduce it and sell it to tourists at from five francs to fifty centimes a copy—I say, consider such a dream dreamed in the hot heart of the day, after certain cups of Vesuvian wine! What a piece of *Katzenjämmer* (I can use no milder term) would that workman think it when he woke again! Alas! what is history and the progress of the arts and sciences but one long *Katzenjämmer*!

Photography cannot give, any more than I, the colors of the frescoes, but it can do the drawing better, and, I suspect, the spirit

also. I used the word workman, and not artist, in speaking of the
decoration of the walls, for in most cases the painter was only an
artisan, and did his work probably by the yard, as the artisan who
paints walls and ceilings in Italy does at this day. But the old
workman did his work much more skillfully and tastefully than
the modern—threw on expanses of mellow color, delicately
paneled off the places for the scenes, and penciled in the figures
and draperies (there are usually more of the one than the other)
with a deft hand. Of course, the houses of the rich were adorned
by men of talent; but it is surprising to see the community of
thought and feeling in all this work, whether it be from cunninger
or clumsier hands. The subjects are nearly always chosen from the
fables of the gods, and they are in illustration of the poets, Homer
and the rest. To suit that soft, luxurious life which people led in
Pompeii, the themes are commonly amorous, and sometimes not
too chaste; there is much of Bacchus and Ariadne, much of Venus
and Adonis, and Diana bathes a good deal with her nymphs,—not
to mention frequent representations of the toilet of that beautiful
monster which the lascivious art of the time loved to depict. One
of the most pleasing of all the scenes is that in one of the houses,
of the Judgment of Paris, in which the shepherd sits upon a bank
in an attitude of ineffable and flattered importance, with one leg
carelessly crossing the other, and both hands resting lightly on his
shepherd's crook, while the goddesses before him await his
sentence. Naturally the painter has done his best for the victress in
this rivalry, and you see

"Idalian Aphrodite beautiful,"

as she should be, but with a warm and piquant spice of girlish
resentment in her attitude, that Paris should pause for an instant,
which is altogether delicious.

"And I beheld great Here's angry eyes."

Awful eyes! How did the painter make them? The wonder of all
these pagan frescoes is the mystery of the eyes—still, beautiful,

unhuman. You cannot believe that it is wrong for those tranquil-eyed men and women to do evil, they look so calm and so unconscious in it all; and in the presence of the celestials, as they bend upon you those eternal orbs, in whose regard you are but a part of space, you feel that here art has achieved the unearthly. I know of no words in literature which give a *sense* (nothing gives the idea) of the *stare* of these gods, except that magnificent line of Kingsley's, describing the advance over the sea toward Andromeda of the oblivious and unsympathizing Nereids. They floated slowly up, and their eyes

"Stared on her, silent and still, like the eyes in the house of the idols."

The colors of this fresco of the Judgment of Paris are still so fresh and bright, that it photographs very well, but there are other frescoes wherein there is more visible perfection of line, but in which the colors are so dim that they can only be reproduced by drawings. One of these is the Wounded Adonis cared for by Venus and the Loves; in which the story is treated with a playful pathos wonderfully charming. The fair boy leans in the languor of his hurt toward Venus; who sits utterly disconsolate beside him, while the Cupids busy themselves with such slight surgical offices as Cupids may render: one prepares a linen bandage for the wound, another wraps it round the leg of Adonis, another supports one of his heavy arms, another finds his own emotions too much for him and pauses to weep. It is a pity that the colors of this beautiful fresco are grown so dim, and a greater pity that most of the frescoes in Pompeii must share its fate, and fade away. The hues are vivid when the walls are first uncovered, and the ashes washed from the pictures, but then the malice of the elements begins anew, and rain and sun draw the life out of tints which the volcano failed to obliterate.

Among the frescoes which told no story but their own, we were most pleased with one in a delicately painted little bed-chamber. This represented an alarmed and furtive man, whom we at once pronounced The Belated Husband, opening a door with a nightlatch. Nothing could have been better than this miserable wretch's cowardly haste and cautious noiselessness in applying his key; apprehension sat upon his brow, confusion dwelt in his guilty eye. He had been out till two o'clock in the morning, electioneering for Pansa, the friend of the people ("Pansa, and Roman gladiators," "Pansa, and Christians to the Beasts," was the platform), and he had left his *placens uxor* at home alone with the children, and now within this door that *placens uxor* awaited him!

V

You have read, no doubt, of their discovering, a year or two since, in making an excavation in a Pompeian street, the moulds of four human bodies, three women and a man, who fell down, blind and writhing, in the storm of fire eighteen hundred years ago; whose shape the settling and hardening ashes took; whose flesh wasted away, and whose bones lay there in the hollow of the matrix till the cunning of this time found them, and, pouring liquid plaster round the skeletons, clothed them with human form again, and drew them forth into the world once more. There are many things in Pompeii which bring back the gay life of the city, but nothing which so vividly reports the terrible manner of her death as these effigies of the creatures that actually shared it. The man in the last struggle has thrown himself upon his back, and taken his doom sturdily—there is a sublime calm in his rigid figure. The women lie upon their faces, their limbs tossed and distorted, their drapery tangled and heaped about them, and in every fibre you see how hard they died. One presses her face into her handkerchief to draw one last breath unmixed with scalding steam; another's arms are wildly thrown abroad to clutch at help; another's hand is appealingly raised, and on her slight fingers you see the silver hoops with which her poor dead vanity adorned them.

The guide takes you aside from the street into the house where they lie, and a dreadful shadow drops upon your heart as you enter their presence. Without, the hell-storms seem to fall again, and the whole sunny plain to be darkened with its ruin, and the city to send up the tumult of her despair. What is there left in Pompeii to speak of after this? The long street of tombs outside the walls? Those that died before the city's burial seem to have scarcely a claim to the solemnity of death. Shall we go see Diomed's Villa, and walk through the freedman's long underground vaults, where his friends thought to be safe, and were smothered in heaps? The garden-ground grows wild among its broken columns with weeds and poplar saplings; in one of the corridors they sell photograpohs, on which, if you please, Ventisei has his bottle, or drink-money. So we escape from the doom of the calamity, and so, at last the severely forbidden *buonamano* is paid.

We return slowly through the city, where we have spent the whole day, from nine till four o'clock. We linger on the way, imploring Ventisei if there is not something to be seen in this or that house; we make our weariness an excuse for sitting down, and cannot rend ourselves from the bliss of being in Pompeii.

At last we leave its gates, and swear each other to come again many times while in Naples, and never go again.

Perhaps it was well. You cannot repeat great happiness.

IX. A HALF-HOUR AT HERCULANEUM

I

THE road from Naples to Herculaneum is, in fact, one long street; it hardly ceases to be city in Naples till it is town at Portici, and in the interval it is suburb running between palatial lines of villas, which all have their names ambitiously painted over their doors. Great part of the distance this street is bordered by the bay, and, as far as this is the case, it is picturesque, as everything is belonging to marine life in Italy. Seafaring people go lounging up and down among the fishermen's boats drawn up on the shore, and among the fishermen's wives making nets, while the fishermen's children play and clamber everywhere, and over all flap and flutter the clothes hung on poles to dry. In this part of the street there are, of course, oysters, and grapes, and oranges, and cactus pulps, and cutlery, and iced drinks to sell at various booths; and Commerce is exceedingly dramatic and boisterous over the bargains she offers; and equally, of course, drinking shops lurk at intervals along the pavement, and lure into their recesses mariners of foreign birth, briefly ashore from their ships. The New York Coffee House is there to attract my maritime fellow-countrymen, and I know that if I look into that place of refreshment I shall see their honest, foolish faces flushed with drink, and with the excitement of buying the least they can for the most money. Poor souls! they shall drink that pleasant morning away in the society of Antonino the best of Neapolitans, and at midnight, emptied of every soldo, shall arise, wrung with a fearful suspicion of treachery, and wander away under Antonino's guidance to seek the protection of the consul; or, taking the law into their own hands, shall proceed to clear out, *more Americano,* the New York Coffee House, when Antonino shall develop into one of the landlords, and deal them the most artistic stab in Naples: handsome, worthy Antonino; tender-eyed, subtle, pitiless!

II

WHERE the road to Herculaneum leaves the bay and its seafaring life, it enters, between the walls of lofty fly-blown houses, a world of maccaroni haunted by foul odors, beggars, and poultry. There were few people to be seen on the street, but through the open doors of the lofty fly-blown houses we saw floury legions at work making maccaroni; grinding maccaroni, rolling it, cutting it, hanging it in mighty skeins to dry, and gathering it when dried, and putting it away. By the frequency of the wine-shops we judged that the legions were a thirsty host, and by the number of the barber-surgeons' shops, that they were a plethoric and too full-blooded host. The latter shops were in the proportion of one to five of the former; and the artist who had painted their signs had indulged his fancy in wild excesses of phlebotomy. We had found that, as we came south from Venice, science grew more and more sanguinary in Italy, and more and more disposed to let blood. At Ferrara, even, the propensity began to be manifest on the barbers' signs, which displayed the device of an arm lanced at the elbow, and jetting the blood by a neatly described curve into a tumbler. Further south the same arm was seen to bleed at the wrist also; and at Naples an exhaustive treatment of the subject appeared, the favorite study of the artist being a nude figure reclining in a genteel attitude on a bank of pleasant greensward, and bleeding from the elbows, wrists, ankles, and feet.

III

IN Naples everywhere one is surprised by the great number of English names which appear on business houses, but it was entirely bewildering to read a bill affixed to the gate of one of the villas on the road: "This Desirable Property for Sale." I should scarcely have cared to buy that desirable property, though the neighborhood seemed to be a favorite summer resort, and there were villas, as I said, nearly the whole way to Portici. Those which stood with their gardens toward the bay would have been tolerable, no doubt, if they could have kept their windows shut to the vile street before their doors, but the houses opposite could have had no escape from its stench and noisomeness. It was absolutely the filthiest street I have seen anywhere outside of New York, excepting only that little street which, in Herculaneum, leads from the theatre to the House of Argo.

This pleasant avenue has a stream of turbid water in its centre, bordered by begging children, and is either fouler or cleaner for the water, but I shall never know which. It is at a depth of some fifty or sixty feet below the elevation on which the present city of Portici is built, and is part of the excavation made long ago to reach the plain on which Herculaneum stands, buried under its half-score of successive layers of lava, and ashes, and Portici. We had the aid of all the poverty and leisure of the modern town—there was a vast deal of both, we found—in our search of the staircase by which you descend to the classic plain, and it proved a discovery involving the outlay of all the copper coin about us, while the sight of the famous theatre of Herculaneum was much more expensive than it would have been had we come there in the old time to see a play of Plautus or Terence.

As for the theatre, "the large and highly ornamented theatre" of which I read, only a little while ago, in an encyclopædia, we found it, by the light of our candles, a series of gloomy hollows, of the general effect of coalbins and potato cellars. It was never perfectly dug out of the lava, and, as is known, it was filled up in the last century, together with other excavations, when they endangered the foundations of worthless Portici overhead. (I am amused to find myself so hot upon the poor property-holders of Portici. I suppose I should not myself, even for the cause of antiquity and the knowledge of classic civilization, like to have my house tumbled about my ears.) But though it was impossible in the theatre of Herculaneum to gain any idea of its size or richness, I remembered there the magnificent bronzes which had been found in it, and paid a hasty reverence to the place. Indeed, it is amazing, when one sees how small a part of Herculaneum has been uncovered, to consider the number of fine works of art in the Museo Nazionale which were taken thence, and which argue a much richer and more refined community than that of Pompeii. A third of the latter city has now been restored to the light of day; but though it has yielded abundance of all the things that illustrate the domestic and public life, and the luxury and depravity of those old times, and has given the once secret rooms of the museum their worst attraction, it still falls far below Herculaneum in the value of its contributions to the treasures of classic art, except only in the variety and beauty of its exquisite frescoes.

The effect of this fact is to stimulate the imagination of the visitor to that degree that nothing short of the instant destruction of Portici and the excavation of all Herculaneum will satisfy him. If the opening of one theatre, and the uncovering of a basilica and two or three houses, have given such riches to us, what delight and knowledge would not the removal of these obdurate hills of ashes and lava bestow!

Emerging from the coalbins and potato cellars, the visitor extinguishes his candle with a pathetic sigh, profusely rewards the custodian (whom he connects in some mysterious way with the

ancient population of the injured city about him), and, thoughtfully removing the tallow from his fingers, follows the course of
the vile stream already sung, and soon arrives at the gate opening
into the exhumed quarter of Herculaneum. And there he finds a
custodian who enters perfectly into his feelings; a custodian who
has once been a guide in Pompeii, but now despises that wretched
town, and would not be guide there for any money since he has
known the superior life of Herculaneum; who, in fine, feels
toward Pompeii as a Bostonian feels toward New York. Yet the
reader would be wrong to form the idea that there is bitterness in
the disdain of this custodian. On the contrary, he is one of the
best-natured men in the world. He is a mighty mass of pinguid
bronze, with a fat lip, and a sunflower smile, and he lectures us
with a vast and genial breadth of manner on the ruins, contra-
dicting all our guesses at things with a sweet "Perdoni, signori!
ma—." At the end, we find that he has some medallions of lava to
sell: there is Victor Emanuel, or, if we are of the *partito d'azione*,
there is Garibaldi; both warm yet from the crater of Vesuvius, and
of the same material which destroyed Herculaneum. We decline to
buy, and the custodian makes the national shrug and grimace
(signifying that we are masters of the situation, and that he washes
his hands of the consequence of our folly) on the largest scale that
we have ever seen: his mighty hands are rigidly thrust forth, his
great lip protruded, his enormous head thrown back to bring his
face on a level with his chin. The effect is tremendous, but we
nevertheless feel that he loves us the same.

IV

THE afternoon on which we visited Herculaneum was in
melancholy contrast to the day we spent in Pompeii. The lingering
summer had at last saddened into something like autumnal
gloom, and that blue, blue sky of Naples was overcast. So, this
second draught of the spirit of the past had not only something of
the insipidity of custom, but brought rather a depression than a
lightness to our hearts. There was so little of Herculaneum: only

a few hundred square yards are exhumed, and we counted the houses easily on the fingers of one hand, leaving the thumb to stand for the few rods of street that, with its flagging of lava and narrow border of foot-walks, lay between; and though the custodian, apparently moved at our dejection, said that the excavation was to be resumed the very next week, the assurance did little to restore our cheerfulness. Indeed, I fancy that these old cities must needs be seen in the sunshine by those who would feel what gay lives they once led; by dimmer light they are very sullen spectres, and their doom still seems to brood upon them. I know that even Pompeii could not have been joyous that sunless afternoon, for what there was to see of mournful Herculaneum was as brilliant with colors as anything in the former city. Nay, I believe that the tints of the frescoes and painted columns were even brighter, and that the walls of the houses were far less ruinous than those of Pompeii. But no house was wholly freed from lava, and the little street ran at the rear of the buildings which were supposed to front on some grander avenue not yet exhumed. It led down, as the custodian pretended, to a wharf, and he showed an iron ring in the wall of the House of Argo, standing at the end of the street, to which, he said, his former fellow-citizens used to fasten their boats, though it was all dry enough there now.

There is evidence in Herculaneum of much more ambitious domestic architecture than seems to have been known in Pompeii. The ground plan of the houses in the two cities is alike; but in the former there was often a second story, as was proven by the charred ends of beams still protruding from the walls, while in the latter there is only one house which is thought to have aspired to a second floor. The House of Argo is also much larger than any in Pompeii, and its appointments were more magnificent. Indeed, we imagined that in this more purely Greek town we felt an atmosphere of better taste in everything than prevailed in the fashionable Roman watering-place, though this, too, was a summer resort of the "best society" of the empire. The mosaic pavements were exquisite, and the little bed-chambers dainty and delicious in their decorations. The lavish delight in color found expression in the vividest hues upon the walls, and not only were the columns of the garden painted, but the foliage of the capitals was variously tinted. The garden of the House of Argo was vaster than any of the classic world which we had yet seen, and was superb with a long colonnade of unbroken columns. Between these and the walls of the houses was a pretty pathway of mosaic, and in the midst once stood marble tables, under which the workmen exhuming the city found certain crouching skeletons. At one end was the dining-room, of course, and painted on the wall was a lady with a parasol.

I thought all Herculaneum sad enough, but the profusion of flowers growing wild in this garden gave it yet more tender and pathetic charm. Here—where so long ago the flowers had bloomed, and perished in the terrible blossoming of the mountain that sent up its fires in the awful similitude of Nature's harmless and lovely forms, and showered its destroying petals all abroad— was it not tragic to find again the soft tints, the graceful shapes, the sweet perfumes of the earth's immortal life? Of them that planted and tended and plucked and bore in their bosoms and twined in their hair these fragile children of the summer, what witness in the world? Only the crouching skeletons under the tables. Alas and alas!

V

THE skeletons went with us throughout Herculaneum, and descended into the cell, all green with damp, under the basilica, and lay down, fettered and manacled in the place of those found there beside the big bronze kettle in which the prisoners used to cook their dinners. How ghastly the thought of it was! If we had really seen this kettle and the skeletons there—as we did not—we could not have suffered more than we did. They took all the life out of the House of Perseus, and the beauty from his pretty little domestic temple to the Penates, and this was all there was left in Herculaneum to see.

"Is there nothing else?" we demanded of the custodian.

"Signori, this is all."

"It is mighty little."

"Perdoni, signore! ma—."

"Well," we said sourly to each other, glancing round at the walls of the pit, on the bottom of which the bit of city stands, "it is a good thing to know that Herculaneum amounts to nothing."

X. CAPRI AND CAPRIOTES

I

WE delayed some days in Naples in hopes of fine weather, and at last chose a morning that was warm and cloudy at nine o'clock, and burst into frequent passions of rain before we reached Sorrento at noon. The first half of the journey was made by rail, and brought us to Castellamare, whence we took carriage for Sorrento, and oranges, and rapture,—winding along the steep shore of the sea, and under the brows of wooded hills that rose high above us into the misty weather, and caught here and there the sunshine on their tops. In that heavenly climate no day can long be out of humor, and at Sorrento we found ours very pleasant, and rode delightedly through the devious streets, looking up to the terraced orange-groves on one hand, and down to the terraced orange-groves on the other, until at a certain turning of the way we encountered Antonino Occhio d'Argento, whom fate had appointed to be our boatman to Capri. We had never heard of Antonino before, and indeed had intended to take a boat from one of the hotels; but when this corsair offered us his services, there was that guile in his handsome face, that cunning in his dark eyes, which heart could not resist, and we halted our carriage and took him at once.

He kept his boat in one of those caverns which honeycomb the cliff under Sorrento, and afford a natural and admirable shelter for such small craft as may be dragged up out of reach of the waves, and here I bargained with him before finally agreeing to go with him to Capri. In Italy it is customary for a public carrier when engaged to give his employer as a pledge the sum agreed upon for the service, which is returned with the amount due him, at the end, if the service has been satisfactory; and I demanded of Antonino this *caparra*, as it is called. "What *caparra*?" said he, lifting the lid of his wicked eye with his forefinger, "this is the best *caparra*," meaning a face as honest and trustworthy as the devil's. The stroke confirmed my subjection to Antonino, and I took his boat without further parley, declining even to feel the muscles of his boatmen's arms, which he exposed to my touch in evidence that they were strong enough to row us swiftly to Capri. The men were only two in number, but they tossed the boat lightly into the surf, and then lifted me aboard, and rowed to the little pier from which the ladies and T. got in.

The sun rose, the water danced and sparkled, and presently we raised our sail, and took the gale that blew for Capri—an oblong height rising ten miles beyond out of the heart of the azure gulf. On the way thither there was little interest but that of natural beauty in the bold, picturesque coast we skirted for some distance; though on one mighty rock there were the ruins of a seaward-looking Temple of Hercules, with arches of the unmistakable Roman masonry, below which the receding waves rushed and poured over a jetting ledge in a thunderous cataract.

Antonino did his best to entertain us, and lectured us unceasingly upon virtue and his wisdom, dwelling greatly on the propriety and good policy of always speaking the truth. This spectacle of veracity became intolerable after a while, and I was goaded to say: "Oh then, if you never tell lies, you expect to go to Paradise." "Not at all," answered Antonino compassionately, "for I have sinned much. But the lie does n't go ahead" (*non va avanti*), added this Machiavelli of boatmen; yet I think he was mistaken, for he deceived us with perfect ease and admirable success. All along he had pretended that we could see Capri, visit the Blue Grotto, and return that day; but as we drew near the island, painful doubts began to trouble him, and he feared the sea would be too rough for the Grotto part of the affair. "But there will be an old man," he said, with a subtile air of prophecy, "waiting for us on the beach. This old man is one of the government guides to the Grotto, and he will say whether it is to be seen to-day."

And certainly there was the old man on the beach—a short patriarch, with his baldness covered by a kind of bloated woolen sock—a blear-eyed sage, and a barelegged. He waded through the surf toward the boat, and when we asked him whether the Grotto was to be seen, he paused knee-deep in the water (at a secret signal from Antonino, as I shall always believe), put on a face of tender solemnity, threw back his head a little, brought his hand to his cheek, expanded it, and said, "No; to-day, no! Tomorrow, yes!" Antonino leaped joyously ashore, and delivered us over to the old man, to be guided to the Hotel di Londra, while he threw his boat upon the land. He had reason to be contented, for this artifice of the patriarch of Capri relieved him from the necessity of verifying to me the existence of an officer of extraordinary powers in the nature of a consul, who, he said, would not permit boats to leave Capri for the mainland after five o'clock in the evening.

When it was decided that we should remain on the island till the morrow, we found so much time on our hands, after bargaining for our lodging at the Hotel di Londra, that we resolved to ascend the mountain to the ruins of the palaces of Tiberius, and to this end we contracted for the services of a certain of the muletresses that had gathered about the inn-gate, clamorously offering their beasts. The muletresses chosen were a matron of mature years and of a portly habit of body; her daughter, a mere child; and her niece, a very pretty girl of eighteen, with a voice soft and sweet as a bird's. They placed the ladies, one on each mule, and then, while the mother and daughter devoted themselves to the hind-quarters of the foremost animal, the lovely niece brought up the rear of the second beast, and the patriarch went before, and T. and I trudged behind. So the cavalcade ascended; first, from the terrace of the hotel overlooking the bit of shipping village on the beach, and next from the town of Capri, clinging to the hillsides, midway between sea and sky, until at last it reached the heights on which the ruins stand. Our way was through narrow lanes, bordered by garden walls; then through narrow streets bordered by dirty houses; and then again by gardens, but now of a better sort than the first, and belonging to handsome villas.

On the road our pretty muletress gossiped cheerfully, and our patriarch gloomily, and between the two we accumulated a store of information concerning the present inhabitants of Capri, which, I am sorry to say, has now for the most part failed me. I remember that they said most of the land-owners at Capri were Neapolitans, and that these villas were their country-houses; though they pointed out one of the stateliest of the edifices as belonging to a certain English physician who had come to visit Capri for a few days, and had now been living on the island twenty years, having married (said the muletress) the prettiest and poorest girl in the town. From this romance—something like which the muletress seemed to think might well happen concerning herself—we passed lightly to speak of kindred things, the muletress responding gayly between the blows she bestowed upon her beast. The accent of these Capriotes has something of German harshness and heaviness: they say *non bosso* instead of *non posso*, and *monto* instead of *mondo*, and interchange the *t* and *d* a good deal; and they use for father the Latin *pater*, instead of *padre*. But this girl's voice, as I said, was very musical, and the island's accent was sweet upon her tongue.

I.—What is your name?

She.—Caterina, little sir (*signorin*).

I.—And how old are you, Caterina?

She.—Eighteen, little sir.

I.—And are you betrothed?

She feigns not to understand; but the patriarch, who has dropped behind to listen to our discourse, explains,—"He asks if you are in love."

She.—Ah, no! little sir, not yet.

I.—No? A little late, it seems to me. I think there must be some good-looking youngster who pleases you—no?

She.—Ah, no! one must work, one cannot think of marrying. We are four sisters, and we have only the *buonamano* from hiring these mules, and we must spin and cook.

The Patriarch.—Don't believe her; she has two lovers.

She.—Ah, no! It is n't true. He tells a fib—he!

But, nevertheless, she seemed to love to be accused of lovers,— such is the guile of the female heart in Capri,—and laughed over the patriarch's wickedness. She confided that she ate maccaroni once a day, and she talked constantly of eating it just as the Northern Italians always talk of *polenta*. She was a true daughter of the isle, and had left it but once in her life, when she went to Naples. "Naples was beautiful, yes; but one always loves one's own country the best." She was very attentive and good, but at the end was rapacious of more and more *buonamano*. "Have patience with her, sir," said the blameless Antonino, who witnessed her greediness; "they do not understand certain matters here, poor little things!"

As for the patriarch, he was full of learning relative to himself and to Capri; and told me with much elaboration that the islanders lived chiefly by fishing, and gained something also by their vineyards. But they were greatly oppressed by taxes and the strict enforcement of the conscriptions, and they had little love for the Italian government, and wished the Bourbons back again. The Piedmontese, indeed, misgoverned them horribly. There was the Blue Grotto, for example: formerly travelers paid the guides five, six, ten francs for viewing it; but now the Piedmontese had made a tariff, and the poor guides could only extract a franc from each person. Things were in a ruinous condition.

By this we had arrived at a little inn on the top of the mountain, very near the ruins of the palaces. "Here," said the patriarch, "it is customary for strangers to drink a bottle of the wine of Tiberius." We obediently entered the hostelry, and the landlord—a white-toothed, brown-faced, good-humored peasant—gallantly ran forward and presented the ladies with bouquets of roses. We thought it a pretty and graceful act, but found later that it was to be paid for, like all pretty and graceful things in Italy; for when we came to settle for the wine, and the landlord wanted more than justice, he urged that he had presented the ladies with flowers,—yet he equally gave me his benediction when I refused to pay for his politeness.

"Now here," again said the patriarch in a solemn whisper, "you can see the Tarantella danced for two francs; whereas down at your inn, if you hire the dancers through your landlord, it will cost you five or six francs." The difference was tempting, and decided us in favor of an immediate Tarantella. The muletresses left their beasts to browse about the door of the inn and came into the little public room, where were already the wife and sister of the landlord, and took their places *vis-à-vis*, while the landlord seized his tambourine and beat from it a wild and lively measure. The women were barefooted and hoopless, and they gave us the Tarantella with all the beauty of natural movement and free floating drapery, and with all that splendid grace of pose which animates the antique statues and pictures of dancers. They swayed themselves in time with the music; then, filled with its passionate impulse, advanced and retreated and whirled away;—snapping their fingers above their heads, and looking over their shoulders with a gay and a laughing challenge to each other, they drifted through the ever-repeated figures of flight and wooing, and wove for us pictures of delight that remained upon the brain like the effect of long-pondered vivid colors, and still return to illumine and complete any representation of that indescribable dance.

Heaven knows what peril there might have been in the beauty and grace of the pretty muletress but for the spectacle of her fat aunt, who burlesqued some of her niece's airiest movements, and whose hard-bought buoyancy was pathetic. She earned her share of the spoils certainly, and she seemed glad when the dance was over, and went contentedly back to her mule.

The patriarch had early retired from the scene as from a vanity with which he was too familiar for enjoyment, and I found him, when the Tarantella was done, leaning on the curb of the precipitous rock immediately behind the inn, over which the Capriotes say Tiberius used to cast the victims of his pleasures after he was sated with them. These have taken their place in the insular imagination as Christian martyrs, though it is probable that the poor souls were anything but Nazarenes. It took a stone thrown from the brink of the rock twenty seconds to send back a response from the water below, and the depth was too dizzying to look into. So we looked instead toward Amalfi, across the Gulf of Salerno, and toward Naples, across her bay. On every hand the sea was flushed with sunset, and an unspeakable calm dwelt upon it, while the heights rising from it softened and softened in the distance, and withdrew themselves into dreams of ghostly solitude and phantom city. The Emperor Tiberius is well known to have been a man of sentiment, and he may often have sought this spot to enjoy the evening hour. It was convenient to his palace, and he could here give a filip to his jaded sensibilities by popping a boon companion over the cliff, and thus enjoy the fine poetic contrast which his perturbed and horrible spirit afforded to that scene of innocence and peace.

The poor patriarch was also a rascal in his small way, and he presently turned to me with a countenance full of cowardly trouble and base remorse. "I pray you, little sir, not to tell the landlord below there that you have seen the Tarantella danced here; for he has daughters and friends to dance it for strangers, and gets a deal of money by it. So, if he asks you to see it, do me the pleasure to say, lest he should take on (*pigliarsi*) with me about it: 'Thanks, but we saw the Tarantella at Pompeii!'"

The patriarch had a curious spice of malice in him, which prompted him to speak evil of all, and to as many as he dared. After we had inspected the ruins of the emperor's villa, a clownish imbecile of a woman, professing to be the wife of the peasant who had made the excavations, came forth out of a cleft in the rock and received tribute of us—why, I do not know. The patriarch abetted the extortion, but Parthianly remarked, as we turned away, "Her husband ought to be here; but this is a *festa* and he is drinking and gaming in the village," while the woman protested that he was sick at home. There was also a hermit living in great publicity among the ruins, and the patriarch did not spare him a sneering comment.[1]

He had even a bad word for Tiberius, and reproached the emperor for throwing people over the cliff. The only human creatures with whom he seemed to be in sympathy were the brigands of the mainland, of whom he spoke poetically as exiles and fugitives.

As for the palace of Tiberius, which we had come so far and so toilsomely to see, it must be confessed there was very little left of it. When he died, the Senate demolished his pleasure-houses at Capri, and left only those fragments of the beautiful brick masonry which yet remain, clinging indestructible to the rocks, and strewing the ground with rubbish. The recent excavations have discovered nothing besides the uninteresting foundations of the building, except a subterranean avenue leading from one part of the palace to another; this is walled with delicate brickwork, and exquisitely paved with white marble mosaic; and this was all that witnessed of the splendor of the wicked emperor. Nature, the all-forgetting, all-forgiving, that takes the red battlefield into her arms and hides it with blossom and harvest, could not remember his iniquity, greater than the multitudinous murder of war. The

---

[1] This hermit I have heard was not brought up to the profession of anchorite, but was formerly a shoemaker, and according to his own confession abandoned his trade because he could better indulge a lethargic habit in the character of religious recluse.

sea, which the despot's lust and fear had made so lonely, slept with the white sails of boats secure upon its breast; the little bays and inlets, the rocky clefts and woody dells had forgotten their desecration; and the gathering twilight, the sweetness of the garden-bordered pathway, and the serenity of the lonely landscape, helped us to doubt history.

We slowly returned to the inn by the road we had ascended, noting again the mansion of the surprising Englishman who had come to Capri for three months and had remained thirty years; passed through the darkness of the village,—dropped here and there with the vivid red of a lamp,—and so reached the inn at last, where wo found the landlord ready to have the Tarantella danced for us. We framed a discreeter fiction than that prepared for us by the patriarch, and went in to dinner, where there were two Danish gentlemen in dispute with as many rogues of boatmen, who, having contracted to take them back that night to Naples, were now trying to fly their bargain and remain at Capri till the morrow. The Danes beat them, however, and then sat down to dinner, and to long stories of the imposture and villainy of the Italians. One of them chiefly bewailed himself that the day before, having unwisely eaten a dozen oysters without agreeing first with the oysterman upon the price, he had been obliged to pay this scamp's extortionate demand to the full, since he was unable to restore him his property. We thought that something like this might have happened to an imprudent man in any country, but we did not the less join him in abusing the Italians—the purpose for which foreigners chiefly visit Italy.

II

STANDING on the height among the ruins of Tiberius's palace, the patriarch had looked out over the waters, and predicted for the morrow the finest weather that had ever been known in that region; but in spite of this prophecy the day dawned stormily, and at breakfast time we looked out doubtfully on waves lashed by driving rain. The entrance to the Blue Grotto, to visit which we had come to Capri, is by a semicircular opening, some three feet in width and two feet in height, and just large enough to admit a small boat. One lies flat in the bottom of this, waits for the impulse of a beneficent wave, and is carried through the mouth of the cavern, and rescued from it in like manner by some receding billow. When the wind is in the wrong quarter, it is impossible to enter the grot at all; and we waited till nine o'clock for the storm to abate before we ventured forth. In the mean time one of the Danish gentlemen, who—after assisting his companion to compel the boatmen to justice the night before—had stayed at Capri, and had risen early to see the grotto, returned from it, and we besieged him with a hundred questions concerning it. But he preserved the wise silence of the boy who goes in to see the six-legged calf, and comes out impervious to the curiosity of all the boys who are doubtful whether the monster is worth their money. Our Dane would merely say that it was now possible to visit the Blue Grotto; that he had seen it; that he was glad he *had* seen it. As to its blueness, Messieurs—yes, it is blue. *C'est à dire.* . . .

The ladies had been amusing themselves with a perusal of the hotel register, and the notes of admiration or disgust with which the different sojourners at the inn had filled it. As a rule, the English people found fault with the poor little hostelry and the French people praised it. Commander Joshing and Lieutenant Pattent, R.N., of the former nation, "were cheated by the donkey women, and thought themselves extremely fortunate to have escaped with their lives from the effects of Capri vintage. The landlord was an old Cossack." On the other hand, we read, "J. Cruttard, homme de lettres, a passé quinze jours ici, et n'a eu que des félicités du patron de cet hôtel et de sa famille." Cheerful man of letters! His good-natured record will keep green a name little known to literature. Who are G. Bradshaw, Duke of New York, and Signori Jones and Andrews, Hereditary Princes of the United States? Their patrician names followed the titles of several English nobles in the register. But that which most interested the ladies in this record was the warning of a terrified British matron against any visit to the Blue Grotto except in the very calmest weather.

The British matron penned her caution after an all but fatal experience. The ladies read it aloud to us, and announced that for themselves they would be contented with pictures of the Blue Grotto and our account of its marvels.

On the beach below the hotel lay the small boats of the guides to the Blue Grotto, and we descended to take one of them. The fixed rate is a franc for each person. The boatmen wanted five francs for each of us. We explained that although not indigenous to Capri, or even Italy, we were not of the succulent growth of travelers, and would not be eaten. We retired to our vantage-ground on the heights. The guides called us to the beach again. They would take us for three francs apiece, or say six francs for both of us. We withdrew furious to the heights again, where we found honest Antonino, who did us the pleasure to yell to his fellow-scoundrels on the beach, "You had better take these signori for a just price. They are going to the syndic to complain of you." At which there arose a lamentable outcry among the boatmen, and they called with one voice for us to come down and go for a franc apiece.

We had scarcely left the landing of the hotel in the boat of the patriarch—for I need hardly say he was first and most rapacious of the plundering crew—when we found ourselves in very turbulent waters, in the face of mighty bluffs, rising inaccessible from the sea. Here and there, where their swarthy fronts were softened with a litle verdure, goat-paths wound up and down among the rocks; and midway between the hotel and the grotto, in a sort of sheltered nook, we saw the Roman masonry of certain antique baths—baths of Augustus, says Valery; baths of Tiberius, say the Capriotes, zealous for the honor of their infamous hero. Howbeit, this was all we saw on the way to the Blue Grotto. Every moment the waves rose higher, emulous of the bluffs, which would not have afforded a foothold, or anything to cling to, had we been upset and washed against them—and we began to talk of the immortality of the soul. As we neared the grotto, the patriarch entertained us with stories of the perilous adventures of people who insisted upon entering it in stormy weather,—especially of a French painter who had been imprisoned in it four days, and kept alive only on rum, which the patriarch supplied him, swimming into the grotto with a bottleful at a time. "And behold us arrived, gentlemen!" said he, as he brought the boat skillfully around in front of the small semicircular opening at the base of the lofty bluff. We lie flat on the bottom of the boat, and complete the immersion of that part of our clothing which the driving torrents of rain had spared. The wave of destiny rises with us upon its breast—sinks, and we are inside of the Blue Grotto. Not so much blue as gray, however, and the water about the mouth of it green rather than azure. They say that on a sunny day both the water and the roof of the cavern are of the vividest cerulean tint—and I saw the grotto so represented in the windows of the paint-shops at Naples. But to my own experience it did not differ from other caves in color or form: there was the customary clamminess in the air; the sound of dropping water; the sense of dull and stupid solitude,—a little relieved in this case by the mighty music of the waves breaking against the rocks outside. The grot is not great in extent, and the roof in the rear shelves gradually down to the water. Valery says that some remains of a gallery have caused the supposition that the grotto was once the scene of Tiberius's pleasures; and the Prussian painter who discovered the cave was led to seek it by something he had read of a staircase by which Barbarossa used to descend into a subterranean retreat from the town of Anacapri on the mountain-top. The slight fragment of ruin which we saw in one corner of the cave might be taken in confirmation of both theories; but the patriarch attributed the work to Barbarossa, being probably tired at last of hearing Tiberius so much talked about.

We returned, soaked and disappointed, to the hotel, where we found Antonino very doubtful about the possibility of getting back that day to Sorrento, and disposed, when pooh-poohed out of the notion of bad weather, to revive the fiction of a prohibitory consul. He was staying in Capri at our expense, and the honest fellow would willingly have spent a fortnight there.

We summoned the landlord to settlement, and he came with all his household to present the account,—each one full of visible longing, yet restrained from asking *buonamano* by a strong sense of previous contact. It was a deadly struggle with them, but they conquered themselves, and blessed us as we departed. The pretty muletress took leave of us on the beach, and we set sail for Sorrento, the ladies crouching in the bottom of the boat, and taking their seasickness in silence. As we drew near the beautiful town, we saw how it lay on a plateau, at the foot of the mountains, but high above the sea. Antonino pointed out to us the house of Tasso,—in which the novelist Cooper also resided when in Sorrento,—a white house not handsomer nor uglier than the rest, with a terrace looking out over the water. The bluffs are pierced by numerous arched caverns, as I have said, giving shelter to the fishermen's boats, and here and there a devious stairway mounts to their crests. Up one of these we walked, noting how in the house above us the people, with that puerility usually mixed with the Italian love of beauty, had placed painted busts of terra-cotta in the windows to simulate persons looking out. There was nothing to blame in the breakfast we found ready at the Hotel Rispoli; or in the grove of slender, graceful orange-trees in the midst of which the hotel stood, and which had lavished the fruit in every direction on the ground.

Antonino attended us to our carriage when we went away. He had kept us all night at Capri, it is true, and he had brought us in at the end for a prodigious *buonamano*; yet I cannot escape the conviction that he parted from us with an unfulfilled purpose of greater plunder, and I have a compassion, which I here declare, for the strangers who fell next into his hands. He was good enough at the last moment to say that his name, Silver-Eye, was a nickname given him according to a custom of the Sorrentines; and he made us a farewell bow that could not be bought in America for money.

At the station of Castellamare sat a curious cripple on the stones,—a man with little, short, withered legs, and a pleasant face. He showed us the ticket-office, and wanted nothing for the politeness. After we had been in the waiting-room a brief time, he came swinging himself in upon his hands, followed by another person, who, when the cripple had planted himself finally and squarely on the ground, whipped out a tape from his pocket and took his measure for a suit of clothes, the cripple twirling and twisting himself about in every way for the tailor's convenience. Nobody was surprised or amused at the sight, and when his measure was thus publicly taken, the cripple gravely swung himself out as he had swung himself in.

XI. BETWEEN ROME AND NAPLES

ONE day it became plain even to our reluctance that we could not stay in Naples forever, and the next morning we took the train for Rome. The Villa Reale put on its most alluring charm to him that ran down before breakfast to thrid once more its pathways bordered with palms and fountains and statues; the bay beside it purpled and twinkled in the light that made silver of the fishermen's sails; far away rose Vesuvius with his nightcap of mist still hanging about his shoulders; all around rang and rattled Naples. The city was never so fair before, nor could ever have been so hard to leave; and at the last moment the landlord of the Hotel Washington must needs add a supreme pang by developing into a poet, and presenting me with a copy of a comedy he had written.

Nobody who cares to travel with decency and comfort can take the second-class cars on the road between Naples and Rome, though these are perfectly good everywhere else in Italy. The Papal city makes her influence felt for shabbiness and uncleanliness wherever she can, and her management seems to prevail on this railway. A glance into the second-class cars reconciled us to the first class,—which in themselves were bad,—and we took our places almost contentedly.

The road passed through the wildest country we had seen in Italy; and presently a rain began to fall and made it drearier than ever. The land was much grown up with thickets of hazel, and was here and there sparsely wooded with oaks. Under these, hogs were feeding upon the acorns, and the wet swineherds were steaming over fires built at their roots. In some places the forest was quite dense; in other places it fell entirely away, and left the rocky hillside bare, and solitary but for the sheep that nibbled at the scanty grass, and the shepherds that leaned upon their crooks and motionlessly stared at us as we rushed by. As we drew near Rome, the scenery grew lonelier yet; the land rose into desolate, sterile, stony heights, without a patch of verdure on their nakedness, and at last abruptly dropped into the gloomy expanse of the Campagna.

The towns along the route had little to interest us in their looks, though at San Germano we caught a glimpse of the famous old convent of Monte-Cassino, perched aloft on its cliff and looking like a part of the rock on which it was built. Fancy now loves to climb that steep acclivity, and wander through the many-volumed library of the ancient Benedictine retreat, and on the whole finds it less fatiguing and certainly less expensive than actual ascent and acquaintance with the monastery would have been. Two Croatian priests, who shared our compartment of the railway carriage, first drew our notice to the place, and were enthusiastic about it for many miles after it was out of sight. What gentle and pleasant men they were, and how hard it seemed that they should be priests and Croats! They told us all about the city of Spalato, where they lived, and gave us such a glowing account of Dalmatian poets and poetry that we began to doubt at last if the seat of literature was not somewhere on the east coast of the Adriatic; and I hope we left them the impression that the literary centre of the world was not a thousand miles from the horse-car office in Harvard Square.

Here and there repairs were going forward on the railroad, and most of the laborers were women. They were straight and handsome girls, and moved with a stately grace under the baskets of earth balanced on their heads. Brave black eyes they had, such as love to look and be looked at; they were not in the least hurried by their work, but desisted from it to gaze at the passengers whenever the train stopped. They all wore their beautiful peasant costume,—the square white linen headdress falling to the shoulders, the crimson bodice, and the red scant skirt; and how they contrived to keep themselves so clean at their work, and to look so spectacular in it all, remains one of the many Italian mysteries.

Another of these mysteries we beheld in the little beggar-boy at Isoletta. He stood at the corner of the station quite mute and motionless during our pause, and made no sign of supplication or entreaty. He let his looks beg for him. He was perfectly beautiful and exceedingly picturesque. Where his body was not quite naked, his jacket and trousers hung in shreds and points; his long hair grew through the top of his hat, and fell over like a plume. Nobody could resist him; people ran out of the cars, at the risk of being left behind, to put coppers into the little dirty hand held languidly out to receive them. The boy thanked none, smiled on none, but looked curiously and cautiously at all, with the quick perception and the illogical conclusions of his class and race. As we started he did not move, but remained in his attitude of listless tranquillity. As we glanced back, the mystery of him seemed to be solved for a moment: he would stand there until he grew up into a graceful, prayerful, pitiless brigand, and then he would rend from travel the tribute now so freely given him. But after all, though his future seemed clear, and he appeared the type of a strange and hardly reclaimable people, he was not quite a solution to the Neapolitan puzzle.

XII. ROMAN PEARLS

I

THE first view of the ruins in the Forum brought a keen sense of disappointment. I knew that they could only be mere fragments and rubbish, but I was not prepared to find them so. I learned that I had all along secretly hoped for some dignity of neighborhood, some affectionate solicitude on the part of Nature to redeem these works of Art from the destruction that had befallen them. But in hollows below the level of the dirty cowfield, wandered over by evil-eyed buffaloes, and obscenely defiled by wild beasts of men, there stood here an arch, there a pillar, yonder a cluster of columns crowned by a bit of frieze; and yonder again, a fragment of temple, half-gorged by the façade of a hideous rococo church; then a height of vaulted brickwork, and, leading on to the Coliseum, another arch, and then incoherent columns overthrown and mixed with dilapidated walls—mere phonographic consonants, dumbly representing the past, out of which all vocal glory had departed. The Coliseum itself does not much better express a certain phase of Roman life than the Arena at

Verona; it is larger only to the foot-rule, and it seemed not grander otherwise, while it is vastly more ruinous. Even the Pantheon failed to impress me at first sight, though I found myself disposed to return to it again and again, and to be more and more affected by it.

Modern Rome appeared, first and last, hideous. It is the least interesting town in Italy, and the architecture is hopelessly ugly—especially the architecture of the churches. The Papal city contrives at the beginning to hide the Imperial city from your thought, as it hides it in such a great degree from your eye, and old Rome only occurs to you in a sort of stupid wonder over the depth at which it is buried. I confess that I was glad to get altogether away from it after a first look at the ruins in the Forum, and to take refuge in the Conservatorio delle Mendicanti, where we were charged to see the little Virginia G. The Conservatorio, though a charitable institution, is not so entirely meant for mendicants as its name would imply, but none of the many young girls there were the children of rich men. They were often enough of parentage actually hungry and ragged, but they were often also the daughters of honest poor folk, who paid a certain sum toward their maintenance and education in the Conservatorio. Such was the case with little Virginia, whose father was at Florence, doubly impeded from seeing her by the fact that he had fought against the Pope for the Republic of 1848, and by the other fact that he had since wrought the Pope a yet deadlier injury by turning Protestant.

Ringing a garrulous bell that continued to jingle some time after we were admitted, we found ourselves in a sort of reception-room, of the temperature of a cellar, and in the presence of a portress who was perceptibly preserved from mould only by the great pot of coals that stood in the centre of the place. Some young girls, rather pretty than not, attended the ancient woman, and kindly acted as the ear-trumpet through which our wishes were conveyed to her mind. The Conservatorio was not, so far, as conventual as we had imagined it; but as the gentleman of the party was strongly guarded by female friends, and asked at once to see the Superior, he concluded that there was, perhaps, something so unusually reassuring to the recluses in his appearance and manner that they had not thought it necessary to behave very rigidly. It later occurred to this gentleman that the promptness with which the pretty mendicants procured him an interview with the Superior had a flavor of self-interest in it, and that he who came to the Conservatorio in the place of a father might have been for a moment ignorantly viewed as a yet dearer and tenderer possibility. From whatever danger there was in this error the Superior soon appeared to rescue him, and we were invited into a more ceremonious apartment on the first floor, and the little Virginia was sent for. The visit of the strangers caused a tumult and interest in the quiet old Conservatorio of which it is hard to conceive now, and the excitement grew tremendous when it appeared that the signori were Americani and Protestanti. We imparted a savor of novelty and importance to Virginia herself, and when she appeared, the Superior and her assistant looked at her with no small curiosity and awe, of which the little maiden instantly became conscious, and began to take advantage. Accompanying us over the building and through the grounds, she cut her small friends wherever she met them, and was not more than respectful to the assistant.

It was from an instinct of hospitality that we were shown the Conservatorio, and instructed in regard to all its purposes. We saw the neat dormitories with their battalions of little white beds; the kitchen with its gigantic coppers for boiling broth, and the refectory with the smell of the frugal dinners of generations of mendicants in it. The assistant was very proud of the neatness of everything, and was glad to talk of that, or, indeed, anything else. It appeared that the girls were taught reading, writing, and plain sewing when they were young, and that the Conservatorio was chiefly sustained by pious contributions and bequests. Any lingering notion of the conventual character of the place was dispelled by the assistant's hurrying to say, "And when we can get the poor things well married, we are glad to do so."

"But how does any one ever see them?"

"Eh! well, that is easily managed. Once a month we dress the marriageable girls in their best, and take them for a walk in the street. If an honest young man falls in love with one of them going by, he comes to the Superior, and describes her as well as he can, and demands to see her. She is called, and if both are pleased, the marriage is arranged. You see it is a very simple affair."

And there was, in the assistant's mind, nothing odd in the whole business, insomuch that I felt almost ashamed of marveling at it.

Issuing from the back door of the convent, we ascended by stairs and gateways into garden spaces, chiefly planted with turnips and other vegetables, and curiosly adorned with fragments of antique statuary, and here and there a fountain in a corner, trickling from moss-grown rocks, and falling into a trough of travertine, about the feet of some poor old goddess or Virtue who had forgotten what her name was.

Once, the assistant said, speaking as if the thing had been within her recollection, though it must have been centuries before, the antiquities of the Conservatorio were much more numerous and striking; but they were now removed to the different museums. Nevertheless they had still a beautiful prospect left, which we were welcome to enjoy if we would follow her; and presently, to our surprise, we stepped from the garden upon the roof of the Temple of Peace. The assistant had not boasted without reason: away before us stretched the Campagna, a level waste, and empty, but for the arched lengths of the aqueducts that seemed to stalk down from the ages across the melancholy expanse like files of giants, with now and then a ruinous gap in the line, as if one had fallen out weary by the way. The city all around us glittered asleep in the dim December sunshine, and far below us—on the length of the Forum over which the Appian Way stretched from the Capitoline Hill under the Arch of Septimius Severus and the Arch of Titus to the Arch of Constantine, leaving the Coliseum on the left, and losing itself in the foliage of the suburbs—the Past seemed struggling to emerge from the ruins, and to shape and animate itself anew. The effort was more successful than that which we had helped the Past to make when standing on the level of the Forum; but Antiquity must have been painfully conscious of the incongruity of the red-legged Zouaves wandering over the grass, and the bewildered tourists trying to make her out with their Murrays.

In a day or two after this we returned again to our Conservatorio, where we found that the excitement created by our first visit had been kept fully alive by the events attending the photographing of Virginia for her father. Not only Virginia was there to receive us, but her grandmother also—an old, old woman, dumb through some infirmity of age, who could only weep and smile in token of her content. I think she had but a dim idea, after all, of what went on beyond the visible fact of Virginia's photograph, and that she did not quite understand how we could cause it to be taken for her son. She was deeply compassionated by the Superior, who rendered her pity with a great deal of gesticulation, casting up her eyes, shrugging her shoulders, and sighing grievously. But the assistant's cheerfulness could not be abated even by the spectacle of extreme age; and she made the most of the whole occasion, recounting with great minuteness all the incidents of the visit to the photographer's, and running to get the dress Virginia sat in, that we might see how exactly it was given in the picture. Then she gave us much discourse concerning the Conservatorio and its usages, and seemed not to wish us to think that life there was altogether eventless. "Here we have a little amusement also," she said. "The girls have their relatives to visit them sometimes, and then in the evening they dance. Oh, they enjoy themselves! I am half old (*mezzo vecchia*). I am done with these things. But for youth, always kept down, something lively is wanted."

When we took leave of these simple folks, we took leave of almost the only natural and unprepared aspect of Italian life which we were to see in Rome; but we did not know this at the time.

II

INDEED, it seems to me that all moisture of romance and adventure has been well-nigh sucked out of travel in Italy, and that compared with the old time, when the happy wayfarer journeyed by vettura through the innumerable little states of the Peninsula,—halted every other mile to show his passport, and robbed by customs officers in every color of shabby uniform and every variety of cocked hat,—the present railroad period is one of but stale and inspid flavor. Much of local life and color remains, of course; but the hurried traveler sees little of it, and, passed from one grand hotel to another, without material change in the cooking or the methods of extortion, he might nearly as well remain at Paris. The Italians, who live to so great extent by the travel through their country, learn our abominable languages and minister to our detestable comfort and propriety, till we have slight chance to know them as we once could,—musical, picturesque, and full of sweet, natural knaveries and graceful falsehood. Rome really belongs to the Anglo-Saxon nations, and the Pope and the Past seem to be carried on entirely for our diversion. Everything is systematized as thoroughly as in a museum where the objects are all ticketed; and our prejudices are consulted even down to almsgiving. Honest Beppo is gone from the steps in the Piazza di Spagna, and now the beggars are labeled like policemen, with an immense plate bearing the image of St. Peter, so that you may know you give to a worthy person when you bestow charity on one of them, and not, alas! to some abandoned impostor, as in former days. One of these highly recommended mendicants gave the last finish to the system, and begged of us in English! No custodian will answer you, if he can help it, in the Italian which he speaks so exquisitely, preferring to speak bad French instead, and in all the shops on the Corso the English tongue is *de rigueur*.

After our dear friends at the Conservatorio, I think we found one of the most simple and interesting of Romans in the monk who showed us the Catacombs of St. Sebastian. These catacombs, he assured us, were not restored like those of St. Calixtus, but were just as the martyrs left them; and, as I do not remember to have read anywhere that they are formed merely of long, low, narrow, wandering underground passages, lined on either side with tombs in tiers like berths on a steamer, and expanding here and there into small square chambers, bearing the traces of ancient frescoes, and evidently used as chapels,—I venture to offer the information here. The reader is to keep in his mind a darkness broken by the light of wax tapers, a close smell, and crookedness and narrowness, or he cannot realize the catacombs as they are in fact. Our monkish guide, before entering the passage leading from the floor of the church to the tombs, in which there was still some "fine small dust" of the martyrs, warned us that to touch it was to incur the penalty of excommunication, and then gently craved pardon for having mentioned the fact. But, indeed, it was only to persons who showed a certain degree of reverence that these places were now exhibited; for some Protestants who had been permitted there had stolen handfuls of the precious ashes, merely to throw away. I assured him that I thought them beasts to do it; and I was afterwards puzzled to know what should attract their wantonness in the remnants of mortality, hardly to be distinguished from the common earth out of which the catacombs were dug.

III

RETURNING to the church above we found, kneeling before one of the altars, two pilgrims,—a man and a woman. The latter was habited in a nun-like dress of black, and the former in a long pilgrim's coat of coarse blue stuff. He bore a pilgrim's staff in his hand, and showed under his close hood a fine, handsome, reverent face, full of a sort of tender awe, touched with the pathos of penitence. In attendance upon the two was a dapper little silk-hatted man, with rogue so plainly written in his devotional countenance that I was not surprised to be told that he was a species of spiritual *valet de place*, whose occupation it was to attend pilgrims on their tour to the Seven Churches at which these devotees pray in Rome, and there to direct their orisons and join in them.

It was not to the pilgrims, but to the heretics that the monk now uncovered the precious marble slab on which Christ stood when he met Peter flying from Rome and turned him back. You are shown the prints of the divine feet, which the conscious stone received and keeps forever; and near at hand is one of the arrows with which St. Sebastian was shot. We looked at these things critically, having to pay for the spectacle; but the pilgrims and their guide were all faith and wonder.

I remember seeing nothing else so finely superstitious at Rome. In a chapel near the Church of St. John Lateran are, as is well known, the marble steps which once belonged to Pilate's house, and which the Saviour is said to have ascended when he went to trial before Pilate. The steps are protected against the wear and tear of devotion by a stout casing of wood, and they are constantly covered with penitents, who ascend and descend them upon their knees. Most of the pious people whom I saw in this act were children, and the boys enjoyed it with a good deal of giggling, as a very amusing feat. Some old and haggard women gave the scene all the dignity which it possessed; but certain well-dressed ladies and gentlemen were undeniably awkward and absurd, and I was led to doubt if there were not an incompatibility between the abandon of simple faith and the care of good clothes.

IV

IN all other parts of Italy one hears constant talk among travelers of the malaria at Rome. But in Rome itself the malaria is laughed at by the foreign residents,—who, nevertheless, go out of the city in midsummer. The Romans, to the number of a hundred thousand or so, remain there the whole year round, and I am bound to say I never saw a healthier, robuster-looking population. The cheeks of the French soldiers, too, whom we met at every turn, were red as their trousers, and they seemed to flourish on the imputed unwholesomeness of the atmosphere. All at Rome are united in declaring that the fever exists at Naples, and that sometimes those who have taken it there come and die in Rome, in order to give the city a bad name; and I think this very likely.

Rome is certainly dirty, however, though there is a fountain in every square, and you are never out of the sound of falling water. The Corso and some of the principal streets do not so much impress you with their filth as with their dullness; but that part of the city where some of the most memorable relics of antiquity are to be found is unimaginably vile. The least said of the state of the archways of the Coliseum the soonest mended; and I have already spoken of the Forum. The streets near the Theatre of Pompey are almost impassable, and the so-called House of Rienzi is a stable, fortified against approach by a *fossé* of excrement. A noisome smell seems to be esteemed the most appropriate offering to the memory of ancient Rome, and I am not sure that the moderns are mistaken in this. In the rascal streets in the neighborhood of the most august ruins, the people turn round to stare at the stranger as he passes them; they are all dirty, and his decency must be no less a surprise to them than the neatness of the French soldiers amid all the filth is a puzzle to him. We wandered about a long time in such places one day, looking for the Tarpeian Rock, less for Tarpeia's sake than for the sake of Hawthorne's Miriam and Donatello and the Model. There are two Tarpeian rocks, between which the stranger takes his choice; and we must have chosen the wrong one, for it seemed but a shallow gulf compared to that in our fancy. We were somewhat disappointed; but then, Niagara disappoints one; and as for Mont Blanc. . . .

v

It is worth while for every one who goes to Rome to visit the Church of St. Peter's; but it is scarcely worth while for me to describe it, or for every one to go up into the bronze globe on the top of the cupola. In fact, this is a great labor, and there is nothing to be seen from the crevices in the ball which cannot be far more comfortably seen from the roof of the church below.

The companions of our ascent to the latter point were an English lady and gentleman, brother and sister, and both Catholics, as they at once told us. The lady and myself spoke for some time in the Tuscan tongue before we discovered that neither of us was Italian, after which we paid each other some handsome compliments upon our fluency and perfection of accent. The gentleman was a pleasant purple porpoise from the waters of

Chili, whither he had wandered from the English coasts in early youth. He had two leading ideas: one concerned the Pope, to whom he had just been presented, and whom he viewed as the best and blandest of beings; the other related to his boy, then in England, whom he called Jack Spratt, and considered the grandest and greatest of boys. With the view from the roof of the church this gentleman did not much trouble himself. He believed Jack Spratt could ride up to the roof where we stood on his donkey. As to the great bronze globe which we were hurrying to enter, he seemed to regard it merely as a rival in rotundity, and made not the slightest motion to follow us.

I should be loath to vex the reader with any description of the scene before us and beneath us, even if I could faithfully portray it. But I recollect, with a pleasure not to be left unrecorded, the sweetness of the great fountain playing in the square before the church, and the harmony in which the city grew in every direction from it, like an emanation from its music, till the last house sank away into the pathetic solitude of the Campagna, with nothing beyond but the snow-capped mountains lighting up the remotest distance. At the same time I experienced a rapture in reflecting that I had underpaid three hackmen during my stay in Rome, and thus contributed to avenge my race for ages of oppression.

The vastness of St. Peter's itself is best felt in looking down upon the interior from the gallery that surrounds the inside of the dome, and in comparing one's own littleness with the greatness of all the neighboring mosaics. But as to the beauty of the temple, I could not find it without or within.

VI

In Rome one's fellow-tourists are a constant source of gratification and surprise. I thought that American travelers were by no means the most absurd among those we saw, nor even the loudest in their approval of the Eternal City. A certain order of German greenness affords, perhaps, the pleasantest pasturage for the ruminating mind. For example, at the Villa Ludovisi there was, beside numerous Englishry in detached bodies, a troop of Germans, chiefly young men, frugally pursuing the Sehenswürdigkeiten in the social manner of their nation. They took their enjoyment very noisily, and wrangled together with furious amiability as they looked at Guercino's "Aurora." Then two of them parted from the rest, and went to a little summer-house in the gardens, while the others followed us to the top of the Casino. There they caught sight of their friends in the arbor, and the spectacle appeared to overwhelm them. They bowed, they took off their hats, they waved their handkerchiefs. It was not eough: one young fellow mounted on the balustrade of the roof at his neck's risk, lifted his hat on his cane, and flourished it in greeting to the heart's-friends in the arbor, from whom he had parted two minutes before.

In strange contrast to the producer of this enthusiasm, so pumped and so unmistakably mixed with beer, a fat and pallid Englishwoman sat in a chair upon the roof and coldly, coldly sketched the lovely landscape. And she and the blonde young English girl beside her pronounced a little dialogue together, which I give, because I saw that they meant it for the public:

The Young Girl.—I wonder, you knoa, you don't draw-ow St. Petuh's!

The Artist.—O ah, you knoa, I can draw-ow St. Petuh's from so mennee powints.

I am afraid that the worst form of American greenness appears abroad in a desire to be perfectly up in critical appreciation of the arts, and to approach the great works in the spirit of the connoisseur. The ambition is not altogether a bad one. A fellow-countryman told me that he had not yet seen Raphael's "Transfiguration," because he wished to prepare his mind for understanding the original by first looking at all the copies he could find.

VII

THE Basilica San Paolo fuori le Mura surpasses everything in splendor of marble and costly stone—porphyry, malachite, alabaster—and luxury of gilding that is to be seen at Rome. But I chiefly remember it because on the road that leads to it, through scenes as quiet and peaceful as if history had never known them, lies the Protestant graveyard in which Keats is buried. Quite by chance the driver mentioned it, pointing in the direction of the cemetery with his whip. We eagerly dismounted and repaired to the gate, where we were met by the son of the sexton, who spoke English through the beauteous line of a curved Hebrew nose. Perhaps a Christian could not be found in Rome to take charge of these heretic graves, though Christians can be got to do almost anything there for money. However, I do not think a Catholic would have kept the place in better order, or more intelligently received our reverent curiosity. It was the new burial-ground which we had entered, and which is a little to the right of the elder cemetery. It was very beautiful and tasteful in every way; the names upon the stones were chiefly English and Scotch, with here and there an American's. But affection drew us to the prostrate tablet inscribed with the words, "Percy Bysshe Shelley, Cor Cordium," and then we were ready to go to the grave of him for whom we all feel so deep a tenderness. The grave of John Keats is one of few in the old burying-ground, and lies almost in the shadow of the pyramid of Caius Cestius; and I could not help thinking of the wonder the Roman would have felt could he have known into what unnamable richness and beauty his Greek faith had ripened in the heart of the poor poet, where it was mixed with so much pain. Doubtless, in his time, a prominent citizen like Caius Cestius was a leading member of the temple in his neighborhood, and regularly attended sacrifice: it would have been but decent; and yet I fancied that a man immersed like him in affairs might have learned with surprise the inner and more fragrant meaning of the symbols with the outside of which his life was satisfied; and I was glad to reflect that in our day a like thing is impossible.

The grave of our beloved poet is sunken to the level of the common earth, and is only marked by the quaintly lettered, simple stone bearing the famous epitaph. While at Rome I heard talk of another and grander monument which some members of the Keats family were to place over the dust of their great kinsman.

But, for one, I hope this may never be done, even though the original stone should also be left there, as was intended. Let the world still keep unchanged this shrine, to which it can repair with at once pity and tenderness and respect. A rose-tree and some sweet-smelling bushes grew upon the grave, and the roses were in bloom. We asked leave to take one of them; but at last could only bring ourselves to gather some of the fallen petals. Our Hebrew guide was willing enough, and unconsciously set us a little example of wantonness; for while he listened to our explanation of the mystery which had puzzled him ever since he had learned English, namely, why the stone should say "*writ* on water," and not *written*, he kept plucking mechanically at one of the fragrant shrubs, pinching away the leaves, and rending the tender twig, till, remembering the once-sensitive dust from which it grew, one waited for the tortured tree to cry out to him with a voice of words and blood, "Perchè mi schianti?"

VIII

One Sunday afternoon we went with some artistic friends to visit the studio of the great German painter, Overbeck; and since I first read Uhland I have known no pleasure so illogical as I felt in looking at this painter's drawings. In the sensuous heart of objective Italy he treats the themes of mediæval Catholicism with the most subjective feeling, and I thought I perceived in his work the enthusiasm which led many Protestant German painters and poets of the romantic school back into the twilight of the Romish faith, in the hope that they might thus realize to themselves something of the earnestness which animated the elder Christian artists.

Walking from the painter's house, two of us parted with the rest on the steps of the Church of Santa Maria Maggiore, and pursued our stroll through the gate of San Lorenzo out upon the Campagna, which tempts and tempts the sojourner at Rome, until at last he must go and see—if it will give him the fever. And, alas! there I caught the Roman fever—the longing that burns one who has once been in Rome to go again—that will not be cured by all the cool contemptuous things he may think or say of the Eternal City; that fills him with fond memories of its fascination, and makes it forever desired.

We walked far down the dusty road beyond the city walls, and then struck out from the highway across the wild meadows of the Campagna. They were weedy and desolate, seamed by shaggy grass-grown ditches, and deeply pitted with holes made in search for catacombs. There was here and there a farmhouse amid the wild lonesomeness, but oftener a round, hollow, roofless tomb, from which the dust and memory of the dead had long been blown away, and through the top of which—fringed and overhung with grasses, and opening like a great eye—the evening sky looked mysteriously sad. One of the fields was full of grim, wide-horned cattle, and in another there were four or five buffaloes lying down and chewing their cuds,—holding their heads horizontally in the air, and with an air of gloomy wickedness which nothing could exceed in their cruel black eyes, glancing about in visible pursuit of some object to toss and gore. There were also many canebrakes, in which the wind made a mournful rustling after the sun had set in golden glitter on the roofs of the Roman churches and the transparent night had fallen upon the scene.

In all our ramble we met not a soul, and I scarcely know what it is makes this walk upon the Campagna one of my vividest recollections of Rome, unless it be the opportunity it gave me to weary myself upon that many-memoried ground as freely as if it had been a woods-pasture in Ohio. Nature, where history was so august, was perfectly simple and motherly, and did so much to make me at home, that, as the night thickened and we plunged here and there into ditches and climbed fences, and struggled, heavy-footed, back through the suburbs to the city gate, I felt as if half my boyhood had been passed upon the Campagna.

IX

Pasquino, like most other great people, is not very interesting upon close approach. There is no trace now in his aspect to show that he has ever been satirical; but the humanity that the sculptor gave him is imperishable, though he has lost all character as a public censor. The torso is at first glance merely a shapeless mass of stone, but the life can never die out of that which has been shaped by art to the likeness of a man, and a second look restores the lump to full possession of form and expression. For this reason I lament that statues should ever be restored except by sympathy and imagination.

X

WHEN the Tiber, according to its frequent habit, rises and inundates the city, the Pantheon is one of the first places to be flooded—the sacristan told us. The water climbs above the altar-tops, sapping, in its recession, the cement of the fine marbles which incrust the columns, so that about their bases the pieces have to be continually renewed. Nothing vexes you so much in the Pantheon as your consciousness of these and other repairs. Bad as ruin is, I think I would rather have the old temple ruinous in every part than restored as you find it. The sacristan felt the wrongs of the place keenly, and said, referring to the removal of the bronze roof, which took place some centuries ago, "They have robbed us of everything" (*Ci hanno levato tutto*); as if he and the Pantheon were of one blood, and he had suffered personal hurt in its spoliation.

What a sense of wildness everywhere lurking about Rome we had given us by that group of peasants who had built a fire of brushwood almost within the portico of the Pantheon, and were cooking their supper at it, the light of the flames luridly painting their swarthy faces!

XI

POOR little Numero Cinque Via del Gambero has seldom, I imagine, known so violent a sensation as that it experienced when, on the day of the Immaculate Conception, the Armenian Archbishop rolled up to the door in his red coach. The master of the house had always seemed to like us; now he appeared with profound respect suffusing, as it were, his whole being, and announced, "Signore, it is Monsignore come to take you to the Sistine Chapel in his carriage," and drew himself up in a line, as much like a series of serving-men as possible, to let us pass out. There was a private carriage for the ladies near that of Monsignore, for he had already advertised us that the sex were not permitted to ride in the red coach. As they appeared, however, he renewed his expressions of desolation at being deprived of their company, and assured them of his good-will with a multiplicity of smiles and nods, intermixed with shrugs of recurrence to his poignant regret. But! In fine, it was forbidden!

Monsignore was in full costume, with his best ecclesiastical clothes on, and with his great gold chain about his neck. The dress was richer than that of the western archbishops; and the long white beard of Monsignore made him look much more like a Scriptural monsignore than these. He lacked, perhaps, the fine spiritual grace of his brother, the Archbishop of Venice, to whose letter of introduction we owed his acquaintance and untiring civilities; but if a man cannot be plump and spiritual, he can be plump and pleasant, as Monsignore was to the last degree. He enlivened our ride with discourse about the Armenians at Venice, equally beloved of us; and, arrived at the Sixtine Chapel, he marshaled the ladies before him, and won them early entrance through the crowd of English and Americans crushing one another at the door. Then he laid hold upon the captain of the Swiss Guard, who was swift to provide them with the best places; and in no wise did he seem one of the uninfluential and insignificant priests that About describes the archbishops at Rome to be. According to this lively author, a Swiss guard was striking back the crowd on some occasion with the butt of his halberd, and smote a cardinal on the breast. He instantly dropped upon his knees with, "Pardon, Eminenza! I thought it was a monsignore!" Even the chief of these handsome fellows had nothing but respect and obedience for our Archbishop.

The gentlemen present were separated from the ladies, and in a very narrow space outside of the chapel men of every nation were penned up together. All talked—several priests as loudly as the rest. But the rudest among them were certain Germans, who not only talked but stood upon a seat to see better, and were ordered down by one of the Swiss with a fierce "*Giù, signori, giù!*" Otherwise the guard kept good order in the chapel, and were no doubt as useful and genuine as anything about the poor old Pope. What gorgeous fellows they were, and, as soldiers, how absurd! The weapons they bore were as obsolete as the Inquisition. It was amusing to pass one of these play-soldiers on guard at the door of the Vatican—tall, straight, beautiful, superb, with his halberd on his shoulder—and then come to a real warrior outside, a little, ugly, red-legged French sentinel, with his Minié on his arm.

Except for the singing of the Pope's choir,—which was angelically sweet, and heavenly far above all praise,—the religious ceremonies affected me as tedious and empty. Each of the cardinals, as he entered the chapel, blew a sonorous nose; and was received standing by his brother prelates—a grotesque company of old-womanish old men in gaudy gowns. From where I stood I saw the Pope's face only in profile: it was gentle and benign enough, but not great in expression, and the smile on it almost degenerated into a simper. His Holiness had a cold; and his *recitative,* though full, was not smooth. He was all *prete* when, in the midst of the service, he hawked, held his handkerchief up before his face, a little way off, and ruthlessly spat in it!

FORZA MAGGIORE

FORZA MAGGIORE

IMAGINE that Grossetto is not a town much known to travel, for it is absent from all the guide-books I have looked at. However, it is chief in the Maremma, where sweet Pia de' Tolommei languished and perished of the poisonous air and her love's cruelty, and where, so many mute centuries since, the Etrurian cities flourished and fell. Further, one may say that Grossetto is on the diligence road from Civita Vecchia to Leghorn, and that in the very heart of the place there is a lovely palm-tree, rare, if not sole, in that latitude. This palm stands in a well-sheltered, dull little court, out of everything's way, and turns tenderly toward the wall that shields it on the north. It has no other company but a beautiful young girl, who leans out of a window high over its head, and I have no doubt talks with it. At the moment we discovered the friends, the maiden was looking pathetically to the northward, while the palm softly stirred and opened its plumes, as a bird does when his song is finished; and there is very little question but it had just been singing to her that song of which the palms are so fond,—

"Ein Fichtenbaum steht einsam
Im Norden auf kahler Höh'."

Grossetto does her utmost to hide the secret of this tree's
existence, as if a hard, matter-of-fact place ought to be ashamed of
a sentimentality of the kind. It pretended to be a very worldly
town, and tried to keep us in the neighborhood of its cathedral,
where the caffè and shops are, and where, in the evening, four or
five officers of the garrison clinked their sabres on the stones, and
promenaded up and down, and as many ladies shopped for
gloves; and as many citizens sat at the principal caffè and drank
black coffee. This was lively enough; and we knew that the
citizens were talking of the last week's news and the Roman
question; that the ladies were really looking for loves, not gloves;
that such of the officers as had no local intrigue to keep their
hearts at rest were terribly bored, and longed for Florence or
Milan or Turin.

Besides the social charms of her piazza, Grossetto put forth
others of an artistic nature. The cathedral was very old and very
beautiful,—built of alternate lines of red and white marble, and
lately restored in the best spirit. But it was not open, and we were
obliged to turn from it to the group of statuary in the middle of the
piazza, representative of the Maremma and Family returning
thanks to the Grand Duke Leopold III. of Tuscany for his
goodness in causing her swamps to be drained. The Maremma
and her children are arrayed in the scant draperies of Allegory, but
the Grand Duke is fully dressed, and is shown looking down with
some surprise at their figures, and with an apparent doubt of the
propriety of their public appearance in that state.

There was also a museum at Grossetto, and I wonder what was
in it?

The wall of the town was perfect yet, though the moat at its feet
had been so long dry that it was only to be known from the
adjacent fields by the richness of its soil. The top of the wall had
been leveled, and planted with shade, and turned into a peaceful
promenade, like most of such mediæval defenses in Italy; though

I am not sure that a little military life did not linger about a bastion here and there. From somewhere, when we strolled out early in the morning, to walk upon the wall, there came to us a throb of drums; but I believe that the only armed men we saw, beside the officers in the piazza, were the numerous sportsmen resorting at that season to Grossetto for the excellent shooting in the marshes. All the way to Florence we continued to meet them and their dogs; and our inn at Grossetto overflowed with abundance of game. On the kitchen floor and in the court were heaps of larks, pheasants, quails, and beccafichi, at which a troop of scullion-boys constantly plucked, and from which the great, noble, beautiful, white-aproned cook forever fried, stewed, broiled, and roasted. We lived chiefly upon these generous birds during our sojourn, and found, when we attempted to vary our bill of fare, that the very genteel waiter attending us had few distinct ideas beyond them. He was part of the repairs and improvements which that hostelry had recently undergone, and had evidently come in with the four-pronged forks, the chromo-lithographs of Victor Emanuel, Garibaldi, Solferino, and Magenta in the large dining-room, and the iron stove in the small one. He had nothing, evidently, in common with the brick floors of the bed-chambers, and the ancient rooms with great fireplaces. He strove to give a Florentine polish to the rusticity of life in the Maremma; and we felt sure that he must know what beefsteak was. When we ordered it, he assumed to be perfectly conversant with it, started to bring it, paused, turned, and, with a great sacrifice of personal dignity, demanded, *"Bifsteca di manzo, o bifsteca di motone?"*—"Beefsteak of beef, or beefsteak of mutton?"

Of Grossetto proper, this is all I remember, if I except a boy whom I heard singing after dark in the streets,—

"Camicia rossa, camicia ardente!"

The cause of our sojourn there was an instance of *forza maggiore*, as the agent of the diligence company defiantly expressed it, in refusing us damages for our overturn into the river. It was in the early part of the winter when we started from Rome for Venice, and we were traveling northward by diligence because the railways were still more or less interrupted by the storms and floods predicted of Matthieu de la Drôme,—the only reliable prophet France has produced since Voltaire;—and if our accident was caused by an overruling Providence, the company, according to the very law of its existence, was not responsible. To be sure, we did not see how an overruling Providence was to blame for loading upon our diligence the baggage of two diligences, or for the clumsiness of our driver; but, on the other hand, it is certain that the company did not make it rain or cause the inundation. And, in fine, although we could not have traveled by railway, we were masters to have taken the steamer instead of the diligence at Civita Vecchia.

The choice of either of these means of travel had presented itself in vivid hues of disadvantage all the way from Rome to the Papal port, where the French steamer for Leghorn lay dancing a hornpipe upon the short, chopping waves, while we approached by railway. We had leisure enough to make the decision, if that was all we wanted. Our engine-driver had derived his ideas of progress from an Encyclical Letter, and the train gave every promise of arriving at Civita Vecchia five hundred years behind time. But such was the desolating and depressing influence of the weather and the landscape, that we reached Civita Vecchia as undecided as we had left Rome. On the one hand, there had been the land, soaked and sodden,—wild, shagged with scrubby growths of timber, and brooded over by sullen clouds, and visibly inhabited only by shepherds, leaning upon their staves at an angle of forty-five degrees, and looking, in their immovable dejection, with their legs wrapped in long-haired goatskins, like satyrs that had been converted, and were trying to do right; turning dim faces to us, they warned us with every mute appeal against the land, as a waste of mud from one end of Italy to the other. On the other hand, there was the sea-wind raving about our train and threatening to blow it over, and whenever we drew near the coast, heaping the waves upon the beach in thundering menace.

We weakly and fearfully remembered our former journeys by diligence over broken railway routes; we recalled our cruel voyage from Genoa to Naples by sea. Still, we might have lingered and hesitated, and perhaps returned to Rome at last, but for the dramatic resolution of the old man who solicited passengers for the diligence, and carried their passports for a final papal *visa* at the police-office. By the account he gave of himself, he was one of the best men in the world, and unique in those parts for honesty; and he besought us, out of that affectionate interest with which our very aspect had inspired him, not to go by steamer, but to go by diligence, which in nineteen hours would land us safe, and absolutely refreshed by the journey, at the railway station in Follonica. And now, once, would we go by diligence? twice, would we go? three times, would we go?

"Signore," said our benefactor angrily, "I lose my time with you;" and ran away, to be called back in the course of destiny, as he knew well enough, and besought to take us as a special favor.

From the passports he learned that there was official dignity among us, and addressed the unworthy bearer of public honors as Eccellenza, and at parting bequeathed his advantage to the conductor, commending us all in set terms to his courtesy. He hovered caressingly about us as long as we remained, straining politeness to do us some last little service; and when the dilgence rolled away, he did all that one man could to give us a round of applause.

At the moment of departure, we were surprised to have enter the diligence a fellow-countryman, whom we had first seen on the road from Naples to Rome. He had since crossed our path with that iteration of travel which brings you again and again in view of the same trunks and the same tourists in the round of Europe, and finally at Civita Vecchia he had turned up, a silent spectator of our scene with the agent of the diligence, and had gone off apparently a confirmed passenger by steamer. Perhaps a nearer view of the sailor's hornpipe, as danced by that vessel in the harbor, shook his resolution. At any rate, here he was again, and with his ticket for Follonica,—a bright-eyed, rosy-cheeked man, and we will say a citizen of Portland, though he was not. For the first time in our long acquaintance with one another's faces, we entered into conversation, and wondered whether we should find brigands or anything to eat on the road, without expectation of finding either. In respect of robbers, we were not disappointed; but shortly after nightfall we stopped at a lonely post-house to change horses, and found that the landlord had so far counted on our appearance as to have, just roasted and fragrantly fuming, a leg of lamb, with certain small fried fish, and a sufficiency of bread. It was a very lonely place as I say; the sky was gloomy overhead; and the wildness of the landscape all about us gave our provision quite a gamy flavor; and brigands could have added nothing to our sense of solitude.

The road creeps along the coast for some distance from Civita Vecchia, within hearing of the sea, and nowhere widely forsakes it, I believe, all the way to Follonica. The country is hilly, and we stopped every two hours to change horses; at which times we looked out, and, seeing that it was a gray and windy night, though not rainy, exulted that we had not taken the steamer. With very little change, the wisdom of our decision in favor of the diligence formed the burden of our talk during the whole night; and to think of eluded seasickness requited us in the agony of our break-neck efforts to catch a little sleep, as, mounted upon our nightmares, we rode steeple-chases up and down the highways and byways of horror. Anything that absolutely awakened us was accounted a blessing; and I remember few things in life with so keen a pleasure as the summons that came to us to descend from our places and cross a river in one boat, while the two diligences of our train followed in another. Here we had time to see our fellow-passengers, as the pulsating light of their cigars illumined their faces, and to discover among them that Italian, common to all large companies, who speaks English, and is very eager to practice it with you,—who is such a benefactor if you do not know his own language, and such a bore if you do. After this, being landed, it was rapture to stroll up and down the good road, and feel it hard and real under our feet, and not an abysmal impalpability, while all the grim shapes of our dreams fled to the spectral line of small boats sustaining the ferry-barge, and swaying slowly from it as the drowned men at their keels tugged them against the tide.

"*S'accommodino, Signori!*" cries the cheerful voice of the conductor, and we ascend to our places in the diligence. The nightmares are brought out again; we mount, and renew the steeple-chase as before.

Suddenly it all comes to an end, and we sit wide awake in the diligence, amid a silence only broken by the hiss of rain against the windows, and the sweep of gusts upon the roof. The diligence stands still; there is no rattle of harness, nor other sound to prove that we have arrived at the spot by other means than dropping from the clouds. The idea that we are passengers in the last diligence destroyed before the Deluge, and are now waiting our fate on the highest ground accessible to wheels, fades away as the day dimly breaks, and we find ourselves planted, as the Italians say, on the banks of another river. There is no longer any visible conductor, the horses have been spirited away, the driver has vanished.

The rain beats and beats upon the roof, and begins to drop through upon us in great, wrathful tears, while the river before us rushes away with a momently swelling flood. Enter now from the depths of the storm a number of rainy peasants, with our conductor and driver perfectly waterlogged, and group themselves on the low, muddy shore, near a flat ferry-barge, evidently wanting but a hint of *forza maggiore* to go down with anything put into it. A moment they dispute in pantomime, sending now and then a windy tone of protest and expostulation to our ears, and then they drop into a motionless silence, and stand there in the tempest, not braving it, but enduring it with the pathetic resignation of their race, as if it were some form of hopeless political oppression. At last comes the conductor to us and says it is impossible for our diligences to cross in the boat, and he has sent for others to meet us on the opposite shore. He expected them long before this, but we see! They are not come. Patience and malediction!

Remaining planted in those unfriendly circumstances from four o'clock till ten, we have still the effrontery to be glad that we did not take the steamer. What a storm that must be at sea! When at last our connecting diligences appear on the other shore, we are almost light-hearted, and make a jest of the Ombrone, as we perilously pass it in the ferry-boat too weak for our diligences. Between the landing and the vehicles there is a space of heavy mud to cross, and when we reach them we find the *coupé* appointed us occupied by three young Englishmen, who insist that they shall be driven to the boat. They keep the seats to which they have no longer any right, while the tempest drenches the ladies to whom the places belong; and it is only by the *forza maggiore* of our conductor that they can be dislodged. In the mean time the Portland man exchanges with them the assurances of personal and national esteem, which that mighty bond of friendship, the language of Shakespeare and Milton, enables us to offer so idiomatically to our transatlantic cousins.

What Grossetto was like, as we first rode through it, we scarcely looked to see. In four or five hours we should strike the railroad at Follonica; and we merely asked of intermediate places that they should not detain us. We dined in Grossetto at an inn of the Larthian period,—a cold inn and a damp, which seemed never to have been swept since the broom dropped from the grasp of the last Etrurian chambermaid,—and we ate with the two-pronged iron forks of an extinct civilization. All the while we dined, a boy tried to kindle a fire to warm us, and beguiled his incessant failures with stories of indundation on the road ahead of us. But we believed him so little, that when he said a certain stream near Grossetto was impassable, our company all but hissed him.

When we left the town and hurried into the open country, we perceived that he had only too great reason to be an alarmist. Every little rill was risen, and boiling over with the pride of harm, and the broad fields lay hid under the yellow waters that here and there washed over the road. Yet the freshet only presented itself to us as a pleasant excitement; and even when we came to a place where the road itself was covered for a quarter of a mile, we scarcely looked outside the diligence to see how deep the water was. We were surprised when our horses were brought to a stand on a rising ground, and the conductor, cap in hand, appeared at the door. He was a fat, well-natured man, full of a smiling good-will; and he stood before us in a radiant desperation.

Would Eccellenza descend, look at the water in the front, and decide whether to go on? The conductor desired to content; it displeased him to delay,—*ma in somma!*—the rest was confided to the conductor's eloquent shoulders and eyebrows.

Eccellenza, descending, beheld a disheartening prospect. On every hand the country was under water. The two diligences stood on a stone bridge spanning the stream, that, now swollen to an angry torrent, brawled over a hundred yards of the road before us. Beyond, the ground rose, and on its slope stood a farmhouse up to its second story in water. Without the slightest hope in his purpose, and merely as an experiment, Eccellenza suggested that a man should be sent in on horseback; which being done, man and horse in a moment floundered into swimming depths.

The conductor, vigilantly regarding Eccellenza, gave a great shrug of desolation.

Eccellenza replied with a foreigner's shrug,—a shrug of sufficiently correct construction, but wanting the tonic accent, as one may say, though expressing, however imperfectly, an equal desolation.

It appeared to be the part of wisdom not to go ahead, but to go back if we could; and we reëntered the water we had just crossed. It had risen a little, meanwhile, and the road could now be traced only by the telegraph poles. The diligence before us went safely through; but our driver, trusting rather to inspiration than to precedent, did not follow it carefully, and directly drove us over the side of a small viaduct. All the baggage of the train having been lodged upon the roof of our diligence, the unwieldy vehicle now lurched heavily, hesitated, as if preparing, like Cæsar, to fall decently, and went over on its side with a stately deliberation that gave us ample time to arrange our plans for getting out.

The torrent was only some three feet deep, but it was swift and muddy, and it was with a fine sense of shipwreck that Eccellenza felt his boots filling with water, while a conviction that it would have been better, after all, to have taken the steamer, struck coldly home to him. We opened the window in the top side of the diligence, and lifted the ladies through it, and the conductor, in the character of life-boat, bore them ashore; while the driver cursed his horses in a sullen whisper, and could with difficulty be diverted from that employment to cut the lines and save one of them from drowning.

Here our compatriot, whose conversation with the Englishman at the Ombrone we had lately admired, showed traits of strict and severe method which afterward came into even bolder relief. The ladies being rescued, he applied himself to the rescue of their hats, cloaks, rubbers, muffs, books, and bags, and handed them up through the window with tireless perseverance, making an effort to wring or dry each article in turn. The other gentleman on top received them all rather grimly, and had not perhaps been amused by the situation but for the exploit of his hat. It was of the sort called in Italian as in English slang a stove-pipe (*canna*), and having been made in Italy, it was of course too large for its wearer. It had never been anything but a horror and reproach to him, and he was now inexpressibly delighted to see it steal out of the diligence in company with one of the red-leather cushions, and glide darkly down the flood. It nodded and nodded to the cushion with a superhuman tenderness and elegance, and had a preposterous air of whispering, as it drifted out of sight,—

> "It may be we shall reach the Happy Isles,—
> It may be that the gulfs shall wash us down."

The romantic interest of this episode had hardly died away, when our adventure acquired an idyllic flavor from the appearance on the scene of four peasants in an ox-cart. These the conductor tried to engage to bring out the baggage and right the fallen diligence; and they, after making him a little speech upon the value of their health which might be injured, asked him, tentatively two hundred francs for the service. The simple incident enforced the fact already known to us,—that if Italians sometimes take advantage of strangers, they are equally willing to prey upon each other; but I doubt if anything could have taught a foreigner the sweetness with which our conductor bore the enormity, and turned quietly from those brigands to carry the Portland man from the wreck, on which he lingered, to the shore.

Here in the gathering twilight the passengers of both diligences grouped themselves, and made merry over the common disaster. As the conductor and the drivers brought off the luggage our spirits rose with the arrival of each trunk, and we were pleased or not as we found it soaked or dry. We applauded and admired the greater sufferers among us: a lady who opened a dripping box was felt to have perpetrated a pleasantry; and a Brazilian gentleman, whose luggage dropped to pieces and was scattered in the flood about the diligence, was looked upon as a very subtile humorist. Our own contribution to these witty passages was the epigrammatic display of a reeking trunk full of the pretty rubbish people bring away from Rome and Naples,—copies of Pompeian frescoes more ruinous than the originals; photographs floating loose from their cards; little earthen busts reduced to the lumpishness of common clay; Roman scarfs stained and blotted out of all memory of their recent hues; Roman pearls clinging together in clammy masses.

We were a band of brothers and sisters, as we all crowded into one diligence and returned to Grossetto. Arrived there, our party, knowing that a public conveyance in Italy always stops at the worst inn in a place, made bold to seek another, and found it without ado, though the person who undertook to show it spoke of it mysteriously and as of difficult access, and tried to make the simple affair as like a scene of grand opera as he could.

We took one of the ancient rooms in which there was a vast fireplace, as already mentioned, and we there kindled such a fire as could not have been known in that fuel-sparing land for ages. The drying of the clothes was an affair that drew out all the energy and method of our compatriot, and at a late hour we left him moving about among the garments that dangled and dripped from pegs and hooks and lines, dealing with them as a physician with his sick, and tenderly nursing his dress-coat, which he wrung and shook and smoothed and pulled this way and that with a never-satisfied anxiety. At midnight, he hired a watcher to keep up the fire and turn the steaming raiment, and returning at four o'clock, found his watcher dead asleep before the empty fireplace. But I rather applaud than blame the watcher for this. He must have been a man of iron nerve to fall asleep amid all that phantasmal show of masks and disguises. What if those reeking silks had forsaken their nails, and, decking themselves with the blotted Roman scarfs and the slimy Roman pearls, had invited the dress-coats to look over the dripping photographs? Or if all those drowned garments had assumed the characters of the people whom they had grown to resemble, and had sat down to hear the shade of Pia de' Tolommei rehearse the story of her sad fate in the Maremma? I say, if a watcher could sleep in such company, he was right to do so.

On the third day after our return to Grossetto we gathered together our damaged effects, and packed them into refractory trunks. Then we held the customary discussion with the landlord concerning the effrontery of his account, and drove off once more toward Follonica. We could scarcely recognize the route for the one we had recently passed over; and it was not until we came to the scene of our wreck, and found the diligence stranded high and dry upon the roadside, that we could believe the whole landscape about us had been flooded three days before. The offending stream had shrunk back to its channel, and now seemed to feign an unconsciousness of its late excess, and had a virtuous air of not knowing how in the world to account for that upturned diligence. The waters, we learned, had begun to subside the night after our disaster; and the vehicle might have been righted and drawn off—

for it was not in the least injured—forty-eight hours previously; but I suppose it was not *en règle* to touch it without orders from Rome. I picture it to myself still lying there, in the heart of the marshes, and thrilling sympathetic travel with the spectacle of its ultimate ruin:—

"Disfecemi Maremma."

We reached Follonica at last, and then the cars hurried us to Leghorn. We were thoroughly humbled in spirit, and had no longer any doubt that we did ill to take the diligence at Civita Vecchia instead of the steamer; for we had been, not nineteen hours, but four days on the road, and we had suffered as aforementioned.

But we were destined to be partially restored to our self-esteem, if not entirely comforted for our losses, when we sat down to dinner in the Hotel Washington, and the urbane head-waiter, catching the drift of our English discourse, asked us,—

"Have the signori heard that the French steamer, which left Civita Vecchia the same day with their diligence, had to put back and lie in port more than two days on account of the storm? She is but now come into Leghorn, after a very dangerous passage."

AT PADUA

AT PADUA

I

THOSE of my readers who have frequented the garden of Doctor Rappaccini no doubt recall with perfect distinctness the quaint old city of Padua. They remember its miles and miles of dim arcade over-roofing the sidewalks everywhere, affording excellent opportunity for the flirtation of lovers by day and the vengeance of rivals by night. They have seen the now vacant streets thronged with maskers, and the Venetian Podestà going in gorgeous state to and from the vast Palazzo della Ragione. They have witnessed ringing tournaments in those sad empty squares, and races in the Prato della Valle, and many other wonders of different epochs, and their pleasure makes me half sorry that I should have lived for several years within an hour by rail from

Padua, and should know little or nothing of those great sights from actual observation. I take shame to myself for having visited Padua so often and so familiarly as I used to do,—for having been bored and hungry there,—for having had toothache there, upon one occasion,—for having rejoiced more in a cup of coffee at Pedrocchi's than in the whole history of Padua,—for having slept repeatedly in the bad-bedded hotels of Padua and never once dreamt of Portia,—for having been more taken by the *salti mortali*[1] of a waiter who summed up my account at a Paduan restaurant, than by all the strategies with which the city has been many times captured and recaptured. Had I viewed Padua only over the wall of Doctor Rappacini's garden, how different my impressions of the city would now be! This is one of the drawbacks of actual knowledge. "Ah! how can you write about Spain when once you have been there?" asked Heine of Théophile Gautier, setting out on a journey thither. Nevertheless it seems to me that I remember something about Padua with a sort of romantic pleasure. There was a certain charm, in sauntering along the top of the old wall of the city, and looking down upon the plumy crests of the Indian corn that flourished up so mightily from the dry bed of the moat. At such times I figured to myself the many sieges that the wall had known, with the fierce assault by day, the secret attack by night, the swarming foe upon the plains below, the bristling arms of the besieged upon the wall, the boom of the great mortars made of ropes and leather and throwing mighty balls of stone, the stormy flight of arrows, the ladders planted against the defenses and staggering headlong into the moat, enriched for future agriculture not only by its sluggish waters, but by the blood of many men. I suppose that most of these visions were old stage spectacles furbished up anew, and that my armies were chiefly equipped with their obsolete implements of warfare from museums of armor and from cabinets of antiquities; but they were very vivid for all that.

---

[1] *Salti mortali* are those prodigious efforts of mental arithmetic by which Italian waiters, in verbally presenting your account, arrive at six as the product of two and two.

I was never able, in passing a certain one of the city gates, to divest myself of an historic interest in the great loads of hay waiting admission on the outside. For an instant they masked again the Venetian troops that, in the War of the League of Cambray, entered the city in the hay-carts, shot down the landsknechts at the gates, and uniting with the citizens, cut the German garrison to pieces. But it was a thing long past. The German garrison was here again; and the heirs of the landsknechts went clanking through the gate to the parade-ground, with that fierce clamor of their kettle-drums which is so much fiercer because unmingled with the noise of fifes. Once more now the Germans are gone, and, let us trust, forever; but when I saw them, there seemed little hope of their going. They had a great Biergarten on the top of the wall, and they had set up the altars of their heavy Bacchus in many parts of the city.

I please myself with thinking that, if I walked on such a spring day as this in the arcaded Paduan streets, I should catch glimpses, through the gateways of the palaces, of gardens full of vivid bloom, and of fountains that tinkle there forever. If it were autumn, and I were in the great market-place before the Palazzo della Ragione, I should hear the baskets of amber-hued and honeyed grapes humming with the murmur of multitudinous bees, and making a music as if the wine itself were already singing in their gentle hearts. It is a great field of succulent verdure, that wide old marklet-place; and fancy loves to browse about among its gay stores of fruits and vegetables, brought thither by the world-old peasant-women who have been bringing fruits and vegetables to the Paduan market for so many centuries. They sit upon the ground before their great panniers, and knit and doze, and wake up with a drowsy, "*Comandala?*" as you linger to look at their grapes. They have each a pair of scales,—the emblem of Injustice,—and will weigh you out a scant measure of the fruit if you like. Their faces are yellow as parchment, and Time has written them so full of wrinkles that there is not room for another line. Doubtless these old parchment visages are palimpsests, and would tell the whole story of Padua if you could get at each successive inscription. Among their primal records there must be some account of the Roman city, as each little contadinella remembered it on market-days; and one might read of the terror of Attila's sack, a little later, with the peasant-maid's personal recollections of the bold Hunnish trooper who ate up the grapes in her basket, and kissed her hard, round red cheeks,—for in that time she was a blooming girl,—and paid nothing for either privilege. What wild and confused reminiscences on the wrinkled visage we should find thereafter of the fierce republican times, of Ecelino, of the Carraras, of the Venetian rule! And is it not sad to think of systems and peoples all passing away, and these ancient women lasting still, and still selling grapes in front of the Palazzo della Ragione? What a long mortality!

The youngest of their number is a thousand years older than the palace, which was begun in the twelfth century, and which is much the same now as it was when first completed. I know that, if I entered it, I should be sure of finding the great hall of the palace—the greatest hall in the world—dim and dull and dusty and delightful, with nothing in it except at one end Donatello's colossal marble-headed wooden horse of Troy, stared at from the other end by the two dog-faced Egyptian women in basalt placed there by Belzoni.

Late in the drowsy summer afternoons I should have the Court of the University all to myself, and might study unmolested the blazons of the noble youth who have attended the school in different centuries ever since 1200, and have left their escutcheons on the walls to commemorate them. At the foot of the stairway ascending to the schools from the court is the statue of the learned lady who was once a professor in the University, and who, if her likeness belie not her looks, must have given a great charm to student life in other times. At present there are no lady professors at Padua any more than at Harvard; and during late years the schools have suffered greatly from the interference of the Austrian government, which frequently closed them for months, on account of political demonstrations among the students. But now there is an end of this and many other stupid oppressions; and the

time-honored University will doubtless regain its ancient importance. Even in 1864 it had nearly fifteen hundred students, and
one met them everywhere under the arcades, and could not well
mistake them, with that blended air of pirate and dandy which the
studious young men loved to assume. They were to be seen a good
deal on the promenades outside the walls, where the Paduan ladies
are driven in their carriages in the afternoon, and where one sees
the blood-horses and fine equipages for which Padua is famous.
There used once to be races in the Prato della Valle, after the
Italian notion of horse-races; but these are now discontinued, and
there is nothing to be found there but the statues of scholars and
soldiers and statesmen, posted in a circle around the old race-
course. If you strolled thither about dusk on such a day as this,
you might see the statues unbend a little from their stony rigidity,
and in the failing light nod to each other very pleasantly through
the trees. And if you stayed in Padua over night, what could be
better to-morrow morning than a stroll through the great Botanical Garden,—the oldest botanical garden in the world,—the
garden which first received in Europe the strange and splendid
growths of our hemisphere,—the garden where Doctor Rappacini
doubtless found the germ of his mortal plant?

The day that we first visited the city was very rainy, and we
spent most of the time in viewing the churches. Their architecture
forms a sort of border-land between the Byzantine of Venice and
the Lombardic of Verona. The superb domes of St. Anthony's
emulate those of St. Mark's; and the porticoes of other Paduan
churches rest upon the backs of bird-headed lions and leopards
that fascinate with their mystery and beauty.

It was the wish to see the attributive Giottos in the Chapter
which drew us first to St. Anthony's, and we saw them with the
satisfaction naturally attending the contemplation of frescoes
discovered only since 1858, after having been hidden under
plaster and whitewash for many centuries; but we could not
believe that Giotto's fame was destined to gain much by their
rescue from oblivion. They are in nowise to be compared with this
master's frescoes in the Chapel of the Annunziata,—which,

indeed, is in every way a place of wonder and delight. You reach it by passing through a garden lane bordered with roses, and a taciturn gardener comes out with clinking keys, and lets you into the chapel, where there is nobody but Giotto and Dante, nor seems to have been for ages. Cool it is, and of a pulverous smell, as a sacred place should be; a blessed benching goes round the walls, and you sit down and take unlimited comfort in the frescoes. The gardener leaves you alone to the solitude and the silence, in which the talk of the painter and the exile is plain enough. Their contemporaries and yours are cordial in their gay companionship: through the half-open doors falls, in a pause in the rain, the same sunshine that they saw lie there; the deathless birds that they heard sing out in the garden trees; it is the fresh sweetness of the grass mown so many hundred years ago that breathes through all the lovely garden grounds.

But in the midst of this pleasant communion with the past you have a lurking pain; for you have hired your brougham by the hour; and you presently quit the Chapel of Giotto on this account.

We had chosen our driver from among many other drivers of broughams in the vicinity of Pedrocchi's, because he had such an honest look, and was not likely, we thought, to deal unfairly with us.

"But first," said the signor who had selected him, "how much is your brougham an hour?"

So and so.

"Show me the tariff of fares."

"There is no tariff."

"There is. Show it to me."

"It is lost, signor."

"I think not. It is here in this pocket. Get it out."

The tariff appears, and with it the fact that he had demanded just what the boatman of the ballad received in gift,—thrice his fee.

The driver mounted his seat, and served us so faithfully that day in Padua that we took him the next day for Arquà. At the end, when he had received his due, and a handsome *mancia* besides, he was still unsatisfied, and referred to the tariff in proof that he had been underpaid. On that confronted and defeated, he thanked us very cordially, gave us the number of his brougham, and begged us to ask for him when we came next to Padua and needed a carriage.

From the Chapel of the Annunziata he drove us to the Church of Santa Giustina, where is a very famous and noble picture by Romanino. But as this writing has nothing in the world to do with art, I here dismiss that subject, and with a gross and idle delight follow the sacristan down under the church to the prison of Santa Giustina.

Of all the faculties of the mind there is none so little fatiguing to exercise as mere wonder; and for my own sake, I try always to wonder at things without the least critical reservation. I therefore, in the sense of deglutition, bolted this prison at once, though subsequent experiences led me to look with grave indigestion upon the whole idea of prisons, their authenticity, and even their existence.

As far as mere dimensions are concerned, the prison of Santa Giustina was not a hard one to swallow, being only three feet wide by about ten feet in length. In this limited space, Santa Giustina passed five years of the reign of Nero and was then brought out into the larger cell adjoining, to suffer a blessed martyrdom. I am not sure now whether the sacristan said she was dashed to death on the stones, or cut to pieces with knives; but whatever the form of martyrdom, an iron ring in the ceiling was employed in it, as I know from seeing the ring,—a curiously well-preserved piece of ironmongery. Within the narrow prison of the saint, and just under the grating, through which the sacristan thrust his candle to illuminate it, was a mountain of candle-drippings,—a monument to the fact that faith still largely exists in this doubting world. My own credulity, not only with regard to this prison, but also touching the coffin of St. Luke, which I saw in the church, had so wrought upon the esteem of the sacristan that he now took me to a well, into which, he said, had been cast the bones of three thousand Christian martyrs. He lowered a lantern into the well, and assured me that, if I looked through a certain screenwork there, I could see the bones. On experiment I could not see the bones, but this circumstance did not cause me to doubt their presence, particularly as I did see upon the screen a great number of coins offered for the repose of the martyrs' souls. I threw down some *soldi*, and thus enthralled the sacristan.

If the signor cared to see prisons, he said, the driver must take him to those of Ecelino, at present the property of a private gentleman near by. As I had just bought a history of Ecelino, at a great bargain, from a second-hand book-stall, and had a lively interest in all the enormities of that nobleman, I sped the driver instantly to the villa of the Signor P——.

It depends here altogether upon the freshness or the mustiness of the reader's historical reading whether he cares to be reminded more particularly who Ecelino was. He flourished balefully in the early half of the thirteenth century as lord of Vicenza, Verona, Padua, and Brescia, and was defeated and hurt to death in an attempt to possess himself of Milan. He was in every respect a remarkable man for that time,—fearless, abstemious, continent, avaricious, hardy, and unspeakably ambitious and cruel. He survived and suppressed innumerable conspiracies, escaping even the thrust of the assassin whom the fame of his enormous wickedness had caused the Old Man of the Mountain to send against him. As lord of Padua he was more incredibly severe and bloody in his rule than as lord of the other cities, for the Paduans had been latest free, and conspired the most frequently against him. He extirpated whole families on suspicion that a single member had been concerned in a meditated revolt. Little children and helpless women suffered hideous mutilation and shame at his hands. Six prisons in Padua were constantly filled by his arrests. The whole country was traversed by witnesses of his cruelties— men and women deprived of an arm or leg, and begging from door to door. He had long been excommunicated; at last the Church proclaimed a crusade against him, and his lieutenant and nephew—more demoniacal, if possible, than himself—was driven out of Padua while he was operating against Mantua. Ecelino retired to Verona, and maintained a struggle against the crusade for nearly two years longer, with a courage which never failed him. Wounded and taken prisoner, the soldiers of the victorious army gathered around him, and heaped insult and reproach upon him; and one furious peasant, whose brother's feet had been cut off by Ecelino's command, dealt the helpless monster four blows upon the head with a scythe. By some, Ecelino is said to have died of these wounds alone; but by others it is related that his death was a kind of suicide, inasmuch as he himself put the case past surgery by tearing off the bandages from his hurts, and refusing all medicines.

II

ENTERING at the enchanted portal of the Villa P——, we found ourselves in a realm of wonder. It was our misfortune not to see the magician who compelled all the marvels on which we looked, but for that very reason, perhaps, we have the clearest sense of his greatness. Everywhere we beheld the evidences of his ingenious but lugubrious fancy, which everywhere tended to a monumental and mortuary effect. A sort of vestibule first received us, and beyond this dripped and glimmered the garden. The walls of the vestibule were covered with inscriptions setting forth the sentiments of the philosophy and piety of all ages concerning life and death; we began with Confucius, and we ended with Benjamino Franklino. But as if these ideas of mortality were not sufficiently depressing, the funereal Signor P—— had collected into earthen *amphoræ* the ashes of the most famous men of ancient and modern times, and arranged them so that a sense of their number and variety should at once strike his visitor. Each jar was conspicuously labeled with the name its illustrious dust had borne in life; and if one escaped with comparative cheerfulness from the thought that Seneca had died, there were in the very next pot the cinders of Napoleon to bully him back to a sense of his mortality.

We were glad to have the gloomy fascination of these objects broken by the custodian, who approached to ask if we wished to see the prisons of Ecelino, and we willingly followed him into the rain out of our sepulchral shelter.

Between the vestibule and the towers of the tyrant lay that garden already mentioned, and our guide led us through ranks of weeping statuary, and rainy bowers, and showery lanes of shrubbery, until we reached the door of his cottage. While he entered to fetch the key to the prisons, we noted that the towers were freshly painted and in perfect repair; and indeed the custodian said frankly enough, on reappearing, that they were merely built over the prisons on the site of the original towers. The storied stream of the Bacchiglione sweeps through the grounds, and now, swollen by the rainfall, it roared, a yellow torrent, under a corner of the prisons. The towers rise from masses of foliage, and form no unpleasing feature of what must be, in spite of Signor P——, a delightful Italian garden in sunny weather. The ground is not so flat as elsewhere in Padua, and this inequality gives an additional picturesqueness to the place. But as we were come in search of horrors, we scorned these merely lovely things, and hastened to immure ourselves in the dungeons below. The custodian, lighting a candle (which ought, we felt, to have been a torch), went before.

We found the cells, though narrow and dark, not uncomfortable, and the guide conceded that they had undergone some repairs since Ecelino's time. But all the horrors for which we had come were there in perfect grisliness, and labeled by the ingenious Signor P—— with Latin inscriptions.

In the first cell was a shrine of the Virgin, set in the wall. Beneath this, while the wretched prisoner knelt in prayer, a trap-door opened and precipitated him upon the points of knives, from which his body fell into the Bacchiglione below. In the next cell, held by some rusty iron rings to the wall, was a skeleton, hanging by the wrists.

"This," said the guide, "was another punishment of which Ecelino was very fond."

A dreadful doubt seized my mind. "Was this skeleton found here?" I demanded.

Without faltering an instant, without so much as winking an eye, the custodian replied, "*Appunto.*"

It was a great relief, and restored me to confidence in the establishment. I am at a loss to explain how my faith should have been confirmed afterwards by coming upon a guillotine—an awful instrument in the likeness of a straw-chopper, with a decapitated wooden figure under its blade—which the custodian confessed to be a modern improvement placed there by Signor P——. Yet my credulity was so strengthened by his candor, that I accepted without hesitation the torture of the water-drop when we came to it. The water-jar was as well preserved as if placed there but yesterday, and the skeleton beneath it—found as we saw it—was entire and perfect.

In the adjoining cell sat a skeleton—found as we saw it—with its neck in the clutch of the garrote, which was one of Ecelino's more merciful punishments; while in still another cell the ferocity of the tyrant appeared in the penalty inflicted upon the wretch whose skeleton had been hanging for ages—as we saw it—head downwards from the ceiling.

Beyond these, in a yet darker and drearier dungeon, stood a heavy oblong wooden box, with two apertures near the top, peering through which we found that we were looking into the eyeless sockets of a skull. Within this box Ecelino had immured the victim we beheld there, and left him to perish in view of the platters of food and goblets of drink placed just beyond the reach of his hands. The food we saw was of course not the original food.

At last we came to the crowning horror of Villa P——, the supreme excess of Ecelino's cruelty. The guide entered the cell before us, and, as we gained the threshold, threw the light of his taper vividly upon a block that stood in the middle of the floor. Fixed to the block by an immense spike driven through from the back was the slender hand of a woman, which lay there just as it had been struck from the living arm, and which, after the lapse of so many centuries, was still as perfectly preserved as if it had been embalmed. The sight had a most cruel fascination; and while one of the horror-seekers stood helplessly conjuring to his vision that scene of unknown dread,—the shrinking, shrieking woman dragged to the block, the wild, shrill, horrible screech following the blow that drove in the spike, the merciful swoon after the mutilation,—his companion, with a sudden pallor, demanded to be taken instantly away.

In their swift withdrawal, they only glanced at a few detached instruments of torture,—all original Ecelinos, but intended for the infliction of minor and comparatively unimportant torments,—and then they passed from that place of fear.

III

In the evening we sat at the Caffè Pedrocchi with an abbate, an acquaintance of ours, who was a professor in the University of Padua. Pedrocchi's is the great caffè of Padua, a granite edifice of Egyptian architecture, which is the mausoleum of the proprietor's fortune. The pecuniary skeleton at the feast, however, does not much trouble the guests. They begin early in the evening to gather into the elegant saloons of the caffè,—somewhat too large for so small a city as Padua,—and they sit there late in the night over their cheerful cups and their ices, with their newspapers and their talk. Not so many ladies are to be seen as at the caffè in Venice, for it is only in the greater cities that they go much to these public places. There are few students at Pedrocchi's, for they frequent the cheaper caffè; but you may nearly always find there some professor of the University, and on the evening of which I speak there were two present besides our abbate. Our friend's great passion was the English language, which he understood too well to venture to speak a great deal. He had been translating from that tongue into Italian certain American poems, and our talk was of these at first.

At last, turning from literature, we spoke with the gentle abbate of our day's adventures, and eagerly related that of the Ecelino prisons. To have seen them was the most terrific pleasure of our lives.

"Eh!" said our friend, "I believe you."

"We mean those under the Villa P——."

"Exactly."

There was a tone of politely suppressed amusement in the abbate's voice; and after a moment's pause, in which we felt our awful experience slipping and sliding away from us, we ventured to say, "You don't mean that those are *not* the veritable Ecelino prisons?"

"Certainly they are nothing of the kind. The Ecelino prisons were destroyed when the Crusaders took Padua, with the exception of the tower, which the Venetian Republic converted into an observatory."

"But at least these prisons are on the site of Ecelino's castle?"

"Nothing of the sort. His castle in that case would have been outside of the old city walls."

"And those tortures and the prisons are all—"

"Things got up for show. No doubt, Ecelino used such things, and many worse, of which even the ingenuity of Signor P—— cannot conceive. But he is an eccentric man, loving the horrors of history, and what he can do to realize them he has done in his prisons."

"But the custodian—how could he lie so?"

Our friend shrugged his shoulders. "Eh! easily. And perhaps he even believed what he said."

The world began to assume an aspect of bewildering ungenuineness, and there seemed to be a treacherous quality of fiction in the ground under our feet. Even the play at the pretty little Teatro Sociale, where we went to pass the rest of the evening, appeared hollow and improbable. We thought the hero something of a bore, with his patience and goodness; and as for the heroine, pursued by the attentions of the rich profligate, we doubted if she were any better than she should be.

PETRARCH'S HOUSE

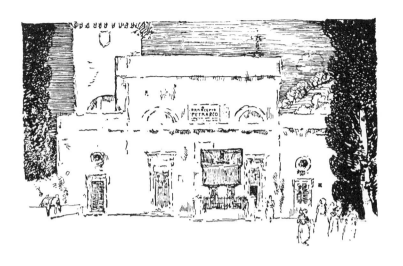

A PILGRIMAGE TO PETRARCH'S HOUSE AT ARQUÀ

I

WE said, during summer days at Venice, when every *campo* was a furnace seven times heated, and every canal was filled with boiling bathers, "As soon as it rains we will go to Arquà." Remembering the ardors of an April sun on the long, level roads of plain, we could not think of them in August without a sense of dust clogging every pore, and eyes that shrank from the vision of their blinding whiteness. So we stayed in Venice, waiting for rain, until the summer had almost lapsed into autumn; and as the weather cooled before any rain reached us, we took the moisture on the mainland for granted, and set out under a cloudy and windy sky.

We had to go to Padua by railway, and take carriage thence to Arquà upon the road to Ferrara. I believe no rule of human experience was violated when it began to rain directly after we reached Padua, and continued to rain violently the whole day. We gave up this day entirely to the rain, and did not leave Padua until

the following morning, when we count that our pilgrimage to
Petrarch's house actually began.

The rain had cooled and freshened the air, but it was already
too late in the season for the summer to recover herself with the
elastic brilliancy that follows the rain of July or early August; and
there was I know not what vague sentiment of autumn in the
weather. There was not yet enough of it to stir the

"Tears from the depth of some divine despair;"

but in here and there a faded leaf in the purple of the ripening
grapes, and in the tawny grass of the pastures, there was autumn
enough to touch our spirits, and, while it hardly affected the tone
of the landscape, to lay upon us the gentle and pensive spell of its
presence. Of all the days in the year I would have chosen this to
go pilgrim to the house of Petrarch.

The Euganean Hills, on one of which the poet's house is built,
are those mellow heights which you see when you look southwest
across the lagoon at Venice. In misty weather they are blue, and in
clear weather silver, and the October sunset loves them. They rise
in tender azure before you as you issue from the southern gate of
Padua, and grow in loveliness as you draw nearer to them from
the rich plain that washes their feet with endless harvests.

Oh beauty that will not let itself be told! Could I not take
warning from another, and refrain from this fruitless effort of
description? A friend in Padua had lent me Disraeli's "Venetia,"
because a passage of the story occurs in Petrarch's house at Arquà,
and we carried the volumes with us on our pilgrimage. I would
here quote the description of the village, the house, and the hills
from this work, as faultlessly true, and as affording no just idea of
either: but nothing of it has remained in my mind except the
geological fact that the hills are a volcanic range. To tell the truth,
the landscape, as we rode along, continually took my mind off the
book, and I could not give that attention, either to the elegant
language of its descriptions or the adventures of its well-born
characters, which they deserved. I was even more interested in the

disreputable looking person who mounted the box beside the driver as soon as we got out of the city gate, and who invariably commits this infringement upon your rights in Italy, no matter how strictly and cunningly you frame your contract that no one else is to occupy any part of the carriage but yourself. He got down, in this instance, just before we reached the little town at which our driver stopped, and asked us if we wished to drink a glass of the wine of the country. We did not, but his own thirst seemed to answer equally well, and he slaked it cheerfully at our cost.

The fields did not present the busy appearance which had delighted us on the same road in the spring, but they had that autumnal charm already mentioned. Many of the vine-leaves were sear; the red grapes were already purple, and the white grapes pearly ripe, and they formed a gorgeous necklace for the trees, around which they clung in opulent festoons. Then, dearer to our American hearts than this southern splendor were the russet fields of Indian corn, and, scattered among the shrunken stalks, great nuggets of the "harmless gold" of pumpkins.

At Battaglia (the village just beyond which you turn off to go to Arquà) there was a fair, on the blessed occasion of some saint's day, and there were many booths full of fruits, agricultural implements, toys, clothes, wooden ware, and the like. There was a great crowd and a noise, but, according to the mysterious Italian custom, nobody seemed to be buying or selling. I am in the belief that a small purchase of grapes we made here on our return was the great transaction of the day, unless, indeed, the neat operation in alms achieved at our expense by a mendicant villager may be classed commercially.

When we turned off from the Rovigo road at Battaglia we were only three miles from Arquà.

II

Now, all the way from this turning to the foot of the hill on which the village was stretched asleep in the tender sunshine, there was on either side of the road a stream of living water. There was no other barrier than this between the road and the fields (unless the vines swinging from tree to tree formed a barrier), and, as if in graceful excuse for the interposition of even these slender streams, Nature had lavished such growth of wild flowers and wild berries on the banks that it was like a garden avenue, through the fragrance and beauty of which we rolled, delighted to silence, almost to sadness.

When we began to climb the hill to Arquà, and the driver stopped to breathe his horse, I got out and finished the easy ascent on foot. The great marvel to me is that the prospect of the vast plain below, on which, turning back, I feasted my vision, should be there yet, and always. It had the rare and melancholy beauty of evanescence, and I wonder did Petrarch walk often down this road from his house just above? I figured him coming to meet me with his book in his hand, in his reverend poetic robes, and with his laurel on, over that curious kind of bandaging which he seems to have been fond of—looking, in a word, for all the world like the neuralgic Petrarch in the pictures.

Drawing nearer, I discerned the apparition to be a robeless, laurelless lout, who belonged to the village inn. Yet this lout, though not Petrarch, had merits. His face and hands, and his legs as seen from his knees down, were richly tanned; he wore a mountain cap with a long tasseled fall to the back of it; his face was comely and his eye beautiful; and he was so nobly ignorant of everything, that a colt or young bullock could not have been better company. He merely offered to guide us to Petrarch's house, and was silent, except when spoken to, from that instant.

I am here tempted to say: Arquà is in the figure of a man stretched upon the hillslope. The head, which is Petrarch's house, rests upon the summit. The carelessly tossed arms lie abroad from this in one direction, and the legs in the opposite quarter. It is a very lank and shambling figure, without elegance or much proportion and the attitude is the last wantonness of loafing. We followed our lout up the right leg, which is a gentle and easy ascent in the general likeness of a street. World-old stone cottages crouch on either side; here and there is a more ambitious house in decay; trees wave over the street, and down its distance comes an occasional donkey-cart very musically and leisurely.

We reached Petrarch's house before the custodian had arrived to admit us, and stood before the high stone wall which shuts in the front of the house, and quite hides it from those without. This wall bears the inscription *Casa Petrarca,* and a marble tablet lettered to the following effect:—

SETI AGITA
SACRO AMORE DI PATRIA
T'INCHINA A QUESTE MURA
OVE SPIRO LA GRAND' ANIMA
IL CANTOR DEI SCIPIONI
E DI LAURA.

Which may be translated: "If thou art stirred by love of country, bow to these walls, whence passed the great soul, the singer of the Scipios and of Laura."

Meanwhile we became the centre of a group of the youths of Arquà, who had kindly attended our progress in gradually increasing numbers from the moment we had entered the village. They were dear little girls and boys, and mountain babies, all with sunburnt faces and the gentle and the winning ways native to this race, which Nature loves better than us of the North. The blonde pilgrim seemed to please them, and they evidently took us for *Tedeschi.* You learn to submit to this fate in Northern Italy, however ungracefully, for it is the one that constantly befalls you outside of the greatest cities. The people know but two varieties of foreigners—the Englishman and the German. If, therefore, you have not *rosbif* expressed in every lineament of your countenance, you must resign yourself to be a German. This is grievous to the soul which loves to spread its eagle in every land and to be known as American, with star-spangled conspicuousness all over the world: but it cannot be helped. I vainly tried to explain the geographical, political, and natural difference between Tedeschi and Americani to the custodian of Petrarch's house. She listened with amiability, shrugged her shoulders hopelessly, and said, in her rude Venetian, *"Mi no so migra"* (I don't know at all).

Before she came, I had a mind to prove the celebrity of the poet on the spot where he lived and died,—on his very hearthstone, as it were. So I asked the lout, who stood gnawing a stick and shifting his weight from one foot to the other,—

"When did Petrarch live here?"

"Ah! I don't remember him."

"Who was he?"

"A poet, signor."

Certainly the first response was not encouraging, but the last revealed that even to the heavy and clouded soul of this lout the divine fame of the poet had penetrated—and he a lout in the village where Petrarch lived and ought to be first forgotten. He did not know when Petrarch had lived there,—a year ago, perhaps, or many centuries,—but he knew that Petrarch was a poet. A weight of doubt was lifted from my spirit, and I responded cheerfully to some observations on the weather offered by a rustic matron who was pitching manure on the little hill-slope near the house. When at last the custodian came and opened the gate to us, we entered a little grassy yard from which a flight of steps led to Petrarch's door. A few flowers grew wild among the grass, and a fig-tree leaned its boughs against the wall. The figs on it were green, though they hung ripe and blackening on every other tree in Arquà. Some ivy clung to the stones, and from this and the fig-tree, as we came away, we plucked memorial leaves, and blended them with flowers which the youth of Arquà picked and forced upon us for remembrance.

A quaint old door opened into the little stone house, and admitted us to a kind of wide passageway with rooms on either side; and at the end opposite to which we entered another door opened upon a balcony. From this balcony we looked down on Petrarch's garden, which, presently speaking, is but a narrow space with more fruit than flowers in it. Did Petrarch use to sit and meditate in this garden? For me I should better have liked a chair on the balcony, with the further and lovelier prospect on every hand of village-roofs, sloping hills all gray with olives, and the broad, blue Lombard plain, sweeping from heaven to heaven below.

The walls of the passageway are frescoed (now very faintly) in illustration of the loves of Petrarch and Laura, with verses from the sonnets he inscribed to explain the illustrations. In all these Laura prevails as a lady of a singularly long waist and stiff movements, and Petrarch, with his face tied up and a lily in his hand, contemplates the flower in mingled botany and toothache. There is occasionally a startling literalness in the way the painter has rendered some of the verses. I remember with peculiar interest the illustration of the lachrymose passage concerning a river of tears, wherein the weeping Petrarch, stretched beneath a tree, had already started a small creek of tears, which was rapidly swelling to a flood with the torrent from his eyes. I attribute these frescoes to a later date than that of the poet's residence, but the portrait over the door of the bedroom inside of the chamber was of his own time, and taken from him—the custodian said. As it seemed to look like all the Petrarchian portraits, I did not remark it closely, but rather turned my attention to the walls of the chamber, which were thickly overscribbled with names. They were nearly all Italian, and none English so far as I saw. This passion for allying oneself to the great, by inscribing one's name on places hallowed by them, is certainly very odd; and (I reflected as I added our names to the rest) it is, without doubt, the most impertinent and idiotic custom in the world. People have thus written themselves down, to the contempt of futurity, all over Petrarch's house.

The custodian insisted that the bedroom was just as in the poet's time; some rooms beyond it had been restored; the kitchen at its side was also repaired. Crossing the passageway, we entered the dining-room, which was comparatively large and lofty, with a generous fireplace at one end, occupying the whole space left by a balcony window. The floor was paved with tiles, and the window-panes were round and small, and set in lead—like the floors and window-panes of all the other rooms. A fresco, representing some indelicate female deity, adorned the front of the fireplace, which sloped expanding from the ceiling and terminated at the mouth without a mantel piece. The chimney was deep, and told of the cold winters in the hills, of which, afterward, the landlady of the village inn prattled less eloquently.

From this dining-room opens, to the right, the door of the room which they called Petrarch's library; and above the door, set in a marble frame, with a glass before it, is all that is mortal of Petrarch's cat, except the hair. Whether or not the fur was found incompatible with the process of embalming, and therefore removed, or whether it has slowly dropped away with the lapse of centuries, I do not know; but it is certain the cat is now quite bald. On the marble slab below there is a Latin inscription, said to be by the great poet himself, declaring this cat to have been "second only to Laura." We may therefore believe its virtues to have been rare enough; and cannot well figure to ourselves Petrarch sitting before that wide-mouthed fireplace, without beholding also the gifted cat that purrs softly at his feet and nestles on his knees, or, with thickened tail and lifted back, parades loftily round his chair in the haughty and disdainful manner of cats.

In the library, protected against the predatory enthusiasm of visitors by a heavy wire netting, are the desk and chair of Petrarch, which I know of no form of words to describe perfectly. The front of the desk is of a kind of mosaic in cubes of wood, most of which have been carried away. The chair is wide-armed and carved, but the bottom is gone, and it has been rudely repaired. The custodian said Petrarch died in this chair while he sat writing at his desk in the little nook lighted by a single window opening on the left from his library. He loved to sit there. As I entered I found he had stepped out for a moment, but I know he returned directly after I withdrew.

On one wall of the library (which is a simple oblong room, in no wise remarkable) was a copy of verses in a frame, by Cesarotti, and on the wall opposite a tribute from Alfieri, both *manu propria*. Over and above these are many other scribblings; and hanging over the door of the poet's little nook was a criminal French lithograph likeness of "Pétrarque" when young. Alfieri's verses are written in ink on the wall, while those of Cesarotti are on paper, and framed. I do not remember any reference to his visit to Petrarch's house in Alfieri's autobiography, though the visit must have taken place in 1783, when he sojourned at Padua, and "made the acquaintance of the celebrated Cesarotti, with whose lively and courteous manners he was no less satisfied than he had always been in reading his (Cesarotti's) most masterly version of 'Ossian.'" It is probable that the friends visited the house together. At any rate, I care to believe that while Cesarotti sat "composing" his tribute comfortably at the table, Alfieri's impetuous soul was lifting his tall body on tiptoe to scrawl its inspirations on the plastering.

After copying these verses we returned to the dining-room, and while one pilgrim strayed idly through the names in the visitor's book, the other sketched Petrarch's cat, before mentioned, and Petrarch's inkstand of bronze. Thus sketching and idling, we held spell-bound our friends the youth of Arquà, as well as our driver, who, having brought innumerable people to see the house of Petrarch, now for the first time, with great astonishment, beheld the inside of it himself.

As to the authenticity of the house I think there can be no doubt, and as to the genuineness of the relics there, nothing in the world could shake my faith in them, though Muratori certainly characterizes them as "superstitions." The great poet was sixty-five years old when he came to rest at Arquà, and when, in his own pathetic words, "there remained to him only to consider and to desire how to make a good end." He says further, at the close of his autobiography: "In one of the Euganean hills, near to ten miles from the city of Padua, I have built me a house, small but pleasant and decent, in the midst of slopes clothed with vines and olives, abundantly sufficient for a family not large and discreet. Here I lead my life, and although, as I have said, infirm of body, yet tranquil of mind, without excitements, without distractions, without cares, reading always, and writing and praising God, and thanking God as well for evil as for good; which evil, if I err not, is trial merely and not punishment. And all the while I pray to Christ that he make good the end of my life, and have mercy on me, and forgive me, and even forget my youthful sins; wherefore, in this solitude, no words are so sweet to my lips as those of the psalm: '*Delicta juventutis meæ, et ignorantias meas ne memineris.*' And with every feeling of the heart I pray God, when it please Him, to bridle my thoughts, so long unstable and erring; and as they have vainly wandered to many things, to turn them all to Him—only true, certain immutable Good."

I venerate the house at Arquà because these sweet and solemn words were written in it. We left its revered shelter (after taking a final look from the balcony down upon "the slopes clothed with vines and olives") and returned to the lower village, where, in the court of the little church, we saw the tomb of Petrarch—"an ark of red stone, upon four columns likewise of marble." The epitaph is this:—

"Frigida Francisci lapis hic tegit ossa Petrarcæ;
Suscipe, Virgo parens, animam; sate Virgine, parce
Fessaque jam terris Cœli requiescat in arce."

A head of the poet in bronze surmounts the ark. The housekeeper of the parish priest, who ran out to enjoy my admiration and bounty, told me a wild local tradition of an attempt on the part of the Florentines to steal the bones of Petrarch away from Arquà, in proof of which she showed me a block of marble set into the ark, whence she said a fragment had been removed by the Florentines. This local tradition I afterwards found verified, with names and dates, in a little "Life of Petrarch," by F. Leoni, published at Padua in 1843. It appears that this curious attempt of the Florentines to do doubtful honor to the great citizen whose hereditary civic rights they restored too late (about the time he was drawing nigh his "good end" at Arquà), was made for them by a certain monk of Portagruaro named Tommaso Martinelli. He had a general instruction from his employers to bring away from Arquà "any important thing of Petrarch's" that he could; and it occurred to this ill-advised friar to "move his bones." He succeeded on a night of the year 1630 in stealing the dead poet's arm. The theft being at once discovered, the Venetian Republic rested not till the thief was also discovered; but what became of the arm or the sacrilegious monk neither the Signor Leoni nor the old women of Arquà give any account. The Republic removed the rest of Petrarch's body, which is now said to be in the Royal Museum of Madrid.

I was willing to know more of this quaint village of Arquà, and I rang at the parish priest's door to beg of him some account of the place, if any were printed. But already at one o'clock he had gone to bed for a nap, and must on no account be roused till four. It is but a quiet life men lead in Arquà, and their souls are in drowsy hands. The amount of sleep which this good man gives himself (if he goes to bed at 9 P.M. and rises at 9 A.M., with a nap of three hours during the day) speaks of a quiet conscience, a good digestion, and uneventful days. As I turned this notion over in my mind, my longing to behold his reverence increased, that I might read life at Arquà in the smooth curves of his well-padded countenance.

Ought I to say here that, on the occasion of a second visit to Arquà, I succeeded in finding this excellent ecclesiastic wide awake at two o'clock in the afternoon, and that he granted me an interview at that hour? Justice to him, I think, demands this admission of me. He was not at all a fat priest, as I had prefigured him, but rather of a spare person, and of a brisk and lively manner. At the village inn, after listening half an hour to a discourse on nothing but white wine from a young priest, who had stopped to drink a glass of it, I was put in the way of seeing the priest of Arquà by his courtesy. Happily enough, his reverence chanced to have the very thing I wanted to see—no other than Leoni's "Life of Petrarch," to which I have already referred. Courtesy is the blood in an Italian's veins, and I need not say that the ecclesiastic of Arquà, seeing my interest in the place, was very polite and obliging. But he continued to sleep throughout our first stay in Arquà, and I did not see him then.

I strolled up and down the lazy, rambling streets, and chiefly devoted myself to watching the young women who were washing clothes at the stream running from the "Fountain of Petrarch." Their arms and legs were bronzed and bare, and they chattered and laughed gayly at their work. Their wash-tubs were formed by a long marble conduit from the fountain; their wash-boards, by the inward-sloping conduit-sides; and they thrashed and beat the garments clean upon the smooth stones. To a girl, their waists were broad and their ankles thick. Above their foreheads the hair was cut short, and their "back hair" was gathered into a mass, and held together by a converging circle of silver pins. The Piazza della Fontana, in Arquà, is a place some fifty feet in length and breadth, and seems to be a favorite place of public resort. In the evening, doubtless, it is alive with gossipers, as now with workers. It may be that then his reverence, risen from his nap, saunters by, and pauses long enough to chuck a pretty girl under the chin or pinch an urchin's cheek.

III

RETURNING, we stopped at the great castle of the Obizzi (now the property of the Duke of Modena), through which we were conducted by a surly and humorous *custode*, whose pride in life was that castle and its treasures, so that he resented as a personal affront the slightest interest in anything else. He stopped us abruptly in the midst of the museum, and, regarding the precious antiques and curiosities around him, demanded,—

"Does this castle please you?" Then, with a scornful glance at us, "Your driver tells me you have been at Arquà? And what did you see at Arquà? A shabby little house and a cat without any hair on. I would not," said this disdainful *custode*, "go to Arquà if you gave me a lemonade."

THE CIMBRI

A VISIT TO THE CIMBRI

I HAD often heard in Venice of that ancient people, settled in the Alpine hills about the pretty town of Bassano, on the Brenta, whom common fame declares to be a remnant of the Cimbrian invaders of Rome, broken up in battle, and dispersed along the borders of North Italy, by Marius, many centuries ago. So once, when the soft September weather came, we sallied out of Venice, in three, to make conquest of whatever was curious in the life and traditions of these mountaineers, who dwell in seven villages, and are therefore called the people of the Sette Communi among their Italian neighbors. We went fully armed with note-book and sketch-book, and prepared to take literary possession of our conquest.

From Venice to the city of Vicenza by railroad it is two hours; and thence one must take a carriage to Bassano (which is an opulent and busy little grain mart, of some twelve thousand souls, about thirty miles north of Venice). We were very glad of the ride across the country. By the time we reached the town it was nine o'clock, and moonlight, and as we glanced out of our windows we saw the quaint up-and-down-hill streets peopled with promenaders, and everybody in Bassano seemed to be making love. Young girls strolled about the picturesque ways with their lovers, and tender couples were cooing at the doorways and windows, and the scene had all the surface of romance with which the Italians contrive to varnish the real commonplaceness of life. Our drive through the twilight landscape had prepared us for the sentiment of Bassano; we had pleased ourselves with the spectacle of the peasants returning from their labor in the fields, led in troops of eight or ten by stalwart, white-teethed, bare-legged maids; and we had reveled in the momentary lordship of an old walled town we passed, which at dusk seemed more Gothic and Middle-Age than anything after Verona, with a fine church, and turrets and battlements in great plenty. What town it was, or what it had been doing there so many ages, I have never sought to know, and I should be sorry to learn anything about it.

The next morning we began those researches for preliminary information concerning the Cimbri which turned out so vain. Indeed, as we drew near the lurking-places of that ancient people, all knowledge relating to them diffused itself into shadowy conjecture. The barber and the bookseller differed as to the best means of getting to the Sette Communi, and the *caffetiere* at whose place we took breakfast knew nothing at all of the road, except that it was up the mountains, and commanded views of scenery which, verily, it would not grieve us to see. As to the Cimbri, he only knew that they had their own language, which was yet harder than the German. The German was hard enough, but the Cimbrian! *Corpo!*

At last, hearing of a famous cave there is at Oliero, a town some miles farther up the Brenta, we determined to go there, and it was a fortunate thought, for there we found a nobleman in charge of the cave who told us exactly how to reach the Sette Communi. You pass a bridge to get out of Bassano—a bridge which spans the crystal swiftness of the Brenta, rushing down to the Adriatic from the feet of the Alps on the north, and full of voluble mills at Bassano. All along the road to Oliero was the finest mountain scenery, Brenta-washed, and picturesque with ever-changing lines. Maize grows in the bottom-lands, and tobacco, which is guarded in the fields by soldiers for the monopolist government. Farm-houses dot the valley, and now and then we passed villages, abounding in blonde girls, so rare elsewhere in Italy, but here so numerous as to give Titian that type from which he painted.

At Oliero we learned not only which was the road to the Sette Communi, but that we were in it, and it was settled that we should come the next day and continue in it, with the custodian of the cave, who for his breakfast and dinner, and what else we pleased, offered to accompany us. We were early at Oliero on the following morning, and found our friend in waiting; he mounted beside our driver, and we rode up the Brenta to the town of Valstagna where our journey by wheels ended, and where we were to take mules for the mountain ascent. Our guide, Count Giovanni Bonato (for I may as well give him his title, though at this stage of our progress we did not know into what patrician care we had fallen), had already told us what the charge for mules would be, but it was necessary to go through the ceremony of bargain with the muleteer before taking the beasts. Their owner was a Cimbrian, with a broad sheepish face, and a heavy, awkward accent of Italian which at once more marked his northern race, and made us feel comparatively secure from plunder in his hands. He had come down from the mountain top the night before, bringing three mules laden with charcoal, and he had waited for us till the morning. His beasts were furnished with comfortable pads, covered with linen, to ride upon, and with halters instead of bridles, and we were prayed to let them have their heads in the ascent, and not to try to guide them.

The leisure of Valstagna (and in an Italian town nearly the whole population is at leisure) turned out to witness the departure of our expedition; the pretty little blonde wife of our innkeeper, who was to get dinner ready against our return, held up her baby to wish us *buon viaggio*, and waved us adieu with the infant as with a handkerchief; the chickens and children scattered to right and left before our advance; and with Ciount Giovanni going splendidly ahead on foot, and the Cimbrian bringing up the rear, we struck on the broad rocky valley between the heights, and presently began the ascent. It was a lovely morning; the sun was on the heads of the hills, and the shadows clothed them like robes to their feet; and I should be glad to feel here and now the sweetness, freshness, and purity of the mountain air, that seemed to bathe our souls in a childlike delight of life. A noisy brook gurgled through the valley; the birds sang from the trees; the Alps rose, crest on crest, around us; and soft before us, among the bald peaks, showed the wooded height where the Cimbrian village of Fozza stood, with a white chapel gleaming from the heart of the lofty grove. Along the mountain sides the smoke curled from the lonely huts of shepherds, and now and then we came upon one of those melancholy refuges which are built in the hills for such travelers as are belated in their ways, or are overtaken there by storms.

The road for the most part winds by the brink of precipices,—walled in with masonry of small stones, where Nature has not shored it up with vast monoliths,—and is paved with limestone. It is, of course, merely a mule-path, and it was curious to see, and thrilling to experience, how the mules, vain of the safety of their foothold, kept as near the border of the precipices as possible. For my own part, I abandoned to my beast the entire responsibility involved by this line of conduct; let the halter hang loose upon his neck, and gave him no aid except such slight service as was occasionally to be rendered by shutting my eyes and holding my breath. The mule of the fairer traveler behind me was not only ambitious of peril like my own, but was envious of my beast's captaincy, and continually tried to pass him on the outside of the path, to the great dismay of the gentle rider; while half-suppressed wails of terror from the second lady in the train gave evidence of equal vanity and daring in her mule. Count Giovanni strode stolidly before, the Cimbrian came behind, and we had little coherent conversation until we stopped under a spreading haw-tree, half way up the mountain, to breathe our adventurous beasts.

Here two of us dismounted, and while one of the ladies sketched the other in her novel attitude of cavalier, I listened to the talk of Count Giovanni and the Cimbrian. The Cimbrian's name in Italian was Lazzaretti, and in his own tongue Brück, which, pronouncing less regularly, we made Brick, in compliment to his qualities of good fellowship. His broad, honest visage was bordered by a hedge of red beard, and a light of dry humor shone upon it: he looked, we thought, like a Cornishman, and the contrast between him and the *viso sciolto, pensieri stretti* expression of Count Giovanni was curious enough. Concerning his people, he knew little; but the Capo-gente of Fozza could tell me everything. Various traditions of their origin were believed among them; Brick himself held to one that they had first come from Denmark.

There was a poor little house of refreshment beside our spreading haw, and a withered old woman came out of it and refreshed us with clear spring water, and our guides and friends with some bitter berries of the mountain, which they admitted were unpleasant to the taste, but declared were very good for the blood. When they had sufficiently improved their blood, we mounted our mules again, and set out with the journey of an hour and a quarter still between us and Fozza.

As we drew near the summit of the mountain our road grew more level, and instead of creeping along by the brinks of precipices, we began to wind through bits of meadow and pleasant valley walled in by lofty heights of rock.

Though September was bland as June at the foot of the mountain, we found its breath harsh and cold on these heights; and we remarked that though there were here and there breadths of wheat, the land was for the most part in sheep pasturage, and the grass looked poor and stinted of summer warmth. We met, at times, the shepherds, who seemed to be of the Italian race, and were of the conventional type of shepherds, with regular faces, and two elaborate curls trained upon their cheeks, as shepherds are always represented in stone over the gates of villas. They bore staves, and their flocks went before them. Encountering us, they saluted us courteously, and when we had returned their greeting, they cried with one voice: "Ah, lords! is not this a miserable country? The people are poor and the air is cold. It is an unhappy land!" And so passed on, profoundly sad; but we could not help smiling at the vehement popular desire to have the region abused. We answered cheerfully that it was a lovely country. If the air was cold, it was also pure.

We now drew in sight of Fozza, and, at the last moment, just before parting with Brick, we learned that he had passed a whole year in Venice, where he brought milk from the mainland and sold it in the city. He declared frankly that he counted that year worth all the other years of his life, and that he would never have come back to his native heights but that his father had died, and left his mother and young brothers helpless. He was an honest soul, and I gave him two florins, which I had tacitly appointed him over and above the bargain, with something for the small Brick-bats at home, whom he presently brought to kiss our hands at the house of the Capo-gente.

The village of Fozza is built on a grassy, oblong plain on the crest of the mountain, which declines from it on three sides, and on the north rises high above it into the mists in bleaker and ruggeder acclivities. There are not more than thirty houses in the village, and I do not think it numbers more than a hundred and fifty souls, if so many. Indeed, it is one of the smallest of the Sette Communi, of which the capital, Asiago, contains some thousands of people, and lies not far from Vicenza. The poor Fozzatti had a church, however, in their village, in spite of its littleness, and they had just completed a fine new bell-tower, which the Capo-gente deplored, and was proud of when I praised it. The church, like all the other edifices, was built of stone; and the village at a little distance might look like broken crags of rock, so well it consorted with the harsh, crude nature about it. Meagre meadowlands, pathetic with tufts of a certain pale blue, tearful flower, stretched about the village and southward as far as to that wooded point which had all day been our landmark in the ascent.

Our train drew up at the humble door of the Capo-gente (in Fozza all doors are alike humble), and, leaving our mules, we entered by his wife's invitation, and seated ourselves near the welcome fire of the kitchen—welcome, though we knew that all the sunny Lombard plain below was purple with grapes and black with figs. Again came from the women here the wail of the shepherds: "Ah, lords! is it not a miserable land?" and I began to doubt whether the love which I had heard mountaineers bore to their inclement heights was not altogether fabulous. They made haste to boil us some eggs, and set them before us with some unhappy wine, and while we were eating, the Capo-gente came in.

He was a very well-mannered person, but had the bashfulness naturally resulting from his lonely life at that altitude, where contact with the world must be infrequent. His fellow-citizens seemed to regard him with a kind of affectionate deference, and some of them came in to hear him talk with the strangers. He stood till we prayed him to sit down, and he presently consented to take some wine with us.

After all, however, he could not tell us much of his people which we had not heard before. A tradition existed among them, he said, that their ancestors had fled to these Alps from Marius, and that they had dwelt for a long time in the hollows and caves of the mountains, living and burying their dead in the same secret places. At what time they had been converted to Christianity he could not tell; they had, up to the beginning of the present century, had little or no intercourse with the Italian population by which they were surrounded on all sides. Formerly, they did not intermarry with that race, and it was seldom that any Cimbrian knew its language. But now intermarriage is very frequent; both Italian and Cimbrian are spoken in nearly all the families, and the Cimbrian is gradually falling into disuse. They still, however, have books of religious instruction in their ancient dialect, and until very lately the services of their church were performed in Cimbrian.

I begged the Capo to show us some of their books, and he

brought us two,—one a catechism for children, entitled "Dar Kloane Catechism vorn Beloseland vortraghet in z' gaprecht von siben Komünen, un vier Halghe Gasang. 1842. Padova." The other book it grieved me to see, for it proved that I was not the only one tempted in recent times to visit these ancient people, ambitious to bear to them the relation of discoverer, as it were. A High-Dutch Columbus, from Vienna, had been before me, and I could only come in for Amerigo Vespucci's tempered glory. This German savant had dwelt a week in these lonely places, patiently compiling a dictionary of their tongue, which, when it was printed, he had sent to the Capo.

Concerning the present Cimbri, the Capo said that in his community they were chiefly hunters, wood-cutters, and charcoal-burners, and that they practiced their primitive crafts in those gloomier and wilder heights we saw to the northward, and descended to the towns of the plains to make sale of their fagots, charcoal, and wild-beast skins. In Asiago and the larger communities they were farmers and tradesmen like the Italians; and the Capo believed that the Cimbri, in all their villages, numbered near ten thousand. He could tell me of no particular customs or usages, and believed they did not differ from the Italians now except in race and language.[1]

They are, of course, subject to the Austrian government, but not

---

[1] The English traveler Rose, who (to my further discomfiture I find) visited Asiago in 1817, mentions that the Cimbri have the Celtic custom of *waking* the dead. "If a traveler dies by the way, they plant a cross upon the spot, and all who pass by cast a stone upon his cairn. Some go in certain seasons in the year to high places and woods, where it is supposed they worshiped their divinities, but the origin of the custom is forgot amongst themselves." If a man dies by violence, they lay him out with his hat and shoes on, as if to give him the appearance of a wayfarer, and "symbolize one surprised in the great journey of life." A woman dying in childbed is dressed for the grave in her bridal ornaments. Mr. Rose is very scornful of the notion that these people are Cimbri, and holds that it is "more consonant to all the evidence of history to say, that the flux and reflux of Teutonic invaders at different periods deposited this backwater of barbarians" in the district they now inhabit. "The whole space, which in addition to the seven burghs contains twenty-four villages, is bounded by rivers, alps, and hills. Its most precise limits are the Brenta to the east, and the Astico to the west."

so strictly as the Italians are; and though they are taxed and made to do military service, they are otherwise left to regulate their affairs pretty much at their pleasure.

The Capo ended his discourse with much polite regret that he had nothing more worthy to tell us; and, as if to make us amends for having come so far to learn so little, he said there was a hermit living near, whom we might like to see, and sent his son to conduct us to the hermitage. It turned out to be the white object which we had seen gleaming in the wood on the mountain from so great distance below, and the wood turned out to be a pleasant beechen grove, in which we found the hermit cutting fagots. He was warmly dressed in clothes without rent, and wore the clerical knee-breeches. He saluted us with a cricket-like chirpiness of manner, and was greatly amazed to hear that we had come all the way from America to visit him. His hermitage was built on the side of a whitewashed chapel of St. Francis, and contained three or four little rooms or cupboards, in which the hermit dwelt and meditated. They opened into the chapel, of which the hermit had the care, and which he kept neat and clean like himself. He told us proudly that once a year, on the day of the titular saint, a priest came and said mass in that chapel, and it was easy to see that this was the great occasion of the old man's life. For forty years, he said, he had been devout; and for twenty-five he had dwelt in this place, where the goodness of God and the charity of the poor people around had kept him from want. Altogether, he was a pleasant enough hermit, not in the least spiritual, but gentle, simple, and evidently sincere. We gave some small coins of silver to aid him to continue his life of devotion, and Count Giovanni bestowed some coppers with the stately blessing, "*Iddio vi benedica, padre mio!*"

So we left the hermitage, left Fozza, and started down the mountain on foot, for no one may ride down those steeps. Long before we reached the bottom, we had learned to loathe mountains and to long for dead levels during the rest of life. Yet the descent was picturesque, and in some things even more interesting than the ascent had been. We met more people: now melancholy shepherds with their flocks; now swineherds and swineherdesses with herds of wild black pigs of the Italian breed; now men driving asses that brayed and woke long, loud, and most musical echoes in the hills; now whole peasant families driving cows, horses, and mules to the plains below. On the way down, fragments of autobiography began, with the opportunities of conversation, to come from the Count Giovanni, and we learned that he was a private soldier at home on that *permesso* which the Austrian government frequently gives its less able-bodied men in times of peace. He had been at home some years, and did not expect to be again called into the service. He liked much better to be in charge of the cave at Oliero than to carry the musket, though he confessed that he liked to see the world, and that soldiering brought one acquainted with many places. He had not many ideas, and the philosophy of his life chiefly regarded deportment toward strangers who visited the cave. He held it an error in most custodians to show discontent when travelers gave them little; and he said that if he received never so much, he believed it wise not to betray exultation. "Always be contented, and nothing more," said Count Giovanni.

"It is what you people always promise beforehand," I said, "when you bargain with strangers, to do them a certain service for what they please; but afterward they must pay what *you* please or have trouble. I know you will not be content with what I give you."

"If I am not content," cried Count Giovanni, "call me the greatest ass in the world!"

And I am bound to say that, for all I could see through the mask of his face, he was satisfied with what I gave him, though it was not much.

He had told us casually that he was nephew of a nobleman of a certain rich and ancient family in Venice, who sent him money while in the army, but this made no great impression upon me; and though I knew there was enough noble poverty in Italy to have given rise to the proverb, *Un conte che non conta, non conta niente*, yet I confess that it was with a shock of surprise I heard our guide and servant saluted by a lounger in Valstagna with *"Sior conte, servitor suo!"* I looked narrowly at him, but there was no ray of feeling or pride visible in his pale languid visage as he responded, *"Buona sera, caro."*

Still, after that revelation we simple plebeians, who had been all day heaping shawls and guidebooks upon Count Giovanni, demanding menial offices from him, and treating him with good-natured slight, felt uncomfortable in his presence, and welcomed the appearance of our carriage with our driver, who, having started drunk from Bassano in the morning, had kept drunk all day at Valstagna, and who now drove us back wildly over the road, and almost made us sigh for the security of mules ambitious of the brinks of precipices.

MINOR TRAVELS

I. PISA

I AM afraid that the talk of the modern railway traveler, if he is
honest, must be a great deal of the custodians, the vetturini,
and the facchini, whose acquaintance constitutes his chief knowledge of the population among which he journeys. We do not
nowadays carry letters recommending us to citizens of the different places. If we did, consider the calamity we should be to the
be-traveled Italian communities we now bless! No, we buy our
through tickets, and we put up at the hotels praised in the
hand-book, and are very glad of a little conversation with any
native, however adulterated he be by contact with the world to
which we belong. I do not blush to own that I love the whole
rascal race which ministers to our curiosity and preys upon us,
and I am not ashamed to have spoken so often in this book of the
lowly and rapacious but interesting porters who opened to me the
different gates of that great realm of wonders, Italy. I doubt if they
can be much known to the dwellers in the land, though they are

the intimates of all sojourners and passengers; and if I have any regret in the matter, it is that I did not more diligently study them when I could.

Among memorable custodians in Italy was one whom we saw at Pisa, where we stopped on our way from Leghorn after our accident in the Maremma, and spent an hour in viewing the Quattro Fabbriche. The beautiful old town, which every one knows from the report of travelers, one yet finds possessed of the incommunicable charm which keeps it forever novel to the visitor. Lying upon either side of the broad Arno, it mirrors in the flood architecture almost as fair and noble as that glassed in the Canalazzo, and its other streets seemed as tranquil as the canals of Venice. Those over which we drove, on the day of our visit, were paved with broad flagstones, and gave out scarcely a sound under our wheels. It was Sunday, and no one was to be seen. Yet the empty and silent city inspired us with no sense of desolation. The palaces were in perfect repair; the pavements were clean; behind those windows we felt that there must be a good deal of easy, comfortable life. It is said that Pisa is one of the few places in Europe where the sweet, but timid spirit of Inexpensiveness— everywhere pursued by Railways—still lingers, and that you find cheap apartments in those well-preserved old palaces. No doubt it would be worth more to live in Pisa than it would cost, for the history of the place would alone be to any reasonable sojourner a perpetual recompense, and a princely income far exceeding his expenditure. To be sure, the Tower of Famine, with which we chiefly associate the name of Pisa, has been long razed to the ground, and built piecemeal into the neighboring palaces, but you may still visit the dead wall which hides from view the place where it stood; and you may thence drive on, as we did, to the great Piazza where stands the most famous group of architecture in the world, after that of St. Mark's Place in Venice. There is the wonderful Leaning Tower, there is the old and beautiful Duomo, there is the noble Baptistery, there is the lovely Campo Santo, and there—somewhere lurking in portal or behind pillar, and keeping out an eagle-eye for ther marveling stranger—is the much-experienced cicerone who shows you through the edifices. Yours is the fourteen-thousandth American family to which he has had the honor of acting as guide, and he makes you feel an illogical satisfaction in thus becoming a contribution to statistics. We entered the Duomo, in our new friend's custody, and we saw the things which it was well to see. There was mass, or some other ceremony, transacting; but as usual it was made as little obtrusive as possible, and there was not much to weaken the sense of proprietorship with which travelers view objects of interest. Then we ascended the Leaning Tower, skillfully preserving its equilibrium as we went by an inclination of our persons in a direction opposed to the tower's inclination, but perhaps not receiving a full justification of the Campanile's appearance in pictures, till we stood at its base, and saw its vast bulk and height as it seemed to sway and threaten in the blue sky above our heads. There the sensation was too terrible for endurance,—even the architectural beauty of the tower could not save it from being monstrous to us,—and we were glad to hurry away from it to the serenity and solemn loveliness of the Campo Santo.

Here are the frescoes painted five hundred years ago to be ruinous and ready against the time of your arrival in 1864, and you feel you are the first to enjoy the joke of the Vergognosa, that cunning jade who peers through her fingers at the shameful condition of deboshed father Noah, and seems to wink one eye of wicked amusement at you. Turning afterward to any book written about Italy during the time specified, you find your impression of exclusive possession of the frescoes erroneous, and your muse naturally despairs, where so many muses have labored in vain, to give a just idea of the Campo Santo. Yet it is most worthy celebration. Those exquisitely arched and traceried colonnades seem to grow like the slim cypresses out of the sainted earth of Jerusalem; and those old paintings, made when Art was—if ever— a Soul, and not as now a mere Intelligence, enforce more effectively than their authors conceived the lessons of life and death; for they are themselves becoming part of the triumphant decay they represent. If it was awful once to look upon that strange scene where the gay lords and ladies of the chase come suddenly upon three dead men in their coffins, while the devoted hermits enjoy the peace of a dismal righteousness on a hill in the background, it is yet more tragic to behold it now when the dead men are hardly discernible in their coffins, and the hermits are but the vaguest shadows of gloomy bliss. Alas! Death mocks even the homage done him by our poor fears and hopes: with dust he covers dust, and with decay he blots the image of decay.

I assure the reader that I made none of these apt reflections in the Campo Santo at Pisa, but have written them out this morning in Cambridge because there happens to be an east wind blowing. No one could have been sad in the company of our cheerful and patient cicerone, who, although visibly anxious to get his fourteen-thousandth American family away, still would not go till he had shown us that monument to a dead enmity which hangs in the Campo Santo. This is the mighty chain which the Pisans, in their old wars with the Genoese, once stretched across the mouth of their harbor to prevent the entrance of the hostile galleys. The Genoese with no great trouble carried the chain away, and kept it ever afterward till 1860, when Pisa was united to the kingdom of Italy. Then the trophy was restored to the Pisans, and with public rejoicings placed in the Campo Santo, an emblem of reconciliation and perpetual amity between ancient foes.[1]

It is not a very good world,—*e pur si muove.*

The Baptistery stands but a step away from the Campo Santo, and our guide ushered us into it with the air of one who had till now held in reserve his great stroke and was ready to deliver it. Yet I think he waited till we had looked at some comparatively trifling sculptures by Nicolò Pisano before he raised his voice and uttered a melodious species of howl. While we stood in some amazement

---

[1] I read in Mr. Norton's *Notes of Travel and Study in Italy,* that he saw in the Campo Santo, as long ago as 1856, "the chains that marked the servitude of Pisa, now restored by Florence," and it is of course possible that our cicerone may have employed one of those chains for the different historical purpose I have mentioned. It would be a thousand pities, I think, if a monument of that sort should be limited to the commemoration of one fact only.

at this, the conscious structure of the dome caught the sound and prolonged it with a variety and sweetness of which I could not have dreamed. The man poured out in quick succession his musical wails, and then ceased, and a choir of heavenly echoes burst forth in response. There was a supernatural beauty in these harmonies of which I despair of giving any true idea: they were of such tender and exalted rapture that we might well have thought them the voices of young-eyed cherubim, singing as they passed through Paradise over that spot of earth where we stood. They seemed a celestial compassion that stooped and soothed, and rose again in lofty and solemn acclaim, leaving us poor and penitent and humbled.

We were long silent, and then broke forth with cries of admiration of which the marvelous echo made eloquence.

"Did you ever," said the cicerone after we had left the building, "hear such music as that?"

"The papal choir does not equal it," we answered with one voice.

The cicerone was not to be silenced even with such a tribute, and he went on:

"Perhaps, as you are Americans, you know Moshu Feelmore, the President? No? Ah, what a fine man! You saw that he had his heart actually in his hand! Well, one day he said to me here, when I told him of the Baptistery echo, 'We have the finest echo in the world in the Hall of Congress.' I said nothing, but for answer I merely howled a little,—thus! Moshu Feelmore was convinced. Said he, 'There is no other echo in the world besides this. You are right.' I am unique," pursued the cicerone, "for making this echo. But," he added with a sigh, "it has been my ruin. The English have put me in all the guide-books, and sometimes I have to howl twenty times a day. When our Victor Emanuel came here I showed him the church, the tower, and the Campo Santo. Says the king, 'Pfui!' "—here the cicerone gave that sweeping outward motion with both hands by which Italians dismiss a trifling subject— 'make me the echo!' I was forced," concluded the cicerone with a strong pretense of injury in his tone, "to howl half an hour without ceasing."

II. TRIESTE

IF you take the midnight steamer at Venice you reach Trieste by
six o'clock in the morning, and the hills rise to meet you as you
enter the broad bay dotted with the sail of fishing-craft. The hills
are bald and bare, and you find, as you draw near, that the city lies
at their feet under a veil or mist, or climbs earlier into view along
their sides. The prospect is singularly devoid of gentle and pleasing
features, and looking at those rugged acclivities, with their aspect
of continual bleakness, you readily believe all the stories you have
heard of that fierce wind called the Bora which sweeps from them

through Trieste at certain seasons. While it blows, ladies walking near the quays are sometimes caught up and set afloat, involuntary Galateas, in the bay, and people keep indoors as much as possible. But the Bora, though so sudden and so savage, does give warning of its rise, and the peasants avail themselves of this characteristic. They station a man on one of the mountain tops, and when he feels the first breath of the Bora, he sounds a horn, which is a signal for all within hearing to lay hold of something that cannot be blown away, and cling to it till the wind falls. This may happen in three days or in nine, according to the popular proverbs. "The spectacle of the sea," says Dall' Ongaro, in a note to one of his ballads, "while the Bora blows, is sublime, and when it ceases the prospect of the surrounding hills is delightful. The air, purified by the rapid current, clothes them with a rosy veil, and the temperature is instantly softened, even in the heart of winter."

The city itself, as you penetrate it, makes good with its stateliness and picturesqueness your loss through the grimness of its environs. It is in great part new, very clean, and full of the life and movement of a prosperous port; but, better than this, so far as the mere sight-seer is concerned, it wins a peculiar charm from the many public staircases by which you ascend and descend its hillier quarters, and which are made of stone, and lightly railed and balustraded with iron.

Something of all this I noticed in my ride from the landing of the steamer to the house of friends in the suburbs, and there I grew better disposed toward the hills, which, as I strolled over them, I found dotted with lovely villas, and everywhere traversed by perfectly kept carriage-roads, and easy and pleasant footpaths. It was in the spring-time, and the peach-trees and almond-trees hung full of blossoms and bees, the lizards lay in the walks absorbing the vernal sunshine, the violets and cowslips sweetened all the grassy borders. The scene did not want a human interest, for the peasant girls were going to market at that hour, and I met them everywhere, bearing heavy burdens on their own heads, or hurrying forward with their wares on the backs of donkeys. They were as handsome as heart could wish, and they wore that Italian costume which is not to be seen anywhere in Italy except at Trieste and in the Roman and Neapolitan provinces,—a bright bodice and gown, with the headdress of dazzling white linen, square upon the crown, and dropping lightly to the shoulders. Later I saw these comely maidens crouching on the ground in the market-place, and selling their wares, with much glitter of eyes, teeth, and earrings, and a continual babble of bargaining.

It seemed to me that the average of good looks was greater among the women of Trieste than among those of Venice, but that the instances of striking and exquisite beauty were rarer. At Trieste, too, the Italian type, so pure at Venice, is lost or continually modified by the mixed character of the population, which is per-haps most noticeable at the Merchants' Exchange. This is a vast edifice roofed with glass, where the traffickers of all races meet daily to gossip over the news and the prices. Here a Greek or Dalmat talks with an eager Italian or a slow, sure Englishman; here the hated Austrian buttonholes the Venetian or the Magyar; here the Jew meets the Gentile on common ground; here Christianity encounters the hoary superstitions of the East, and makes a good thing out of them in cotton or grain. All costumes are seen here, and all tongues are heard, the native Triestines contributing almost as much to the variety of parlance as the foreigners. "In regard to language," says Cantù, "though the country is peopled by Slavonians, yet the Italian tongue is spreading into the remotest villages where a few years since it was not understood. In the city it is the common and familiar language; the Slavonians of the North use the German for the language of ceremony; those of the South, as well as the Israelites, the Italian; while the Protestants use the German, the Greeks the Hellenic and Illyric, the *employés* of the civil courts the Italian or the German, the schools now German and now Italian, the bar and the pulpit Italian. Most of the inhabitants, indeed, are bi-lingual, and very many tri-lingual, without counting French, which is un-derstood and spoken from infancy. Italian, German, and Greek are written, but the Slavonic little, this having remained in the condi-tion of a vulgar tongue. But it would be idle to distinguish the population according to language, for the son adopts a language different from the father's, and now prefers one language and now another; the women incline to the Italian; but those of the upper class prefer now German, now French, now English, as, from one decade to another, affairs, fashions, and fancies change. This in the salons; in the squares and streets, the Venetian dialect is heard." And with the introduction of the Venetian dialect, Venetian discontent seems also to have crept in, and I once heard a Triestine declaim against the Imperial government quite in the manner of Venice. It struck me that this desire for union with Italy, which he declared prevalent in Trieste, must be of very recent growth, since even so late as 1848 Trieste had refused to join Venice in the expulsion of the Austrians. Indeed, the Triestines have fought the Venetians from the first; they stole the Brides of Venice in one of their piratical cruises in the lagoons; gave aid and comfort to those enemies of Venice, the Visconti, the Carraras, and the Genoese; revolted from St. Mark whenever subjected to his banner, and finally, rather than remain under his sway, gave themselves five centuries ago to Austria.

The objects of interest in Trieste are not many. There are remains of an attributive temple of Jupiter under the Duomo, and there is near at hand the Museum of Classical Antiquities founded in honor of Winckelmann, murdered at Trieste by Ancangeli, who had seen the medals bestowed on the antiquary by Maria Theresa and believed him rich. There is also a scientific museum founded by the Archduke Maximilian, and, above all, there is the beautiful residence of that ill-starred prince,—the Miramare, where the half-crazed Empress of the Mexicans vainly waits her husband's return from the experiment of paternal government in the New World. It would be hard to tell how Art has charmed rock and wave at Miramare until the spur of one of those rugged Triestine hills, jutting into the sea, has been made the seat of ease and luxury, but the visitor is aware of the magic as soon as he passes the gate of the palace grounds. These are in great part perpendicular, and are over clambered with airy stairways climbing to pensile arbors. Where horizontal, they are diversified with mimic seas for swans to sail upon, and summer-houses for people to lounge in and look at the swans from. On the point of land farthest from the aclivity stands the Castle of Miramare, half at sea, and half adrift in the clouds above:—

> "And fain it would stoop downward
> To the mirrored wave below;
> And fain it would soar upward
> In the evening's crimson glow."

I remember that a little yacht lay beside the pier at the castle's foot, and lazily flapped its sail, while the sea beat inward with as languid a pulse. That was some years ago, before Mexico was dreamed of at Miramare: now, perchance, she who is one of the most unhappy among women looks down distraught from those high windows, and finds in the helpless sail and impassive wave the images of her baffled hope, and that immeasurable sea which gives back its mariners neither to love nor sorrow. I think though she be the wife and daughter of princes, we may pity this poor Empress at least as much as we pity the Mexicans to whom her dreams brought so many woes.

It was the midnight following my visit to Miramare when the fiacre in which I had quitted my friend's house was drawn up by its greatly bewildered driver on the quay near the place where the steamer for Venice should be lying. There was no steamer for Venice to be seen. The driver swore a little in the polyglot profanities of his native city, and descending from his box, went and questioned different lights—blue lights, yellow lights, green lights—to be seen at different points. To a light, they were ignorant, though eloquent, and to pass the time, we drove up and down the quay, and stopped at the landings of all the steamers that touch at Trieste. It was a snug fiacre enough, but I did not care to spend the night in it, and I urged the driver to further inquiry. A wanderer whom we met declared that it was not the night for the Venice steamer; another admitted that it might be; a third conversed with the driver in low tones, and then leaped upon the box. We drove rapidly away, and before I had, in view of this mysterious proceeding, composed a fitting paragraph for the *Fatti Diversi* of the "Osservatore Triestino," descriptive of the state in which the Guardie di Polizia should find me floating in the bay, exanimate and evidently the prey of a *triste evenimento*—the driver pulled up once more, and now beside a steamer. It was the steamer for Venice, he said, in precisely the tone which he would have used had he driven me directly to it without blundering. It was breathing heavily, and was just about to depart, but even in the hurry of getting on board, I could not help noticing that it seemed to have grown a great deal since I had last voyaged on it. There was not a soul to be seen except the mute steward who took my satchel, and guiding me below into an elegant saloon, instantly left me alone. Here again the steamer was vastly enlarged. These were not the narrow quarters of the Venice steamer, nor was this lamp, shedding a soft light on cushioned seats and paneled doors and wainscotings the sort of illumination usual in that humble craft. I rang the small silver bell on the long table, and the mute steward appeared.

Was this the steamer for Venice?

Sicuro!

All that I could do in comment was to sit down; and in the mean time the steamer trembled, groaned, choked, cleared its throat, and we were under way.

"The other passengers have all gone to bed, I suppose," I argued acutely, seeing none of them. Nevertheless, I thought it odd, and it seemed a shrewd means of relief to ring the bell, and pretending drowsiness, to ask the steward which was my stateroom.

He replied with a curious smile that I could have any of them. Amazed, I yet selected a stateroom, and while the steward was gone for the sheets and pillow-cases, I occupied my time by opening the doors of all the other staterooms. They were empty.

"Am I the only passenger?" I asked, when he returned, with some anxiety.

"Precisely," he answered.

I could not proceed and ask if he composed the entire crew—it seemed too fearfully probable that he did.

I now suspected that I had taken passage with the Olandese
Volante. There was nothing in the world for it, however, but to go
to bed, and there, with the accession of a slight seasickness, my
views of the situation underwent a total change. I had gone down
into the Maelstrom with the Ancient Mariner—I was a Manuscript Found in a Bottle!

Coming to the surface about six o'clock A.M., I found a daylight
as cheerful as need be upon the appointments of the elegant
saloon, and upon the good-natured face of the steward when he
brought me the *caffè latte*, and the buttered toast for my
breakfast. He said "*Servitor suo!*" in a loud and comfortable
voice, and I perceived the absurdity of having thought that he was
in any way related to the Nightmare-Death-in-life-that-thicks-
man's-blood-with-cold.

"This is not the regular Venice steamer, I suppose," I remarked
to the steward as he laid my breakfast in state upon the long table.

No. Properly, no boat should have left for Venice last night,
which was not one of the times of the tri-weekly departure. This
was one of the steamers of the line between Trieste and Alexan-
dria, and it was going at present to take on an extraordinary
freight at Venice for Egypt. I had been permitted to come on board
because my driver said I had a return ticket, and would go.

Ascending to the deck I found nothing whatever mysterious in the
management of the steamer. The captain met me with a bow in the
gangway; seamen were coiling wet ropes at different points, as they
always are; the mate was promenading the bridge, and taking the
rainy weather as it came, with his oil-cloth coat and hat on.

We were in sight of the breakwater outside Malamocco, and a
pilot-boat was making us from the land. Even at this point the
innumerable fortifications of the Austrians began, and they mul-
tiplied as we drew near Venice, till we entered the lagoon, and
found it a nest of fortresses one with another.

Unhappily the day being rainy, Venice did not spring resplendent from the sea, as I had always read she would. She rose slowly
and languidly from the water,—not like a queen, but like the gray,
slovenly, bedrabbled, heart-broken old slave she really was.

III. BASSANO

I HAVE already told, in recounting the story of our visit to the Cimbri, how full of courtship we found the little city of Bassano on the evening of our arrival there. Bassano is the birthplace of the painter Jacopo da Ponte, who was one of the first Italian painters to treat scriptural story as accessory to mere landscape, and who had a peculiar fondness for painting Entrances into the Ark, for in these he could indulge without stint the taste for pairing-off early acquired from observation of local customs in his native town. This was the theory offered by one who had imbibed the spirit of subtle speculation from Ruskin, and I think it reasonable. At least it does not conflict with the fact that there is at Bassano a most excellent gallery of paintings entirely devoted to the works of Jacopo da Ponte, and his four sons, who are here to be seen to better advantage than anywhere else. As few strangers visit Bassano, the gallery is little frequented. It is in the charge of a very strict old man, who will not allow people to look at the pictures till he has shown them the adjoining cabinet of geological specimens. It is in vain that you assure him of your indifference to these scientific *seccature*; he is deaf, and you are not suffered to escape a single fossil. He asked us a hundred questions, and understood nothing in reply, insomuch that when he came to his last inquiry, "Have the Protestants the same God as the Catholics?" we were rather glad that he should be obliged to settle the fact for himself.

Underneath the gallery was a school of boys, whom as we entered we heard humming over the bitter honey which childhood is obliged to gather from the opening flowers of orthography. When we passed out, the master gave these poor busy bees an atom of holiday, and they all swarmed forth together to look at the strangers. The teacher was a long, lank man, in a black threadbare coat, and a skull-cap—exactly like the schoolmaster in "The Deserted Village." We made a pretense of asking him our way to somewhere, and went wrong, and came by accident upon a wide flat space, bare as a brick-yard, beside which was lettered on a fragment of the old city wall, "Giuoco di Palla." It was evidently the playground of the whole city, and it gave us a pleasanter idea of life in Bassano than we had yet conceived, to think of its entire population playing ball there in the spring afternoons. We respected Bassano as much for this as for her diligent remembrance of her illustrious dead, of whom she has very great numbers. It appeared to us that nearly every house bore a tablet announcing that "Here was born," or "Here died," some great or good man of whom no one out of Bassano ever heard. There is enough celebrity in Bassano to supply the world; but as laurel is a thing that grows anywhere, I covet rather from Bassano the magnificent ivy that covers the portions of her ancient wall yet standing. The wall, where visible, is seen to be of a pebbly rough-cast, but it is clad almost from the ground in glossy ivy, that glitters upon it like chain-mail upon the vast shoulders of some giant warrior. The moat beneath is turned into a lovely promenade bordered by quiet villas, with rococo shepherds and shepherdesses in marble on their gates; where the wall is built on the verge of the high ground on which the city stands, there is a swift descent to the wide valley of the Brenta waving in corn and vines and tobacco.

We went up the Brenta one day as far as Oliero, to visit the famous cavern already mentioned, out of which, from the secret heart of the hill, gushes one of the foamy affluents of the river. It is reached by passing through a paper-mill, fed by the stream, and then through a sort of ante-grot whence stepping-stones are laid in the brawling current through a succession of natural compartments with dome-like roofs. From the hill overhead hang stalactites of all grotesque and fairy shapes, and the rock underfoot is embroidered with fantastic designs wrought by the water in the silence and darkness of the endless night. At a considerable distance from the mouth of the cavern is a wide lake, with a boat upon it, and voyaging to the centre of the pool your attention is drawn to the dome above you, which contracts into a shaft rising upward to a height as yet unmeasured and even unpierced by light. From somewhere in its mysterious ascent, an auroral boy, with a tallow candle, produces a so-called effect of sunrise, and sheds a sad, disheartening radiance on the lake and the cavern sides, which is to sunlight about as the blind creatures of subterranean waters are to those of waves that laugh and dance above ground. But all caverns are much alike in their depressing and gloomy influences, and since there is so great opportunity to be wretched on the surface of the earth, why do people visit them? I do not know that this is more dispiriting or its stream more Stygian than another.

The wicked memory of the Ecelini survives everywhere in this part of Italy, and near the entrance of the Oliero grotto is a hollow in the hill something like the apsis of a church, which is popularly believed to have been the hiding-place of Cecilia da Baone, one of the many unhappy wives of the many miserable members of the Ecelino family. It is not quite clear when Cecilia should have employed this as a place of refuge, and it is certain that she was not the wife of Ecelino da Romano, as the neighbors believe at Oliero, but of Ecelino il Monaco, his father; yet since her name is associated with the grot, let us have her story, which is curiously illustrative of the life of the best society in Italy during the thirteenth century. She was the only daughter of the rich and potent lord, Manfredo, Count of Baone and Abano, who died leaving his heiress to the guardianship of Spinabello da Xendrico. When his ward reached womanhood, Spinabello cast about him to find a suitable husband for her, and it appeared to him that a match with the son of Tiso da Camposampiero promised the greatest advantages. Tiso, to whom he proposed the affair, was delighted, but desiring first to take counsel with his friends upon so important a matter, he confided it for advice to his brother-in-law and closest intimate, Ecelino Balbo. It had just happened that Balbo's son, Ecelino il Monaco, was at that moment disengaged, having been recently divorced from his first wife, the lovely but light Speronella; and Balbo falsely went to the greedy guardian of Cecilia, and offering him better terms than he could hope for from Tiso, secured Cecilia for his son. At this treachery the Camposampieri were furious; but they dissembled their anger till the moment of revenge arrived, when Cecilia's rejected suitor encountering her upon a journey beyond the protection of her husband, violently dishonored his successful rival. The unhappy lady returning to Ecelino at Bassano, recounted her wrong, and was with a horrible injustice repudiated and sent home, while her husband arranged schemes of vengeance in due time consummated. Cecilia next married a Venetian noble, and being in due time divorced, married yet again, and died the mother of a large family of children.

This is a very old scandal, yet I think there was an *habitué* of the caffè in Bassano who could have given some of its particulars from personal recollection. He was an old and smoothly shaven gentleman, in a scrupulously white waistcoat, whom we saw every evening in a corner of the caffè playing solitaire. He talked with no one, saluted no one. He drank his glasses of water with anisette, and silently played solitaire. There is no good reason to doubt that he had been doing the same thing every evening for six hundred years.

IV. POSSAGNO, CANOVA'S BIRTHPLACE

IT did not take a long time to exhaust the interest of Bassano, but we were sorry to leave the place because of the excellence of the inn at which we tarried. It was called "Il Mondo," and it had everything in it that heart could wish. Our rooms were miracles of neatness and comfort; they had the freshness, not the rawness, of recent repair, and they opened into the dining-hall, where we were served with indescribable salads and risotti. During our sojourn we simply enjoyed the house; when we were come away we wondered that such perfection of hotel could exist in so small a town as Bassano. It is one of the pleasures of byway travel in Italy, that you are everywhere introduced in character, that you become fictitious and play a part as in a novel. To this inn of The World, our driver had brought us with a clamor and rattle proportioned to the fee received from us, and when, in response to his haughty summons, the cameriere, who had been gossiping with the cook, threw open the kitchen door, and stood out to welcome us in a broad square of forth-streaming ruddy light, amid the lovely odors of broiling and roasting, our driver saluted him with, "Receive these gentle folks, and treat them to your very best. They are worthy of anything." This at once put us back several centuries, and we never ceased to be lords and ladies of the period of Don Quixote as long as we rested in that inn.

It was a bright and breezy Sunday when we left "Il Mondo," and gayly journeyed toward Treviso, intending to visit Possagno, the birthplace of Canova, on our way. The road to the latter place passes through a beautiful country, that gently undulates on either hand till in the distance it rises into pleasant hills and green mountain heights. Possagno itself lies upon the brink of a declivity, down the side of which drops terrace after terrace, all planted with vines and figs and peaches, to a watercourse below. The ground on which the village is built, with its quaint and antiquated stone cottages, slopes gently northward, and on a little rise upon the left hand of us coming from Bassano we saw that stately edifice with which Canova has honored his humble birthplace. It is a copy of the Pantheon, and it cannot help being beautiful and imposing, but it would be utterly out of place in any other than an Italian village. Here, however, it consorted well enough with the lingering qualities of the old pagan civilization still perceptible in Italy. A sense of that past was so strong with us as we ascended the broad stairway leading up the slope from the village to the level on which the temple stands at the foot of a mountain, that we might well have believed we approached an altar devoted to the elder worship: through the open doorway and between the columns of the portico we could see the priests moving to and fro, and the voice of their chanting came out to us like the sound of hymns to some of the deities long disowned; and I remember how Padre L—— had said to me in Venice, "Our blessed saints are only the old gods baptized and christened anew." Within as without, the temple resembled the Pantheon, but it had little to show us. The niches designed by Canova for statues of the saints are empty yet; but there are busts by his own hand of himself and his brother, the Bishop Canova. Among the people was the sculptor's niece, whom our guide pointed out to us, and who was evidently used to being looked at. She seemed not to dislike us, and stared back at us amiably enough, being a good-natured, plump, comely dark-faced lady of perhaps fifty years.

Possagno is nothing if not Canova, and our guide, a boy, knew all about him,—how, more especially, he had first manifested his wonderful genius by modeling a group of sheep out of the dust of the highway, and how an Inglese happening along in his carriage, saw the boy's work and gave him a plateful of gold napoleons. I dare say this is as near the truth as most facts. And is it not better for Canova to have begun in this way than to have poorly picked up the rudiments of his art in the workshop of his father, a maker of altar-pieces and the like for country churches? The Canova family has intermarried with the Venetian nobility, and will not credit those stories of Canova's beginnings which his townsmen so fondly cherish. I believe they would even distrust the butter lion with which the boy sculptor is said to have adorned the table of the noble Falier, and first won his notice.

Besides the temple at Possagno, there is a very pretty gallery containing casts of all Canova's works. It is an interesting place, where Psyches and Cupids flutter, where Venuses present themselves in every variety of attitude, where Sorrows sit upon hard, straight-backed classic chairs, and mourn in the society of faithful Storks; where the Bereft of this century surround deathbeds in Greek costume appropriate to the scene; where Muses and Graces sweetly pose themselves and insipidly smile, and where the Dancers and Passions, though nakeder, are no wickeder than the Saints and Virtues. In all, there are a hundred and ninety-five pieces in the gallery, and among the rest the statue named George Washington, which was sent to America in 1820, and afterwards destroyed by fire in the Capitol. The figure is in a sitting posture;

naturally, it is in the dress of a Roman general; and if it does not look much like George Washington, it does resemble Julius Cæsar.

The custodian of the gallery had been Canova's body-servant, and he loved to talk of his master. He had so far imbibed the family spirit that he did not like to allow that Canova had ever been other than rich and grand, and he begged us not to believe the idle stories of his first essays in art. He was delighted with our interest in the Cæsarean Washington, and our pleasure in the whole gallery, which we viewed with the homage due to the man who had rescued the world from Swaggering in sculpture. When we were satisfied, he invited us, with his mistress's permission, into the house of the Canovas adjoining the gallery; and there we saw many paintings by the sculptor,—pausing longest in a lovely little room decorated after the Pompeian manner with *scherzi* in miniature panels representing the jocose classic usualities: Cupids escaping from cages, and being sold from them, and playing many pranks and games with Nymphs and Graces.

Then Canova was done, and Possagno was finished; and we resumed our way to Treviso, a town nearly as much porticoed as Padua, and having a memory and hardly any other consciousness. The Duomo, which is perhaps the ugliest duomo in the world, contains an "Annunciation" by Titian, one of his best paintings; and in the Monte di Pietà is the beautiful "Entombment" by which Giorgione is perhaps most worthily remembered. The church of San Nicolò is interesting from its quaint frescoes by the school of Giotto. At the railway station an admirable old man sells the most delicious white and purple grapes.

V. COMO

MY visit to Lake Como has become to me a dream of summer,—a vision that remains faded the whole year round, till the blazing heats of July bring out the sympathetic tints in which it was vividly painted. Then I behold myself again in burning Milan, amidst noises and fervors and bustle that seem intolerable after my first six months in tranquil, cool, mute Venice. Looking at the great white Cathedral, with its infinite pinnacles piercing the cloudless blue, and gathering the fierce sun upon it, I half expect to see the whole mass calcined by the heat, and crumbling, statue by statue, finial by finial, arch by arch, into a vast heap of lime on the Piazza, with a few charred English tourists blackening here and there upon the ruin, and contributing a smell of burnt leather and Scotch tweed to the horror of the scene. All round Milan smokes the great Lombard plain, and to the north rises Monte Rosa, her dark head coifed with tantalizing snows as with a peasant's white linen kerchief. And I am walking out upon that fuming plain as far as to Arco della Pace, on which the bronze horses may melt any minute; or am I sweltering through the city's noonday streets, in search of Sant' Ambrogio, or the Cenacolo of Da Vinci, or what know I? Coming back to our hotel, "Alla Bella Venezia," and greeted on entering by the immense fresco which covers one whole side of the court, it appeared to my friend and me no wonder that Garibaldi should look so longingly from the prow of a gondola toward the airy towers and balloon-like domes that swim above the unattainable lagoons of Venice, where the Austrian then lorded it in coolness and quietness, while hot, red-shirted Italy was shut out upon the dusty plains and stony hills. Our desire for water became insufferable; we paid our modest bills, and at six o'clock took the train for Como, where we arrived about the hour when Don Abbondio, walking down the lonely path with his book of devotions in his hand, gave himself to the Devil on meeting the bravos of Don Rodrigo. I counsel the reader to turn to "I Promessi Sposi," if he would know how all the lovely Como country looks at that hour. For me the ride through the evening landscape, and the faint sentiment of pensiveness provoked by the smell of the ripening maize, which exhales the same sweetness on the way to Como that it does on any Ohio bottom-land, have given me an appetite, and I am to dine before wooing the descriptive Muse.

After dinner, we find at the door of the hotel an English architect whom we know, and we take a boat together for a moonlight row upon the lake, and voyage far up the placid water through air that bathes our heated senses like dew. How far we have left Milan behind! On the lake lies the moon, but the hills are held by mysterious shadows, which for the time are as substantial to us as the hills themselves. Hints of habitation appear in the twinkling lights along the water's edge, and we suspect an alabaster lamp in every casement, and in every invisible house a villa such as Claude Menotte described to Pauline,—and some one mouths that well-worn fustian.

The town of Como lies, a swarm of lights, behind us; the hills and shadows gloom around; the lake is a sheet of tremulous silver. There is no telling how we get back to our hotel, or with what satisfied hearts we fall asleep in our room there. The steamer starts for the head of the lake at eight o'clock in the morning, and we go on board at that hour.

There is some pretense of shelter in the awning stretched over the after part of the boat; but we do not feel the need of it in the fresh morning air, and we get as near the bow as possible, that we may be the very first to enjoy the famous beauty of the scenes opening before us. A few sails dot the water, and everywhere there are small, canopied rowboats, such as we went pleasuring in last night. We reach a bend in the lake, and all the roofs and towers of the city of Como pass from view, as if they had been so much architecture painted on a scene and shifted out of sight at a theatre. But other roofs and towers constantly succeed them, not less lovely and picturesque than they, with every curve of the many-curving lake. We advance over charming expanses of water lying between lofty hills; and as the lake is narrow, the voyage is like that of a winding river. Wherever the hills do not descend sheer into Como, a pretty town nestles on the brink, or, if not a town, then a villa, or else a cottage, if there is room for nothing more. Many little towns climb the heights half way, and where the hills are green and cultivated in vines or olives, peasants' houses scale them to the crest. They grow loftier and loftier as we leave our starting-place farther behind, and as we draw near Colico they wear light wreaths of cloud and snow. So cool a breeze has drawn down between them all the way that we fancy it to have come from them till we stop at Colico, and find that, but for the efforts of our honest engine, sweating and toiling in the dark below, we should have had no current of air. A burning calm is in the atmosphere, and on the broad, flat valley,—out of which a marshy stream oozes into the lake,—and on the snow-crowned hills upon the left, and on the dirty village of Colico upon the right, and on the indolent beggars waiting to welcome us, and sunning their goitres at the landing.

The name Colico, indeed, might be literally taken in English as descriptive of the local insalubrity. The place was once large, but it has fallen away much from sickness, and we found a bill posted in its public places inviting emigrants to America on the part of a German steamship company. And yet Colico, though undeniably hot, and openly dirty, and tacitly unhealthy, had merits, though the dinner we got there was not among its virtues. It had an accessible country about it; that is, its woods and fields were not impenetrably walled in from the vagabond and after we had dined we went and lay down under some greenly waving trees beside a field of corn, and heard the plumed and panoplied maize talking to itself of its kindred in America. It always has a welcome for tourists of our nation where it finds us in Italy; and sometimes its sympathy, expressed in a rustling and clashing of its long green blades, or in its strong sweet perfume, has, as already hinted, made me homesick, though I have been uniformly unaffected by potato-patches and tobacco-fields.

From where we lay beside the cornfield, we could see, through the twinkling leaves and the twinkling atmosphere, the great hills across the lake, taking their afternoon naps, with their clouds drawn like handkerchiefs over their heads. It was very hot, and the red and purple ooze of the unwholesome river below "burnt like a witch's oils." It was indeed but a fevered joy we snatched from Nature there; and I am afraid that we got nothing more comfortable from sentiment, when, rising, we wandered off through the un-guarded fields toward a ruined tower on a hill. It must have been a relic of feudal times, and I could easily believe it had been the hold of one of those wicked lords who used to rule in the terror of the people beside peaceful and happy Como. But the life, good or bad, was utterly gone out of it now, and what was left of the tower was a burden to the sense. A few scrawny blackberries and other brambles grew out of its fallen stones; harsh, dust-dry mosses painted its weather-worn walls with their blanched gray and yel-low. From its foot, looking out over the valley, we saw the road to the Splügen Pass lying white-hot in the valley; and while we looked, the diligence appeared, and dashed through the dust that rose like a flame before. After that it was a relief to stroll in dirty byways, past cottages of saffron peasants, and poor stony fields that begrudged them a scanty vegetation, back to the steamer blistering in the sun.

Now indeed we were glad of the awning, under which a silent crowd of people with sunburnt faces waited for the departure of the boat. The breeze rose again as the engine resumed its unappreciated labors, and, with our head toward Como, we pushed out into the lake. The company on board was such as might be expected. There was a German landscape-painter, with three heart's-friends beside him; there were some German ladies; there were the unfailing Americans and the unfailing Englishman; there were some French people; there were Italians from the meridional provinces, dark, thin, and enthusiastic, with fat silent wives, and a rhythmical speech; there were Milanese with their families, out for a holiday,—round-bodied men, with blunt square features, and hair and vowels clipped surprisingly short; there was a young girl whose face was of the exact type affected in rococo sculpture, and at whom one gazed without being able to decide whether she was a nymph descended from a villa gate, or a saint come from under a broken arch in a church.

STOPPING AT VICENZA, VERONA, AND PARMA

STOPPING AT VICENZA, VERONA, AND PARMA

I

IT was after sunset when we arrived in the birthplace of Palladio, which we found a fair city in the lap of caressing hills. There are pretty villas upon these slopes, and an abundance of shaded walks and drives about the houses which were pointed out to us, by the boy who carried our light luggage from the railway station, as the property of rich citizens "but little less than lords" in quality. A lovely grove lay between the station and the city, and our guide not only took us voluntarily by the longest route through this, but after reaching the streets led us by labyrinthine ways to the hotel, in order, he afterwards confessed, to show us the city. He was a poet, though in that lowly walk of life, and he had done well. No other moment of our stay would have served us so well for a first general impression of Vicenza as that twilight hour. In its uncertain glimmer we seemed to get quite back to the dawn of feudal civilization, when Theodoric founded the great Basilica of the city; and as we stood before the famous Clock Tower, which rises light and straight as a mast eighty-two metres into the air from a base of seven metres, the wavering obscurity enhanced the effect by half concealing the tower's crest, and letting it soar endlessly upward in the fancy. The Basilica is greatly restored by Palladio, and the cold hand of that friend of virtuous poverty in architecture lies heavy upon his native city in many places. Yet there is still a great deal of Lombardic architecture in Vicenza; and we walked through one street of palaces in which Venetian Gothic prevailed, so that it seemed as if the Grand Canal had but just shrunk away from their bases. When we threw open our window at the hotel, we found that it overlooked one of the city gates, from which rose a Ghibelline tower with a great bulging cornice, full of the beauty and memory of times long before Palladio.

They were rather troublous times, and not to be recalled here in all their circumstance; but I think it due to Vicenza, which is now little spoken of, even in Italy, and is scarcely known in America, where her straw-braid is bought for that of Leghorn, to remind the reader that the city was for a long time a republic of very warlike stomach. Before she arrived at that state, however, she had undergone a great variety of fortunes. The Gauls founded the city (as I learn from "The Chronicles of Vicenza," by Battista Pagliarino, published at Vicenza in 1563) when Gideon was Judge in Israel, and were driven out by the Romans some centuries later. As a matter of course, Vicenza was sacked by Attila and conquered by Alboin; after which she was ruled by some lords of her own, until she was made an imperial city by Henry I. Then she had a government more or less republican in form till Frerderick Barbarossa burnt her, and "wrapped her in ashes," and gave her to his vicar Ecelino da Romano, who "held her in cruel tyranny" from 1236 to 1259. The Paduans next ruled her forty years, and the Veronese seventy-seven, and the Milanese seventeen years; then she reposed in the arms of the Venetian Republic till these fell weak and helpless from all the Venetian possessions at the threat of Napoleon. Vicenza belonged again to Venice during the brief Republic of 1848, but the most memorable battle of that heroic but unhappy epoch gave her back to Austria. Now at last, and for the first time, she is Italian.

Vicenza is

"Of kindred that have greatly expiated
And greatly wept,"

and but that I so long fought against Ecelino da Romano, and the imperial interest in Italy, I could readily forgive her all her past errors. To us of the Lombard League, it was grievous that she should remain so doggishly faithful to her tyrant; though it is to be granted that perhaps fear had as much to do with her devotion as favor. The defense of 1848 was greatly to her honor, and she took an active part in that demonstration against the Austrians which endured from 1859 till 1866.

Of the demonstration we travelers saw an amusing phase at the opera which we attended the evening of our arrival in Vicenza. "Nabucodonosor" was the piece to be given in the new open-air theatre outside the city walls, whither we walked under the starlight. It was a pretty structure of fresh white stucco, oval in form, with some graceful architectural pretensions without, and within very charmingly galleried; while overhead it was roofed with a blue dome set with such starry mosaic as never covered temple or theatre since they used to leave their houses of play and worship open to the Attic skies. The old Hebrew story had, on this stage brought so near to Nature, effects seldom known to opera, and the scene evoked from far-off days the awful interest of the Bible histories,—the vague, unfigured oriental splendor—the desert—the captive people by the waters of the river of Babylon—the shadow and mystery of the prophecies. When the Hebrews, chained and toiling on the banks of the Euphrates, lifted their voices in lamentation, the sublime music so transfigured the commonplace words that they meant all deep and unutterable affliction, and for a while swept away whatever was false and tawdry in the show, and thrilled our hearts with a rapture rarely felt. Yet, as but a moment before we had laughed to see Nebuchadnezzar's crown shot off his head by a squib visibly directed from the side scenes,—at the point when, according to the libretto, "the thunder roars, and a bolt descends upon the head of the king,"—so but a moment after some new absurdity marred the illusion, and we began to look about the theatre at the audience. We then beheld that act of *dimostrazione* which I have mentioned. In one of the few boxes sat a young and very beautiful woman in a dress of white, with a fan which she kept in constant movement. It was red on one side, and green on the other, and gave, with the white dress, the forbidden Italian colors, while, looked at alone, it was innocent of offense. I do not think a soul in the theatre was ignorant of the demonstration. A satisfied consciousness was reflected from the faces of the Italians, and I saw two Austrian officers exchange looks of good-natured intelligence, after a glance at the fair patriot. I wonder what these poor people do, now they are free, and deprived of the sweet, perilous luxury of defying their tyrants by constant acts of subtle disdain? Life in Venetia must be very dull: no more explosion of pasteboard petards; no more treason in bouquets; no more stealthy inscriptions on the walls—it must be insufferably dull. *Ebbene, pazienza!* Perhaps Victor Emanuel may betray them yet.

A spirit of lawlessness, indeed, seemed to pervade the whole audience in the theatre that night at Vicenza, and to extend to the ministers of the law themselves. There were large placards everywhere posted, notifying the people that it was forbidden to smoke in the theatre, and that smokers were liable to expulsion; but except for ourselves, and the fair patriot in the box, I think everybody there was smoking, and the policemen set the example of an anarchy by smoking the longest and worst cigars of all. I am sure that the captive Hebrews all held lighted cigarettes behind their backs, and that Nebuchadnezzar, condemned to the grass of the field, conscientiously gave himself up to the Virginia weed behind the scenes.

Before I fell asleep that night, the moon rose over the top of the feudal tower in front of our hotel, and produced some very pretty effects with the battlements. Early in the morning a regiment of Croats marched through the gate below the tower, their band playing "The Young Recruit." These advantages of situation were not charged in our bill; but, even if they had been, I should still advise my reader to go, when in Vicenza, if he loves a pleasant landlord and a good dinner, to the Hotel de la Ville, which he will find almost at his sole disposition for however long time he may stay. His meals will be served him in a vast dining-hall, as bare as a barn or a palace, but for the pleasant, absurd old paintings on the wall, representing, as I suppose, Cleopatra applying the Asp, Susannah and the Elders, the Roman Lucrezia, and other moral and appetizing histories. I take it there is a quaint side-table or two lost midway of the wall, and that an old woodcut picture of the Most Noble City of Venice hangs over each. I know that there is a screen at one end of the apartment behind which the landlord invisibly assumes the head waiter; and I suspect that at the moment of sitting down at meat, you hear two Englishmen talking—as they pass along the neighboring corridor—of wine, in dissatisfied chest-tones. This hotel is of course built round a court, in which there is a stable and—exposed to the weather—a diligence, and two or three carriages and a driver, and an ostler chewing straw, and a pump and a grape-vine. Why the hotel, therefore, does not smell like a stable, from garret to cellar, I am utterly at a loss to know. I state the fact that it does not, and that every other hotel in Italy does smell of stable as if cattle had been immemorially pastured in its halls, and horses housed in its bed-chambers—or as if its only guests were centaurs on their travels.

From the Museo Civico, whither we repaired first in the morning, and where there are some beautiful Montagnas, and an assortment of good and bad works by other masters, we went to the Campo Santo, which is worthy to be seen, if only because of the beautiful Laschi monument by Vela. It is nothing more than a very simple tomb, at the door of which stands a figure in flowing drapery, with folded hands and uplifted eyes in an attitude exquisitely expressive of grief. The figure is said to be the portrait of the widow of him within the tomb, and the face is very beautiful. We asked if the widow was still young, and the custodian answered us in terms that ought to endear him to all women, if not to our whole mortal race,—"Oh, quite young, yet. She is perhaps fifty years old."

After the Campo Santo one ought to go to that theatre which Palladio built for the representation of classic tragedy, and which tries to be a perfect reproduction of the Greek theatre. Alfieri is the only poet of modern times whose works have been judged worthy of this stage, and no drama has been given on it since 1857, when the "Œdipus Tyrannus" of Sophocles was played. We found it very silent and dusty, and were much sadder as we walked through its gayly frescoed, desolate anterooms than we had been in the Campo Santo. Here used to sit, at coffee and bassett, the merry people who owned the now empty seats of the theatre,— lord, and lady, and abbé,—who affected to be entertained by the scenes upon the stage. Upon my word, I should like to know what has become, in the other world, of those poor pleasurers of the past whose memory makes one so sad upon the scenes of their enjoyment here! I suppose they have something quite as unreal, yonder, to satisfy them as they had on earth, and that they still play at happiness in the old rococo way, though it is hard to conceive of any fiction outside of Italy so perfect and so entirely suited to their unreality as this classic theatre. It is a Greek theatre, for Greek tragedies; but it could never have been for popular amusement, and it was not open to the air, though it had a sky skillfully painted in the centre of the roof. The proscenium is a Greek façade, in three stories, such as never was seen in Greece; and the architecture of the three streets running back from the proscenium, and forming the one unchangeable scene of all the dramas, is—like the statues in the niches and on the gallery inclosing the auditorium—Greek in the most fashionable Vicentine taste. It must have been but an operatic chorus that sang in the semicircular space just below the stage and in front of the audience. Admit and forget these small blemishes and aberrations, however, and what a marvelous thing Palladio's theatre is! The sky above the stage is a wonderful trick, and those three streets— one in the centre and serving as entrance for the royal persons of the drama, one at the right for the nobles, and one at the left for the citizens—present unsurpassed effects of illusion. They are not painted, but modeled in stucco. In perspective they seem each half a mile long, but entering them you find that they run back from the proscenium only some fifteen feet, the fronts of the houses and the statues upon them decreasing in recession with a well-ordered abruptness. The semicircular gallery above the auditorium is of stone, and forty statues of marble crown its colonnade, or occupy niches between the columns.

II

It was curious to pass, with the impression left by this costly and ingenious toy upon our minds, at once to the Arena in Verona, which, next to the Coliseum, has, of all the works bequeathed us by the ancient Roman world, the greatest claim upon the wonder and imagination. Indeed, it makes even a stronger appeal. We know who built the Coliseum, but in its unstoried origin, the Veronese Arena has the mystery of the Pyramids. Was its founder Augustus, or Vitellius, or Antoninus, or Maximian, or the Republic of Verona? Nothing is certain but that it was conceived and reared by some mighty prince or people, and that it yet remains in such perfection that the great shows of two thousand years ago might take place in it to-day. It is so suggestive of the fierce and splendid spectacles of Roman times that the ring left by a modern circus on the arena, and absurdly dwarfed by the vast space of the oval, had an impertinence which we hotly resented, looking down on it from the highest grade of the interior. It then lay fifty feet below us, in the middle of an elipse five hundred feet in length and four hundred in breadth, and capable of holding fifty thousand spectators. The seats that the multitudes pressed of old are perfect yet; scarce a stone has been removed from the interior; the ædile and the prefect might take their places again in the balustraded tribunes above the great entrance at either end of the arena, and scarcely see that they were changed. Nay, the victims and the gladiators might return to the cells below the seats of the people, and not know they had left them for a day; the wild beasts might leap into the arena from dens as secure and strong as when first built. The ruin within seems only to begin with the aqueduct, which was used to flood the arena for the naval shows, but which is now choked with the dust of ages. Without, however, is plain enough the doom which is written against all the work of human hands, and which, unknown of the builders, is among the memorable things placed in the corner-stone of every edifice. Of the outer wall that rose high over the highest seats of the amphitheatre, and encircled it with stately corridors, giving it vaster amplitude and grace, the earthquake of six centuries ago spared only a fragment that now threatens above one of the narrow Veronese streets. Blacksmiths, wagon-makers, and workers in clangorous metals have made shops of the lower corridors of the old arena, and it is friends and neighbors with the modern life about it, as such things usually are in Italy. Fortunately for the stranger, the Piazza Brà flanks it on one hand, and across this it has a magnificent approach. It is not less happy in being little known to sentiment, and the traveler who visits it by moonlight, has a full sense of grandeur and pathos, without any of the sheepishness attending homage to that battered old coquette, the Coliseum, which so many emotional people have sighed over, kissing and afterwards telling.

But he who would know the innocent charm of a ruin as yet almost wholly uncourted by travel, must go to the Roman theatre in Verona. It is not a favorite of the hand-books; and we were decided to see it chiefly by a visit to the Museum, where, besides an admirable gallery of paintings, there is a most interesting collection of antiques in bronze and marble found in excavating the theatre. The ancient edifice had been completely buried, and a quarter of the town was built over it, as Portici is built over Herculaneum, and on the very top stood a Jesuit convent. One day, some children, playing in the garden of one of the shabby houses, suddenly vanished from sight. Their mother ran like one mad (I am telling the story in the words of the peasant who related it to me) to the spot where they had last been seen, and fell herself into an opening of the earth there. The outcry raised by these unfortunates brought a number of men to their aid, and in digging to get them out, an old marble staircase was discovered. This was about twenty-five years ago. A certain gentleman named Monga owned the land, and he immediately began to make excavations. He was a rich man, but considered rather whimsical (if my peasant represented the opinion of his neighbors), and as the excavation ate a great deal of money (*mangiava molti soldi*), his sons discontinued the work after his death, and nothing has been done for some time, now. The peasant in charge was not a person of imaginative mind, though he said the theatre (supposed to have been built in the time of Augustus) was completed two thousand years before Christ. He had a fine conventional admiration of the work, which he expressed at regular intervals, by stopping short in his course, waving both hands over the ruins, and crying in a sepulchral voice, *"Qual' opera!"*

We crossed three or four streets, and entered at several different gates, in order to see the uncovered parts of the work, which could have been but a small proportion of the whole. The excavation has been carried down thirty and forty feet below the foundations of the modern houses, revealing the stone seats of the auditorium, the corridors beneath them, and the canals and other apparatus for naval shows, as in the great Arena. These works are even more stupendous than those of the Arena, for in many cases they are not constructed, but hewn out of the living rock, so that in this light the theatre is a gigantic sculpture. Below all are cut channels to collect and carry off the water of the springs in which the rock abounds. The depth of one of these channels near the Jesuit convent must be fifty feet below the present surface. Only in one place does the ancient edifice rise near the top of the ground, and there is uncovered the arched front of what was once a family-box at the theatre, with the owner's name graven upon the arch. Many poor little houses have of course been demolished to carry on the excavations, and to the walls that joined them cling memorials of the simple life that once inhabited them. To one of the buildings hung a melancholy fireplace left blackened with smoke, and battered with use, but witnessing that it had once been the heart of a home. It was far more touching than anything in the elder ruin; and I think nothing could have so vividly expressed the difference which, in spite of all the resemblances noticeable in Italy, exists between the ancient and modern civilization, as that family-box at the theatre and this simple fireside.

I do not now remember what fortunate chance it was that discovered to us the house of the Capulets, and I incline to believe that we gravitated toward it by operation of well-known natural principles which bring travelers acquainted with improbabilities wherever they go. We found it a very old and time-worn edifice, built round an ample court, and we knew it, as we had been told we should, by the cap carven in stone above the interior of the grand portal. The family, anciently one of the principal of Verona, has fallen from much of its former greatness. On the occasion of our visit, Juliet, very dowdily dressed, looked down from the top of a long, dirty staircase which descended into the court, and seemed interested to see us; while her mother caressed with one hand a large yellow mastiff, and distracted it from its first impulse to fly upon us poor children of sentiment. There was a great deal of stable litter, and many empty carts standing about in the court; and if I might hazard the opinion formed upon these and other appearances, I should say that old Capulet had now gone to keeping a hotel, united with the retail liquor business, both in a small way.

Nothing could be more natural, after seeing the house of the Capulets, than a wish to see Juliet's Tomb, which is visited by all strangers, and is the common property of the hand-books. It formerly stood in a garden, where, up to the beginning of this century, it served, says my "Viaggio in Italia," "for the basest uses,"—just as the sacred prison of Tasso was used for a charcoal bin. We found the sarcophagus under a shed in one corner of the garden of the Orfanotrofio delle Franceschine, and had to confess to each other that it looked like a horse-trough roughly hewn out of stone. The garden, said the boy in charge of the moving monument, had been the burial-place of the Capulets, and this tomb being found in the middle of the garden, was easily recognized as that of Juliet. Its genuineness, as well as its employment in the ruse of the lovers, was proved beyond cavil by a slight hollow cut for the head to rest in, and a hole at the foot "to breathe through," as the boy said. Does not the fact that this relic has to be protected from the depradations of travelers, who could otherwise carry it away piecemeal, speak eloquently of a large amount of vulgar and rapacious innocence drifting about the world?

It is well to see even such idle and foolish curiosities, however, in a city like Verona, for the mere going to and fro in search of them through her streets is full of instruction and delight. To my mind, no city has a fairer place than she that sits beside the eager Adige, and breathes the keen air of mountains white with snows in winter, green and purple with vineyards in summer, and forever rich with marble. Around Verona stretch those gardened plains of Lombardy, on which Nature, who dotes on Italy, and seems but a stepmother to all transalpine lands, has lavished every gift of beauty and fertility. Within the city's walls, what store of art and history! Her market-places have been the scenes of a thousand tragic or ridiculous dramas; her narrow streets are ballads and legends full of love-making and murder; the empty, grass-grown piazzas before her churches are tales that are told of municipal and ecclesiastical splendor. Her nobles sleep in marble tombs so beautiful that the dust in them ought to be envied by living men in Verona; her lords lie in perpetual state in the heart of the city, in magnificent sepulchres of such grace and opulence, that, unless a language be invented full of lance-headed characters, and Gothic vagaries of arch and finial, flower and fruit, bird and beast, they can never be described. Sacred be their rest from pen of mine, Verona! Nay, while I would fain bring the whole city before my reader's fancy, I am loath and afraid to touch anything in it with my poor art: either the tawny river, spanned with many beautiful bridges, and murmurous with mills afloat and turned by the rapid current; or the thoroughfares with their passengers and bright shops and caffès; or the grim old feudal towers; or the age-embrowned palaces, eloquent in their haughty strength of the times when they were family fortresses; or the churches with the red pillars of their porticoes resting upon the backs of eagle-headed lions; or even the white-coated garrison (now there no more), with its heavy-footed rank and file, its resplendent officers, its bristling fortifications, its horses and artillery, crowding the piazzas of churches turned into barracks. Verona is an almost purely Gothic city in her architecture, and her churches are more worthy to be seen than any others in North Italy, outside of Venice. San Zenone, with the bronzes on its doors representing in the rudeness of the first period of art the incidents of the Old Testament and the miracles of the saints—with the allegorical sculptures surrounding the interior and exterior of the portico, and illustrating, among other things, the creation of Eve with absolute literalness—with its fine solemn crypt in which the dust of the titular saint lies entombed—with its minute windows, and its massive columns sustaining the roof upon capitals of every bizarre and fantastic device—is doubtless most abundant in that Gothic spirit, now grotesque and now earnest, which somewhere appears in all the churches of Verona; which has carven upon the façade of the Duomo the statues of Orlando and Oliviero, heroes of romance, and near them has placed the scandalous figure of a pig in a monk's robe and cowl, with a breviary in its paw; which has reared the exquisite monument of Guglielmo da Castelbarco before the church of St. Anastasia, and has produced the tombs of the Scaligeri before the chapel of Santa Maria Antica.

I have already pledged myself not to attempt any description of these tombs, and shall not fall now. But I bought in the English tongue, as written at Verona, some "Notices" kept for sale by the sacristan, "of the Ancient Churg of our Lady, and of the Tombs of the most illustrious Family Della-Scala," and from these I think it no dereliction to quote *verbatim*. First is the tomb of Can

Francesco, who was "surnamed the Great by reason of his valor." "With him the Great Alighieri and other exiles took refuge. We see his figure extended upon a bed, and above his statue on horsebac with the vizor down, and his crest falling behind his shoulders, his horse covered with mail. The columns and capitals are wonderful." "Within the Cemetery to the right leaning against the walls of the church is the tomb of John Scaliger." "In the side of this tomb near the wall of Sacristy, you see the urn that encloses the ashes of Martin I.," "who was traitorously killed on the 17th of October 1277, by Scaramello of the Scaramelli, who wished to revenge the honor of a young lady of his family." "The Mausoleum that is in the side facing the Place encloses the Martin II.'s ashes. . . . This building is sumptuous and wonderful because it stands on four columns, each of which has an architrave of nine feet. On the beams stands a very large square of marble that forms the floor, on which stands the urn of the Defunct. Four other columns support the vault that covers the urn; and the rest is adorned by facts of Old Testament. Upon the Summit is the equestrian statue as large as life." Of "Can Signorius," whose tomb is the most splendid of all, the "Notices" say: "He spent two thousand florins of gold, in order to prepare his own sepulchre while he was yet alive, and to surpass the magnificence of his predecessors. The monument is as magnificent as the contracted space allows. Six columns support the floor of marble on which it stands covered with figures. Six other columns support the top, on that is the Scaliger's statues. . . . The monument is surrounded by an enclosure of red marble, with six pillars, on which are square capitols with armed Saints. The rails of iron with the Arms of the Scala are worked with a beauty wonderful for that age," or, I may add, for any age. These "rails" are an exquisite network of iron wrought by hand, with an art emulous of that of Nicolò Caparra at Florence. The chief device employed is a ladder (*scala*) constantly repeated in the centres of quatre-foils; and the whole fabric is still so flexible and perfect, after the lapse of centuries, that the net may be shaken throughout by a touch. Four other tombs of the Scaligeri are here, among which the "Notices" particularly mention that of Alboin della Scala: "He was one of the Ghibelline party, as the arms on his urn schew, that is a staircase risen by an eagle—wherefore Dante said, *In sulla Scala porta il santo Uccello.*"

I should have been glad to meet the author of these delightful histories, but in his absence we fared well enough with the sacristan. When, a few hours before we left Verona, we came for a last look at the beautiful sepulchres, he recognized us, and seeing a sketch-book in the party, he invited us within the inclosure again, and then ran and fetched chairs for us to sit upon—nay, even placed chairs for us to rest our feet on. Winning and exuberant courtesy of the Italian race! If I had never acknowledged it before, I must do homage to it now, remembering the sweetness of the sacristans and custodians of Verona. They were all men of the most sympathetic natures. He at San Zenone seemed never to have met with real friends till we expressed pleasure in the magnificent Mantegna, which is the pride of his church. "What coloring!" he cried, and then triumphantly took us into the crypt: "What a magnificent crypt! What works they executed in those days, there!" At San Giorgio Maggiore, where there are a Tintoretto and a Veronese, and four horrible swindling big pictures by Romanino, I discovered to my great dismay that I had in my pocket but five soldi, which I offered with much abasement and many apologies to the sacristan; but he received them as if they had been so many napoleons, prayed me not to speak of embarrassment, and declared that his labors in our behalf had been nothing but pleasure. At Santa Maria in Organo, where are the wonderful *intagli* of Fra Giovanni da Verona, the sacristan fully shared our sorrow that the best pictures could not be unveiled, as it was Holy Week. He was also moved at the gradual decay of the *intagli*, and led us to believe that, to a man of so much sensibility, the general ruinous state of the church was an inexpressible affliction; and we rejoiced for his sake that it should possess at least one piece of art in perfect repair. This was a modern work, that day exposed for the first time, and it represented in a group of wooden figures The Death of St. Joseph. The

Virgin and Christ supported the dying saint on either hand; and as the whole was vividly colored, and rays of glory in pink and yellow gauze descended upon Joseph's head, nothing could have been more impressive.

III

PARMA is laid out with a regularity which may be called characteristic of the great ducal cities of Italy, and which it fully shares with Mantua, Ferrara, and Bologna. The signorial cities, Verona, Vicenza, Padua, and Treviso, are far more picturesque, and Parma excels only in the number and beauty of her fountains. It is a city of gloomy aspect, says Valery, who possibly entered it in a pensive frame of mind, for its sadness did not impress us. We had just come from Modena, where the badness of our hotel enveloped the city in an atmosphere of profound melancholy. In fact, it will not do to trust to travelers in anything. I, for example, have just now spoken of the many beautiful fountains in Parma because I think it right to uphold the statement of M. Richard's hand-book; but I only remember seeing one fountain, passably handsome, there. My Lord Corke, who was at Parma in 1754, says nothing of fountains, and Richard Lasells, Gent., who was there a century earlier, merely speaks of the fountains in the Duke's gardens, which, together with his Grace's "wild beasts" and "exquisite coaches," and "admirable Theater to exhibit Operas in," "the Domo, whose Cupola was painted by the rare hand of Correggio," and the church of the Capuchins, where Alexander Farnese is buried, were "the Chief things to be seen in Parma" at that day.

The wild beasts have long run away with the exquisite coaches, but the other wonders named by Master Lasells are still extant in Parma, together with some things he does not name. Our minds, in going thither, were mainly bent on Correggio and his works, and while our dinner was cooking at the admirable Albergo della Posta, we went off to feast upon the perennial Hash of Frogs in the dome of the Cathedral. This is one of the finest Gothic churches in

Italy, and vividly recalls Verona, while it has a quite unique and
most beautiful feature in the three light-columned galleries, that
traverse the façade one above another. Close at hand stands the
ancient Baptistery, hardly less peculiar and beautiful; but, after
all, it is the work of the great painter which gives the temple its
chief right to wonder and reverence. We found the fresco, of
course, much wasted, and at first glance, before the innumerable
arms and legs had time to order and attribute themselves to their
respective bodies, we felt the justice of the undying spite which
called this divinest of frescoes a *guazzetto di rane*. But in another
moment it appeared to us the most sublime conception of the
Assumption ever painted, and we did not find Caracci's praise too
warm where he says: "And I still remain stupefied with the sight
of so grand a work—everything so well conceived—so well seen
from below—with so much severity, yet with so much judgment
and so much grace; with a coloring which is of very flesh." The
height of the fresco above the floor of the church is so vast that it
might well appear like a heavenly scene to the reeling sense of the
spectator. Brain, nerve, and muscle were strained to utter exhaus-
tion in a very few minutes, and we came away with our
admiration only half satisfied, and resolved to ascend the cupola
next day, and see the fresco on something like equal terms. In one
sort we did thus approach it; and as we looked at the gracious
floating figures of the heavenly company through the apertures of
the dome, they did seem to adopt us and make us part of the
painting. But the tremendous depth, over which they drifted so
lightly, it dizzied us to look into; and I am not certain that I should
counsel travelers to repeat our experience. Where still perfect, the
fresco can only gain from close inspection,—it is painted with
such exquisite and jealous perfection,—yet the whole effect is now
better from below, for the decay is less apparent; and besides, life
is short, and the stairway by which one ascends to the dome is in
every way too exigent. It is with the most astounding sense of
contrast that you pass from the Assumption to the contemplation
of that other famous roof frescoed by Correggio, in the Monastero
di San Paolo. You might almost touch the ceiling with you hand,

it hovers so low with its counterfeit of vine-clambered trellis-
work, and its pretty boys looking roguishly through the embo-
wering leaves. It is altogether the loveliest room in the world; and
if the Diana in her car on the chimney is truly a portrait of the
abbess for whom the chamber was decorated, she was altogether
worthy of it, and one is glad to think of her enjoying life in the
fashion amiably permitted to nuns in the fifteenth century. What
curious scenes the gayety of this little chamber conjures up, and
what a vivid comment it is upon the age and people that produced
it! This is one of the things that makes a single hour of travel
worth whole years of study, and which casts its light upon all
future reading. Here, no doubt, the sweet little abbess, with the
noblest and prettiest of her nuns about her, received the polite
world, and made a cheerful thing of devotion, while all over
transalpine Europe the sour-hearted Reformers were destroying
pleasant monasteries like this. The light-hearted lady-nuns and
their gentleman friends looked on heresy as a deadly sin, and they
had little reason to regard it with favor. It certainly made life
harder for them in time, for it made reform within the Church as
well as without, so that at last the lovely Chamber of St. Paul was
closed against the public for more than two centuries.

All Parma is full of Correggio, as Venice is of Titian and
Tintoretto, as Naples of Spagnoletto, as Mantua of Giulio Romano, as Vicenza of Palladio, as Bassano of Da Ponte, as Bologna
of Guido Reni. I have elsewhere noticed how ineffaceably and
exclusively the manner of the masters seems to have stamped itself
upon the art of the cities where they severally wrought,—how at
Parma Correggio yet lives in all the sketchy mouths of all the
pictures painted there since his time. One might almost believe,
hearing the Parmesans talk, that his manner had infected their
dialect, and that they fashioned their lazy, incomplete utterance
with the careless lips of his nymphs and angels. They almost
entirely suppress the last syllable of their words, and not with a
quick precision, as people do in Venice or Milan, but with an
ineffable languor, as if language were not worth the effort of
enunciation; while they rise and lapse several times in each

sentence, and sink so sweetly and sadly away upon the closing vocable that the listener can scarcely repress his tears. In this melancholy rhythm, one of the citizens recounted to me the whole story of the assassination of the last Duke of Parma in 1850; and left me as softly moved as if I had been listening to a tale of hapless love. Yet it was an ugly story, and after the enchantment of the recital passed away, I perceived that when the Duke was killed justice was done on one of the maddest and wickedest tyrants that ever harassed an unhappy city.

The Parmesans remember Maria Louisa, Napoleon's wife, with pleasant enough feelings, and she seems to have been good to them after the manner of sovereigns, enriching their city with art, and beautifying it in many ways, besides doing works of private charity and beneficence. Her daughter by a second marriage, the Countess Sanvitali, still lives in Parma; and in one of the halls of the academy of Fine Arts the Duchess herself survives in the marble of Canova. It was she who caused the two great pictures of Correggio, the St. Jerome and the Madonna della Scodella, to be placed alone in separate apartments hung with silk, in which the painter's initial A is endlessly interwoven. "The Night," to which the St. Jerome is "The Day," is in the Gallery at Dresden, but Parma could have kept nothing more representative of her great painter's power than this "Day." It is "the bridal of the earth and sky," and all sweetness, brightness, and tender shadow are in it. Many other excellent works of Correggio, Caracci, Parmigianino, and masters of different schools are in this gallery, but it is the good fortune of travelers, who have to see so much, that the memory of the very best alone distinctly remains. Nay, in the presence of prime beauty nothing else exists, and we found that the church of the Steccata, where Parmigianino's sublime "Moses breaking the Tables of the Law" is visible in the midst of a multitude of other figures on the vault, really contained nothing at last but that august presence.

The great Farnese Theatre was, as we have seen, admired by Lasells; but Lord Cooke found it a "useless structure" though immense. "The same spirit that raised the Colossus at Rhodes," he says, "raised the theatre at Parma; that insatiable spirit and lust of Fame which would brave the Almighty by fixing eternity to the name of a perishable being." If it was indeed this spirit, I am bound to say that it did not build so wisely at Parma as at Rhodes. The playhouse that Ranuzio I. constructed in 1628, to do honor to Cosimo II. de' Medici (pausing at Parma on his way to visit the tomb of San Carlo Borromeo), and that for a century afterward was the scene of the most brilliant spectacles in the world, is now one of the dismalest and dustiest of ruins. This *Theatrum orbis miraculum* was built and ornamented with the most perishable materials, and even its size has shrunken as the imaginations of men have contracted under the strong light of later days. When it was first opened, it was believed to hold fourteen thousand spectators; at a later *fête* it held only ten thousand; the last published description fixes its capacity at five thousand; and it is certain that for many and many a year it has held only the stray tourists who have looked in upon its desolation. The gay paintings hang in shreds and tatters from the roof; dust is thick upon the seats and in the boxes, and on the leads that line the space once flooded for naval games. The poor plaster statues stand naked and forlorn amid the ruin of which they are part; and the great stage, from which the curtain has rotted away, yawns dark and empty before the empty auditorium.

DUCAL MANTUA

DUCAL MANTUA

IN that desperate depth of Hell where Dante beholds the
Diviners doomed to pace with backward-twisted faces, and
turn forever on the past the rainy eyes once bent too daringly on
the future, the sweet guide of the Tuscan poet points out among
the damned the daughter of a Theban king, and discourses to his
charge:—

> Manto was she: through many lands she went
>   Seeking, and paused where I was born, at last.
>   Therefore I choose thou be on me intent
> A little. When from life her father passed,
>   And they of Bacchus' city became slaves,
>   Long time about the world the daughter cast.
> Up in fair Italy is a lake that laves
>   The feet of Alps that lock in Germany:
>   Benaco called. . . .
> And Peschiera in strong harness sits
>   To front the Brescians and the Bergamasques,
>   Where one down-curving shore the other meets.

There all the gathered waters outward flow
That may not in Benaco's bosom rest,
And down through pastures green a river go.

. . . .

As far as to Governo, where, its quest
Ended at last, it falls into the Po.
But far it has not sought before a plain
It finds and floods, out-creeping wide and slow
To be the steaming summer's offense and bane.
Here passing by, the fierce, unfriendly maid
Saw land in the middle of the sullen main,
Wild and unpeopled, and here, unafraid
Of human neighborhood, she made her lair,
Rested, and with her menials wrought her trade,
And lived, and left her empty body there.
Then the sparse people that were scattered near
Gathered upon that island, everywhere
Compassed about with swamps and kept from fear.
They built their city above the witch's grave,
And for her sake that first made dwelling there
The name of Mantua to their city gave.

To this account of the first settlement of Mantua Virgil adds a warning to his charge to distrust all other histories of the city's foundation; and Dante is so thoroughly persuaded of its truth, that he declares all other histories shall be to him as so many listless embers. Nevertheless, divers chroniclers of Mantua reject the tradition here given as fabulous; and the carefullest and most ruthless of these traces the city's origin, not to the unfriendly maid, but to the Etruscan King Ocno, fixing the precise date of its foundation at thirty years before the Trojan war, one thousand five hundred and thirty-nine years after the creation of the world, three hundred years before Rome, and nine hundred and fifteen years after the flood, while Abimelech was judge in Israel. "And whoever," says the compiler of the "Flower of the Mantuan Chroniclers" (it is a very dry and musty flower, indeed), citing doughty authorities for all his facts and figures,—"whoever wishes to understand this more curiously, let him read the said authors, and he will be satisfied."

But I am as little disposed to unsettle the reader's faith in the Virgillian tradition, as to part with my own; and I therefore candidly hold back the names of the authorities cited. This tradition was in fact the only thing concerning Mantuan history present to my thoughts as I rode toward the city, one afternoon of a pleasant Lombard spring; and when I came in sight of the ancient hold of sorcery, with the languid waters of its lagoons lying sick at its feet, I recognized at least the topographical truth of Virgil's description. But old and mighty walls now surround the spot which Manto found sterile and lonely in the heart of the swamp formed by the Mincio, no longer Benaco; and the dust of the witch is multitudinously hidden under the edifices of a city whose mighty domes, towers, and spires make its approach one of the stateliest in the world. It is a prospect on which you may dwell long as you draw toward the city, for the road from the railway station winds through some two miles of flat meadowland before it reaches the gate of the stronghold which the Italians call the first hope of the winner of the land, and the last hope of the loser of Italy. Indeed, there is no haste in any of the means of access to Mantua. It lies scarce forty miles south of Verona, and you are three hours in journeying this distance in the placid railway train,—a distance which Romeo, returning to Verona from his exile in Mantua, no doubt traveled in less time. There is abundant leisure to study the scenery on the way; but it scarcely repays the perusal, for it lacks the beauty of the usual Lombard landscape. The soil is red, stony, and sterile; the orchard trees are scant and slender, and not wedded with the caressing vines which elsewhere in North Italy garland happier trees and stretch gracefully from trunk to trunk. Especially the landscape looks sad and shabby about the little village of Villafranca, where, in 1864, the dejected prospect seemed incapable of a smile even in spring; as if it had lost all hope and cheerfulness since the peace was made which confirmed Venetia to the alien. It said as plainly as real estate could express the national sentiment, "Come si fa? Ci vuol pazienza!" and crept sullenly out of sight, as our pensive train resumed its meditative progress. No doubt this poor landscape *was* imbued, in its dull, earthy way, with a feeling that the coming of Garibaldi would irrigate and fertilize it into a paradise; as at Venice the gondoliers believed that his army would bring in its train cheap wine and hordes of rich and helpless Englishmen bent on perpetual tours of the Grand Canal without agreement as to price.

But within and without Mantua was a strong argument against possibility of change in the political condition of this part of Italy. Compassed about by the corruption of the swamps and the sluggish breadth of the river, the city is no less mighty in her artificial defenses than in this natural strength of her position; and the Croats of her garrison were as frequent in her sad, handsome streets as the priests in Rome. Three lakes secure her from approach upon the east, north, and south; on the west is a vast intrenched camp, which can be flooded at pleasure from one of the lakes; while the water runs three fathoms deep at the feet of the solid brick walls all round the city. There are five gates giving access by drawbridges from the town to the fortressed posts on every side, and commanding with their guns the roads that lead to them. The outlying forts, with the citadel, are four in number, and are each capable of holding from two to three thousand men. The intrenched camp, for cavalry and artillery, and the barracks of the city itself, can receive a garrison of from thirty to forty thousand men; and the measureless depths of the air are full of the fever that fights in defense of Mantua, and serves with equal zeal whoever is master of the place, let him be French, Italian, or Austrian, so only that he have an unacclimated enemy before him.

The place seemed sunken, that dull April evening of our visit, into an abiding lethargy; as if perfect repose, and oblivion from the many troubled past,—from the renown of all former famine, fire, intrigue, slaughter, and sack,—were to be preferred by the ghost of a once populous and haughty capital to the most splendid memories of national life. Certainly, the phantom of bygone Mantuan greatness did not haunt the idle tourists who strolled through her wide streets, enjoying their quiet beauty and regularity, and finding them, despite their empty, melancholy air, full of something that reminded of home. Coming from a land where there is a vast deal of length, breadth, and rectitude in streets, as well as human nature, they could not, of course, feel that wonder in the Mantuan avenues which inspired a Venetian ambassador, two centuries since, to write the Serenest Senate in praise of their marvelous extent and straightness; but they were still conscious of a certain expansive difference from Gothic Verona and narrow Venice. The windows of the ground floors were grated to the prison-like effect common throughout Italy; but people evidently lived upon the ground floors, and at many of the iron-barred windows fair young prisoners sat and looked out upon the streets, or laughed and chatted together. About the open doorways, moreover, people lounged gossiping; and the interiors of the entry-halls, as they appeared to the passing glance, were clean, and had not that forbidding, inhospitable air characteristic of most house-entrances in North Italy. But sculptured Venice and Verona had unfitted the travelers for pleasure in the stucco of Mantua; and they had an immense scorn for the large and beautiful palaces of which the before-quoted ambassador speaks, because they found them faced with cunningly moulded plaster instead of carven stone. Nevertheless, they could not help a kind of half-tender respect for the old town. It shares the domestic character of its scenes with the other ducal cities, Modena, Parma, and Ferrara; and this character is perhaps proper to all long and intensely municipalized communities. But Mantua has a ghostly calm wholly its own; and this was not in the least broken that evening by the chatters at thresholds, and pretty laughters at grated windows. It was very, very quiet. Perhaps half a score of carriages rumbled by us in our long walk, and we met some scattered promenaders. But for the most part the streets were quite empty; and even in the chief piazza, where there was still some belated show of buying and selling, and about the doors of the caffès, where there was a good deal of languid loafing, there was no indeceny of noise or bustle. There were visibly few people in the place, and it was in decay; but it was not squalid in its lapse. The streets were scrupulously neat and clean, and the stuccoed houses were all painted of that pale saffron hue which gives such unquestionable respectability to New England towns. Before we returned to our lodgings, Mantua had turned into twilight; and we walked homeward through a placid and dignified gloom, nowhere broken by the flare of gas, and only remotely affected, here and there, by the light of lamps of oil, faintly twinkling in a disheartened Mantuan fashion.

If you turn this pensive light upon the yellow pages of her old chroniclers, it reveals pictures fit to raise both pity and wonder for the past of this city,—pictures full of the glory of struggles for freedom, of the splendor of wise princes, of the comfort of a prosperous and contented people, of the grateful fruits of protected arts and civilization; but likewise stained with images of unspeakable filth and wickedness, baseness and cruelty, incredible shame, suffering, and sin.

Long before the birth of Christ, the Gauls drive out the Etruscans from Mantua, and aggrandize and beautify the city, to be in their turn expelled by the Romans, under whom Mantua again waxes strong and fair. In this time, the wife of a farmer not far from the city dreams a marvelous dream of bringing forth a laurel bough, and in due time bears into the world the chiefest of the Mantuans, with a smile upon his face. This is a poet, and they call his name Virgil. He goes from his native city to Rome, when ripe for glory, and has there the good fortune to win back his father's farm, which the greedy veterans of Augustus, then settled in the Cremonese, had annexed to the spoils bestowed upon them by the Emperor. Later in this Roman time, and only three years after the death of Him whom the poet all but prophesied, another grand event marks an epoch in Mantuan history. According to the pious legend, the soldier Longinus, who pierced the side of Christ as he hung upon the cross, has been converted by a miracle; wiping away that precious blood from his spear-head, and then drawing his hand across his eyes, he is suddenly healed of his near-sightedness, and stricken with the full wonder of conviction. He gathers anxiously the drops of blood from his weapon into the phial from which the vinegar mixed with gall was poured, and, forsaking his life as a soldier, he wanders with his new-won faith and his priceless treasure to Mantua, where it is destined to work famous miracles, and to be the most valued possession of the city to all after-time. The saint himself, preaching the Gospel of Christ, suffers martyrdom under Tiberius; his tongue is cut out, and his body is burnt; and his ashes are buried at Mantua, forgotten, and found again in after ages with due signs and miraculous portents. The Romans give a civil tranquillity to Mantua; but it is not till three centuries after Christ that the persecutions of the Christians cease. Then the temples of the gods are thrown down, and churches are built; and the city goes forward to share the destinies of the Christianized empire, and be spoiled by the barbarians. In 407 the Goths take it, and the Vandals in their turn sack and waste it, and scatter its poeople, who return again after the storm, and rebuild their city. Attila, marching to destroy it, is met at Governo (as you see in Raphael's fresco in the Vatican) by Pope Leo I., who conjures him to spare the city, and he threatens him with Divine vengeance if he refuse; above the pontiff's head two wrathful angels, bearing drawn swords, menace the Hun with death if he advance; and, thus miraculously admonished, he turns aside from Mantua and spares it. The citizens successfully resist an attack of Alboin; but the Longobards afterwards, unrestrained by the visions of Attila, beat the Mantuans and take the city. From the Lombards the Greeks, sent thither by the Exarch of Ravenna, capture Mantua about the end of the sixth century; and then, the Lombards turning immediately to besiege it again, the Greeks defend their prize long and valiantly, but in the end are overpowered. They are allowed to retire with their men and arms to Ravenna, and the Lombards dismantle the city.

Concerning our poor Mantua under Lombard rule there is but little known, except that she went to war with the Cremonese; and it may be fairly supposed that she was, like her neighbors, completely involved in foreign and domestic discords of every kind. That war with the Cremonese was about the possession of the river Ollio; and the Mantuans came off victors in it, slaying immense numbers of the enemy, and taking some thousands of them prisoners, whom their countrymen ransomed on condition of building one of the gates of Mantua with materials from the Cremonese territory, and mortar mixed with water from the disputed Ollio. The reader easily conceives how bitter a pill this must have been for the proud Cremonese gentlemen of that day.

When Charlemagne made himself master of Italy, the Mantuan lands and Mantuan men were divided up among the brave soldiers who had helped to enslave the country. These warriors of Charlemagne became counts; and the *contadini,* or inhabitants of each *contado* (county), became absolutely dependent on their will and pleasure. It is recorded (to the confusion of those who think primitive barbarism is virtue) that the corruption of those rude and brutal times was great, that all classes were sunk in vice, and that the clergy were especially venal and abominable. After the death of Charlemagne, in the ninth century, wars broke out all over Italy between the factions supporting different aspirants to his power; and we may be sure that Mantua had some share in the common quarrel. As I have found no explicit record of this period, I distribute to the city, as her portion of the calamities, at least two sieges, one capture and sack, and a decimation by famine and pestilence. We certainly read that, fifty years later, the Emperor Rudolph attacked it with his Hungarians, took it, pillaged it, and put great part of its people to the sword. During the siege, some pious Mantuans had buried (to save them from the religious foe) the blood of Christ, and part of the sponge which had held the gall and vinegar, together with the body of St. Longinus. Most unluckily, however, these excellent men were put to the sword, and all knowledge of the place of sepulture perished with them.

At the end of these wars Mantua received a lord, by appointment of the Emperor, and the first lord's son married the daughter of the Duke of Lorraine, from which union was born the great Countess Matilda. Boniface was the happy bridegroom's name, and the wedding had a wild splendor and profuse barbaric jollity about it which it is pleasant enough to read of after so much cutting and slashing. The viands were passed round on horseback to the guests, and the horses were shod with silver shoes loosely nailed on, that they might drop off and be scrambled for by the people. Oxen were roasted whole, and wine was drawn from wells with buckets hung on silver chains. It was the first great display of that magnificence of which after princes of Mantua were so fond; and the wretched hinds out of whose sweat it came no doubt thought it very fine.

Of course Lord Boniface had his wars. There was a plot to depose him discovered in Mantua, and the plotters fled to Verona. Boniface demanded them; but the Veronese answered stoutly that theirs was a free city, and no man should be taken from it against his will. Boniface marched to attack them; and the Veronese were such fools as to call the Duke of Austria to their aid, promising submission to his government in return for his help. It was then that Austria first put her finger into the Italian *pasticcio*, where she kept it so many centuries. But the Austrian governor whom the duke set over the Veronese made himself intolerable,—the Austrian governor always does,—and they drove him out of the city. On this the duke turns about, unites with Boniface, takes Verona, and sacks it.

An altogether pleasanter incident of Boniface's domination was the miraculous discovery of the sacred relics, buried and lost during the sack of Mantua by the Hungarians. The place of sepulture was revealed thrice to a blind pauper in a dream. People dug where he bade them and found the relics. Immediately on its exhumation the Blood wrought innumerable miracles; and the fame of it grew so great that the Pope came to see it, attended by such a concourse of the people that they were obliged to sleep in the streets.

After the death of Boniface the lordship'of Mantua fell to his famous daughter, Matilda, of whom most have heard. She was a woman of strong will and strong mind; she held her own, and rent from others, till she had united nearly all of Lombardy under her rule. She was not much given to the domestic affections; she had two husbands (successively), and, if the truth must be told, divorced them both: one because he wished to share her sovereignty, perhaps usurp it; and the other because he was not warm

enough friend of religion. She was a great friend of learning,—
founded libraries, established the law schools at Bologna, caused
the codification of the canon law, corresponded with distant
nations, and spoke all the different languages of her soldiers.
More than literature, however, she loved the Church; and fought
on the side of Pope Gregory VII. in his wars with the Emperor
Henry IV. Henry therefore took Mantua from her in 1091, and up
to the year 1111 the city enjoyed a kind of republican government
under his protection. In that year Henry made peace with Matilda,
and appointed her his vice-regent in Italy; but the Mantuans, after
twenty years of freedom, were in no humor to feel the weight of
the mailed hand of this strong-minded lady. She was then,
moreover, nigh to her death; and hearing that her physicians had
given her up, the Mantuans refused submission. The great countess rose irefully from her death-bed, and gathering her army, led
it in person, as she always did, laid siege to Mantua by land and
water, entered the city in 1114, and did not die till a year after.
Such is female resolution.

The Mantuans now founded a republican government, having
unlimited immunities and privileges from the Emperor, whose
power over them extended merely to the investiture of their
consuls. Their republic was democratic, the legislative council of
nine rectors and three curators being elective by the whole people.
This government, or something like it, endured for more than a
century, during which period the Mantuans seems to have done
nothing but war with their neighbors in every direction,—with the
Veronese chiefly, with the Cremonese a good deal, with the
Paduans, with the Ferrarese, with the Modenese and the Bolognese: indeed, we count up twelve years of these wars. Like the
English of their time, the Mantuans were famous bowmen, and
their shafts took flight all over Lombardy. At the same time they
did not omit to fight each other at home; and it must have been a
dullish kind of day in Mantua when there was no street battle
between families of the factious nobility. Dante has peopled his
Hell from the Italy of this time, and he might have gone farther
and fared worse for a type of the infernal state. The spectacle of

these countless little Italian powers, racked, and torn, and blazing with pride, aggression, and disorder, within and without,—full of intrigue, anguish, and shame,—each with its petty chief of victorious faction making war upon the other, and bubbling over with local ambitions, personal rivalries, and lusts,—is a spectacle which the traveler of to-day, passing over the countless forgotten battlefields, and hurried from one famous city to another by railroad, can scarcely conjure up. Parma, Modena, Bologna, Ferrara, Padua, Mantua, Vicenza, Verona, Bassano,—all are now at peace with each other, and firmly united in the national sentiment that travelers were meant to be eaten alive by Italians. Poor old cities! it is hard to conceive of their bygone animosities; still harder to believe that all the villages squatting on the long white roads, and waking up to beg of you as your diligence passes, were once embroiled in deadly and incessant wars.

Besides their local wars and domestic feuds, the Mantuans had troubles on a much larger scale,—troubles, indeed, which the Emperor Barbarossa laid out for all Italy. In Carlyle's "History of Frederick the Great" you can read a pleasanter account of the Emperor's business at Roncaglia about this time than our Italian chroniclers will give you. Truly, one would hardly guess, from that picture of Frederick Redbeard at Roncaglia, with the standard set before his tent, inviting all men to come and have justice done them, that the Emperor was actually at Roncaglia for the purpose of conspiring with his Diet to take away every vestige of liberty and independence from miserable Italy. Among other cities Mantua lost her freedom at this Diet, and was ruled by an imperial governor and by consuls of Frederick's nomination till 1167, when she joined the Lombard League against him. The leagued cities beat the Emperor at Legnano, and received back their liberties by the treaty of Costanza in 1183, after which, Frederick having withdrawn to Germany, they fell to fighting among themselves again with redoubled zeal, and rent their league into as many pieces as there had been parties to it. In 1236 the Germans again invaded Lombardy, under Frederick II.; and aided by the troops of the Ghibelline cities, Verona, Padua, Vicenza, and

Treviso, besieged Mantua, which surrendered to this formidable union of forces, thus becoming once more an imperial city, and irreparably fracturing the Lombard League. It does not appear, however, that her ancient liberties were withdrawn by Frederick II.; and we read that the local wars went on after this with as little interruption as before. The wars went on as usual, and on the old terms with Verona and Cremona, and there is little in their history to interest us. But in 1256 the famous tyrant of Padua, Ecelino da Romano, who aspired to the dominion of Lombardy, gathered his forces and went and sat down before Mantua. The Mantuans refused to surrender at his summons; and Ecelino, who had very little notion of what the Paduans were doing in his absence, swore that he would cut down the vines in those pleasant Mantuan vineyards, plant new ones, and drink the wine of their grapes before ever he raised the siege. But meantime that conspiracy which ended in Ecelino's ruin had declared itself in Padua, and the tyrant was forced to abandon the siege and look to his dominion of other cities.

After which there was something like peace in Mantua for twenty years, and the city waxed prosperous. Indeed, neither industry nor learning had wholly perished during the wars of the republic, and the people built grist-mills on the Mincio, and cultivated belles-lettres to some degree. Men of heavier science likewise flourished, and we read of jurists and astronomers born in those troublous days, as well as of a distinguished physician, who wrote a ponderous dictionary of simples, and dedicated it to King Robert of Naples. But by far the greatest Mantuan of this time was he of whom readers have heard something from a modern poet. He is the haughty Lombard soul, "in the movement of the eyes honest and slow," whom Dante, ascending the heights of Purgatory, beheld; and who summoning all himself, leaped to the heart of Virgil when he named Mantua: "O Mantuan! I am Sordello of thine own land!"

Of Virgil the superstition of the Middle Ages had made a kind of wizard, and of Sordello the old writers fable all manner of wonders; he is both knight and poet, and has adventures scarcely less surprising than those of Amadis of Gaul. It is pretty nearly certain that he was born in 1189 of the Visconti di Goito, in the Mantuan country, and that he married Beatrice, a sister of Ecelino, and had amours with the youngest sister of this tyrant, the pretty Cunizza, whom Dante places in his "Paradiso." This final disposition of Cunizza, whom we should hardly think now of assigning a position among the blest, susprised some people even in that day, it seems; for an old commentator defends it, saying: "Cunizza was always, it is true, tender and amorous, and properly called a daughter of Venus; but she was also compassionate, benign, and merciful toward those unhappy ones whom her brother cruelly tormented. Therefore the poet is right in feigning to find her in the sphere of Venus. *For if the gentle Cyprians deified their Venus, and the Romans their Flora, how much more honestly may a Christian poet save Cunizza.* The lady, whose salvation is on these grounds inexpugnably accomplished, was married to Count Sanbonifazio of Padua, in her twenty-fourth year; and Sordello was early called to this nobleman's court, having already given proofs of his poetic genius. He fell in love with Cunizza, whom her lord, becoming the enemy of the Ecelini, began to ill-treat. A curious glimpse of the manners and morals of that day is afforded by the fact that the brothers of Cunizza conspired to effect her escape with Sordello from her husband's court, and that, under the protection of Ecelino da Romano, the lovers were left unmolested.

It was probably after this amour ended that Sordello set out upon his travels, visiting most courts, and dwelling long in Provence, where he learned to poetize in the Provençal tongue, in which he thereafter chiefly wrote, and composed many songs. He did not, however, neglect his Lombard language, but composed in it a treatise on the art of defending towns. The Mantuan historian, Volta, says that some of Sordello's Provençal poems exist in manuscript in the Vatican and Chigi libraries at Rome, in the Laurentian at Florence, and at the Estense at Modena. He was versed in arms as well as letters, and he caused Mantua to be surrounded with fosses five miles beyond her walls; and the republic having lodged sovereign powers in his hands when Ecelino besieged the city, Sordello conducted the defense with great courage and ability, and did not at all betray the place to his obliging brother-in-law, as the latter expected. Verci, in his "History of the Ecelini," says: "The writers represent this Sordello as the most polite, the most gentle, the most generous man of his time, of middle stature, of beautiful aspect and fine person, of lofty bearing, agile and dexterous, instructed in letters, and a good poet, as his Provençal poems manifest. To these qualities he united military valor in such degree that no knight of his time could stand before him." He was properly the first lord of Mantua, and the republic seems to have died with him in 1284.

The madness which comes upon a people about to be enslaved commonly makes them the agents of their own undoing. The time had now come for the destruction of the last vestiges of liberty in Mantua, and the Mantuans, in their assembly of the Four Hundred and Ninety, voted full power into the hands of their destroyer. That Pinamonte Bonacolsi whom Dante mentions in the twentieth canto of the "Inferno," had been elected captain of the republic, and, feigning to fear aggression from the Marquis of Ferrara, he demanded of the people the right to banish all enemies of the state. This reasonable demand was granted, and the captain banished, as is well known, all enemies of Pinamonte Bonacolsi. After that, having things his own way, he began to favor public tranquillity, abolished family feuds and the ancient amusement of street-battles, and led his enslaved country in the paths of material prosperity; for which he was no doubt lauded in his day by those who thought the Mantuans were not prepared for freedom. He resolved to make the captaincy of the republic hereditary in the Bonacolsi family; and when he died, in 1293, his power descended to his son Bordellone. This Bordellone seems to have been a generous and merciful captain enough, but he loved ease and pleasure; and a rough nephew of his, Guido Botticella, conspired against him to that degree that Bordellone thought best, for peace and quietness' sake, to abdicate in his favor. Guido had the customary war with the Marquis of Ferrara, and then died, and was succeeded by his brother Passerino, a very bad person, whose son at last brought his whole family to grief. The Emperor made him vicar of Modena; and he used the Modenese very cruelly, and shut up Francesco Pico and his sons in a tower, where he starved them, as the Pisans did Ugolino. In those days, also, the Pope was living at Avignon, and people used to send him money and other comforts there out of Italy. An officer of Passerino's, being of Ghibelline politics, attacked one of these richly laden emissaries, and took his spoils, dividing them with Passerino. For this the Pope naturally excommunicated the captain of Mantua, and thereupon his neighbors made a great deal of pious war upon him. But he beat the Bolognese, the most pious of his foes, near Montevoglio, and with his Modenese took from them that famous bucket, about which Tassoni made his great Bernesque epic, "The Rape of the Bucket" (*La Secchia Rapita*), and which still hangs in the tower of the Duomo at Modena. Meantime, while Passerino had done everything to settle himself comfortably and permanently in the tyranny of Mantua, his worthless son Francesco fell in love with the wife of Filippino Gonzaga.

According to the old Mantuan chronicles the Gonzagas were of a royal German line, and had fixed themselves in the Mantuan territory in 770, where they built a castle beyond Po, and began at once to take part in public affairs. They had now grown to be a family of such consequence that they could not be offended with impunity, and it was a great misfortune to the Bonacolsi that Francesco happened to covet Filippino Gonzaga's wife. The insult sank deep into the bitter hearts of the Gonzagas; and the head of that proud race, Filippino's uncle, Luigi Gonzaga, resolved to avenge the family dishonor. He was a secret and taciturn man, and a pious adulator of his line has praised him for the success with which he dissembled his hatred of the Bonacolsi, while conspiring to sweep them and their dominion away. He won over adherents among the Mantuans, and then made a league with Can Grande of Verona to divide the spoils of the Bonacolsi; and so, one morning, having bribed the guards to open the city gates, he entered Mantua at the head of the banded forces. The population was roused with patriotic cries of "Long live the Mantuan people!" and, as usual, believed, poor souls, that some good was meant them by those who came to overthrow their tyrants. The Bonacolsi were dreaming that pleasant morning of anything but ruin, and they offered no resistance to the insurrection till it burst out in the great square before the Castello di Corte. They then made a feeble sally from the castle, but were swiftly driven back, and Passerino, wounded to death under the great Gothic archway of the palace, as he retreated, dropped from his languid hands the bridle-rein of his charger and the reins of that government with which he had so long galled Mantua. The unhappy Francesco fled to the cathedral for protection; but the Gonzagas slew him at the foot of the altar. Passerino's brother, a bishop, was flung into a tower to starve, that the Picos might be avenged; and the city of Mantua was liberated.

In that day, when you freed a city from a tyrant, you gave it up to be pillaged by the army of liberation; and Mantua was now sacked by her deliverers. Can Grande's share of the booty alone amounted to a hundred thousand gold florins (about two hundred and fifty thousand dollars). The Mantuans, far from imitating the ungrateful Paduans, who, when the Crusaders liberated them from Ecelino, grudged these brave fellows three days' pillage of their city, and even wished back their old tyrant,—the Mantuans, we say, seemed not in the least to mind being devoured, but gratefully elected the Gonzaga their captain-general, and purchased him absolution from the Pope for his crimes committed in the sack. They got this absolution for twenty thousand gold florins; and the Pope probably sold it cheap, remembering his old grudge against the Bonacolsi, whom the Gonzaga had overthrown. All this was in the year of grace 1328.

When Luigi Gonzaga was made lord of Mantua, he left his castle beyond Po, to dwell in the city. In this castle he had dwelt, like other lords of his time, in the likeness of a king, spending regally, and keeping state and open house in an edifice strongly built about with walls, encircled with ditches passable by a single drawbridge, and guarded day and night, from castle moat to castle crest, by armed vassals. Hundreds ate daily at his board, which was heaped with a rude and rich profusion, and furnished with carven goblets and plate of gold and silver. In fair weather the banquet-hall stood open to all the winds that blew; in foul, the guests were sheltered from the storm by curtains of oiled linen, and the place was lighted with torches borne by splendidly attired pages. The great saloons of the castle were decked with tapestries of Flanders and Damascus, and the floor was strewn with straw or rushes. The bed in which the lord and lady slept was the couch of a monarch; the household herded together in the empty chambers, and lay upon the floor like swine. The garden-fields about the castle smiled with generous harvests; the peasant lay down after his toil, at night, in deadly fear of invasion from some neighboring state, which should rob him of everything, dishonor his wife and daughters, and slay him upon the smoking ruins of his home.

In the city to which this lord repaired, the houses were built here and there at caprice, without numbers or regularity, and only distinguished by the figure of a saint, or some pious motto painted above the door. Cattle wandered at will through the crooked, narrow, and filthy streets, which rang with the clamor of frequent feud, and reeked with the blood of the embattled citizens; over all the squalor and wickedness rose the loveliest temples that ever blossomed from man's love of the beautiful to the honor and glory of God.

It was a time ignorant of the simplest comfort, but debauched with the vices of luxury; in which cities repressed the license of their people by laws regulating the length of women's gowns and the outlays at weddings and funerals. Every wild misdeed and filthy crime was committed, and punished by terrible penalties, or atoned for by fines. A fierce democracy reigned, banishing nobles, razing their palaces, and ploughing up the salt-sown sites; till at last, in a paroxysm of madness, it delivered itself up to lords to be defended from itself, and was crushed into slavery. Literature and architecture flourished, and the sister arts were born amid the struggles of human nature convulsed with every abominable passion.

For nearly four hundred years the Gonzagas continued to rule the city, which the first prince of their line, having well-nigh destroyed, now rebuilt and restored to greater splendor than ever; and it is the Mantua of the Gonzagas which travelers of this day look upon when they visit the famous old city. Their pride and their wealth adorned it; their wisdom and prudence made it rich and prosperous; their valor glorified it; their crimes stain its annals with infamy; their wickedness and weakness ruined it and brought it low. They were a race full of hereditary traits of magnificence, but one reads their history, and learns to love, of all their long succession, only one or two in their pride, learns to pity only one or two in their fall. They were patriotic, but the patriotism of despotic princes is self-love. They were liberal—in spending the revenues of the state for the glory of their family. They were brave, and led many nameless Mantuans to die in forgotten battles for alien quarrels which they never understood.

The succession of the Gonzagas was of four captains, ending in 1407; four marquises, ending in 1484; and ten dukes, ending in 1708.

The first of the captains was Luigi, as we know. In his time the great Gothic fabric of the Castello di Corte was built; and having rebuilt the portions of the city wasted by the sack, he devoted himself, as far as might be in that age, to the arts of peace; and it is remembered of him that he tried to cure the Mantuan air of its feverish unwholesomeness by draining the swampy environs. During his time, Petrarch, making a sentimental journey to the birthplace of Virgil, was splendidly entertained and greatly honored by him. For the rest, Can Grande of Verona was by no means content with his hundred thousand florins of spoil from the sack of the city, but aspired to its sovereignty, declaring that he had understood Gonzaga to have promised him it as the condition of alliance against the Bonacolsi. Gonzaga construed the contract differently, and had so little idea of parting with his opinion, that he fought the Scaligero on this point of difference till he died, which befell thirty years after his election to the captaincy.

Him his son Guido succeeded,—a prince already old at the time

of his father's death, and of feeble spirit. He shared his dominion
with his son Ugolino, excluding the younger brothers from the
dominion. These, indignant at the partiality, one night slew their
brother Ugolino at a supper he was giving; and being thereupon
admitted to a share in their father's government, had no trouble in
obtaining the pardon of the Pope and Emperor. One of the
murderers died before the father; the other, named Ludovico, was,
on the death of Guido, in 1370, elected to the captaincy, and ruled
long, wisely, and well. He loved a peaceful life; and though the
Emperor confirmed him in the honors conferred on him by the
Mantuans, and made him vicar imperial, Ludovico declined to
take part with Ghibellines against Guelphs, remained quietly at
home, and spent himself much in good works, as if he would thus
expiate his bloody crime. He gathered artists, poets, and learned
men about him, and did much to foster all arts. In his time,
Mantua had rest from war, and grew to have twenty-eight
thousand inhabitants; but it was not in the nature of a city of the
Middle Ages to be long without a calamity of some sort, and it is
a kind of relief to know that Mantua, under this peaceful prince,
was well-nigh depopulated by a pestilence.

In 1381 he died, and with his son Francesco the blood-letting
began again. Indeed, this captain spent nearly his whole life in war
with those pleasant people, the Visconti of Milan. He had married
the daughter of Barnabo Visconti, but discovering her to be
unfaithful to him, or believing her so, he caused her to be put to
death, refusing all her family's intercessions for mercy. After that,
a heavy sadness fell upon him, and he wandered aimlessly about
in many Italian cities, and at last married a second time, taking to
wife Margherita Malatesta. He was a prince of high and generous
soul and of manly greatness rare in his time. There came once a
creature of the Visconti to him, with a plot for secretly taking off
his masters; but the Gonzaga (he must have been thought an
eccentric man by his neighbors) dismissed the wretch with horror.
I am sure the reader will be glad to know that he finally beat the
Visconti in fair fight, and (the pest still raging in Mantua) lived to
make a pilgrimage to the Holy Land. When he returned, he

compiled the city's statutes, divided the town into four districts, and named its streets. So he died.

And after this prince had made his end, there came another Francesco, or Gianfrancesco, who was created Marquis of Mantua by the Emperor Sigismund. He was a friend of war, and having been the ward of the Venetian Republic he became the leader of her armies on the death of Carmagnola. The Gonzaga took Verona and Padua for the republic, and met the Milanese in many battles. Venice was then fat with the spoils of the Orient, and it is probable that the Marquis of Mantua acquired there that taste for splendor which he introduced into his hitherto frugal little state. We read of his being in Venice in 1414, when the Jewelers and Goldsmiths' Guild gave a tournament in the Piazza San Marco, offering as prizes to the victorious lances a collar enriched with pearls and diamonds, the work of the jewelers, and two helmets excellently wrought by the goldsmiths. On this occasion the Gonzaga, with two hundred and sixty Mantuan gentlemen, mounted on superb horses, contested the prizes with the Marquis of Ferrara, at the head of two hundred Ferrarese, equally mounted, and attended by their squires and pages, magnificently dressed. There were sixty thousand spectators of the encounter. "Both the marquises," says Mutinelli in his "Annali Urbani," "being each assisted by fourteen well-armed cavaliers, combated valorously at the barrier, and were both judged worthy of the first prize: a Mantuan cavalier took the second."

The Marquis Gonzaga was the first of his line who began that royal luxury of palaces with which Mantua was adorned. He commenced the Ducal Palace; but before he went far with the work he fell a prey to the science then much affected by Italian princes, but still awaiting its last refinement from the gifted Lucrezia Borgia. The poor marquis was poisoned by his wife's paramour, and died in the year 1444. Against this prince is recorded the vandalism of causing to be thrown down and broken in pieces the antique statue of Virgil which stood in one of the public places of Mantua, and of which the head is still shown in the Museum of the city. In all times, the Mantuans had honored, in divers ways, their great poet, and at certain epochs had coined money bearing his face. With the common people he had a kind of worship (more likely as wizard than as poet), and they celebrated annually some now-forgotten event by assembling with songs and dances about the statue of Virgil which was destroyed by the uncle of the marquis, Malatesta, rather than by the marquis's own order. This ill-conditioned person is supposed to have been "vexed because our Mantuan people thought it their highest glory to be fellow-citizens of the prince of poets."

Francesco having consented, by his acceptance of the marquisate, to become a prince of the Roman Empire, Mantua was thus subjected to the Emperors, but liberty had long been extinguished; and the voluntary election of the Council, which bestowed the captaincy on each succeeding generation of the Gonzagas, was a mere matter of form, and of course.

The next prince, Lodovico Gonzaga, was an austere man, and had been bred in a hard school, if I may believe some of the old chroniclers, whom, indeed, I sometimes suspect of not being altogether faithful. It is said that his father loved his younger brother better than him, and that Lodovico ran away in his boyhood, and took refuge with his father's hereditary enemies, the Visconti. To make dates agree, it must have been the last of these, for the line failed during Lodovico's time, and he had wars with the succeeding Sforza. In the day of his escapade, Milan was at war with Mantua and with Venice, and the Marquis Gonzaga was at the head of the united armies, as we have already seen. So the father and son met in several battles; though the Visconti, out of love for the boy, and from a sentiment of piety somewhat amazing in them, contrived that he should never actually encounter his parent face to face. Lodovico came home after the wars, wearing a long beard; and his mother called her son "the Turk," a nickname that he never lost.

Il Turco was a lover of the arts and of letters, and he did many works to enrich and beautify the city. He established the first printing-office in Mantua, where the first book printed was the "Decamerone" of Boccaccio. He founded a college of advocates, and he dug canals for irrigation; and the prosperity of Mantuan manufacturers in his time may be inferred from the fact that when the King of Denmark paid him a visit, in 1474, the merchants decked their shops with five thousand pieces of fine Mantuan cloth.

The marquis made his brilliant little court the resort of the arts and letters; and hither from Florence came once the elegant Politian, who composed his tragedy of "Orfeo" in Mantua, and caused it to be first represented before Lodovico. But it must be confessed that this was a soil in which art flourished better than literature, and that even born Mantuan poets went off, after a while, and flourished in other air. The painter Mantegna, whom the marquis invited from Padua, passed his whole life here, painting for the marquis in the palaces and churches. The prince loved him, and gave him a house, and bestowed other honors upon him; and Mantegna executed for Lodovico his famous pictures representing the Triumph of Julius Cæsar.[1] It was divided into nine compartments, and, as a frieze, went round the upper part of Lodovico's newly erected palace of San Sebastian. Mantegna also painted a hall in the Castello di Corte, called the Stanza di Mantegna, and there, among other subjects of fable and of war, made the portraits of Lodovico and his wife. It was partly the wish to see such works of Mantegna as still remained in Mantua that took us thither; and it was chiefly this wish that carried us, the morning after our arrival, to the Castello di Corte, or the Ducal Palace.

If the reader cares to fancy a wide piazza, or open square, with a church upon the left hand, immense, uninteresting edifices on the right, and an ugly bishop's palace of Renaissance taste behind him, he may figure before him as vastly and magnificently as he pleases the superb Gothic front of the Castello di Corte. This façade is the only one in Italy that reminds you of the Ducal Palace at Venice; and it does this merely by right of its short pillars and deep Gothic arches in the ground story, and the great breadth of

---

[1] Now at Hampton Court, in England.

wall that rises above them, unbroken by the second line of columns which relieves and lightens this wall in the Venetian palace. It stands at an extremity of the city, upon the edge of the broad fresh-water lagoon, and is of such extent as to include within its walls a whole court-city of theatre, church, stables, playground, course for riding, and several streets. There is a far older edifice adjoining the Castello di Corte, which Guido Bonacolsi began, and which witnessed the bloody end of his line, when Louis Gonzaga surprised and slew his last successor. But the palace itself is all the work of the Gonzagas, and it remains the monument of their kingly state and splendid pride.

But it is known that the works of Mantegna suffered grievously in the wars of the last century, and his memory has faded so dim in this palace where he wrought, that the guide could not understand the curiosity of the foreigners concerning the old painter; and certainly Giulio Romano has stamped himself more ineffaceably than Mantegna upon Mantua.

In the Ducal Palace are seen vividly contrasted the fineness and strength, the delicacy and courage of the fancy, which, rather than the higher gift of imagination, characterize Giulio's work. There is such an airy refinement and subtile grace in the pretty grotesques with which he decorates a chamber; there is such daring luxury of color and design in the pictures for which his grand halls are merely the frames. No doubt I could make fine speeches about these paintings; but who, not seeing them, would be the wiser, after the best description and the choicest critical disquisition? In fact, our travelers themselves found it pleasanter, after a while, to yield to the guidance of the custode, and to enjoy the stupider marvels of the place, than to do the set and difficult admiration of the works of art. So, passing the apartments in good preservation (the Austrian emperors had taken good care of some parts of the palace of one of their first Italian possessions), they did justice to the splendor of the satin beds and the other upholstery work; they admired rich carpentering and costly toys; they dwelt on marvelous tapestries (among which the tapestry copies of Raphael's cartoons, woven at Mantua in the fifteenth century, are certainly worthy of wonder); and they expressed the proper amazement at the miracles of art which caused figures frescoed in the ceilings to turn with them, and follow and face them from whatever part of the room they chose to look. Nay, they even enjoyed the Hall of the Rivers, on the sides of which the usual river-gods were painted, in the company of the usual pottery, from which they pour their founts, and at the end of which there was an abominable little grotto of what people call, in modern landscape-gardening, rock-work, out of the despair with which its unmeaning ugliness fills them. There was, besides all this, a hanging garden in this small Babylon which occupied a spacious oblong, and had a fountain and statues, trees and flowers, and would certainly have been taken for the level of the earth, had not the custode proudly pointed out that it was on a level with the second floor, where they stood.

After that they wandered through a series of unused, dismantled apartments and halls, melancholy with faded fresco, dropping stucco, and mutilated statues of plaster, and came at last upon a balcony overlooking the Cavallerizza, which one of the early dukes built after a design by the inevitable Giulio Romano. It is a large square, and was meant for the diversion of riding on horseback. Balconies go all round it between those thick columns, finely twisted, as we see them in that cartoon of Raphael, "The Healing of the Lame Man at the Beautiful Gate of the Temple;" and here once stood the jolly dukes and the ladies of their light-hearted court, and there below rode the gay, insolent, intriguing courtiers, and outside groaned the city under the heavy extortions of the tax-gatherers. It is all in weather-worn stucco, and the handsome square is planted with trees. The turf was now cut and carved by the heavy wheels of the Austrian baggage-wagons constantly passing through the court to carry munitions to the fortress outside, whose black guns grimly overlook the dead lagoon. A sense of desolation had crept over the sight-seers, with that strange sickness of heart which one feels in the presence of ruin not to be lamented, and which deepened into actual pain as the custode clapped his hands and the echo buffeted itself against the forlorn stucco, and up from the trees rose a score of sullen, slumberous owls, and flapped heavily across the lonesome air with melancholy cries. It only needed, to crush these poor strangers, that final touch which the custode gave, as they passed from the palace through the hall in which are painted the Gonzagas, and in which he pointed to the last Duke of Mantua, saying he was deposed by the Emperor for felony, and somehow conveying the idea of horse-stealing and counterfeiting on the part of his Grace. A very different man from this rogue was our old friend Lodovico, who also, however, had his troubles. He was an enemy of the Ghibellines, and fought them a great deal. Of course he had the habitual wars with Milan, and he was obliged to do battle with his own brother Carlo to some extent. This Gonzaga had been taken prisoner by the Sforza; and Lodovico, having paid for him a ransom of sixty thousand florins of gold (which Carlo was scarcely worth), seized the fraternal lands, and held them in pledge of repayment. Carlo could not pay, and tried to get back his possessions by war. Vexed with these and other contentions, Lodovico was also unhappy in his son, whose romance I may best tell in the words of the history[1] from which I take it.

"Lodovico Gonzaga, having agreed with the Duke of Bavaria to take his daughter Margherita as wife for his (Lodovico's) first-born, Federico, and the young man having refused her, Lodovico was so much enraged that he sought to imprison him; but the Marchioness Barbara, mother of Federico, caused him to fly from the city till his father's anger should be abated. Federico departed with six attendants;[2] but this flight caused still greater displeasure to his father, who now declared him banished, and threatened with heavy penalties any one who should give him help or favor. Federico, therefore, wandered about with these six attendants in divers places, and finally arrived in Naples; but having already spent all his substance, and not daring to make himself known for fear of his father, he fell into great want, and so into severe

---

[1] Volta, *Storia di Mantova.*
[2] The *Fioretto delle Cronache* says "persons of gentle condition."

sickness. His companions having nothing wherewith to live, and not knowing any trade by which to gain their bread, did menial services fit for day-laborers, and sustained their lord with their earnings, he remaining hidden in a poor woman's house where they all dwelt.

"The Marchioness had sent many messengers in divers provinces with money to find her son, but they never heard any news of him; so that they thought him dead, not hearing anything, either, of his attendants. Now it happened that one of those who sought Federico came to Naples, and presented himself to the king with a letter from the said lady, praying that he should make search in his territory for a company of seven men, giving the name and description of each. The king caused this search to be made by the heads of the district; and one of these heads told how in his district there were six Lombard men (not knowing of Federico, who lay ill), but that they were laborers and of base condition. The king determined to see them; and they being come before him, he demanded who they were, and how many; as they were not willing to discover their lord, on being asked their names they gave others, so that the king, not being able to learn anything, would have dismissed them. But the messenger sent by the Marchioness knew them, and said to the king, 'Sire, these are the attendants of him whom I seek; but they have changed their names.' The king caused them to be separated one from another, and then asked them of their lord; and they, finding themselves separated, minutely narrated everything; and the king immediately sent for Federico, whom his officers found miserably ill on a heap of straw. He was brought to the palace, where the king ordered him to be cared for, sending the messenger back to his mother to advise her how the men had been found and in what great misery. The Marchioness went to her husband, and, having cast herself at his feet, besought him of a grace. The Marquis answered that he would grant everything, so it did not treat of Federico. Then the lady opened him the letter of the king of Naples, which had such effect that it softened the soul of the Marquis, showing him in how great misery his son had been; and so, giving the letter to the

Marchioness, he said, 'Do that which pleases you.' The Marchioness straightway sent the prince money, and clothes to clothe him, in order that he should return to Mantua; and having come, the son cast himself at his father's feet, imploring pardon for himself and for his attendants; and he pardoned them, and gave those attendants enough to live honorably and like noblemen, and they were called The Faithful of the House of Gonzaga, and from them come the *Fedeli* of Mantua.

"The Marquis then, not to break faith, caused Federico to take Margherita, daughter of the Duke of Bavaria, for his wife, and celebrated the nuptials splendidly; so that there remained the greatest love between father and son."

The son succeeded to the father's dominion in 1478; and it is recorded of him in the "Flower of the Chronicles," that he was a hater of idleness, and a just man, greatly beloved by his people. Federico was marquis only six years and died in 1484, leaving his marquisate to his son Francesco, the most ambitious, warlike, restless, splendid prince of his magnificent race. This Gonzaga wore a beard, and brought the custom into fashion in Italy again. He founded the famous breed of Mantuan horses and gave them about free-handedly to other sovereigns of his acquaintance. To the English king he presented a steed which, if we may trust history, could have been sold for almost its weight in gold. He was so fond of hunting that he kept two hundred dogs of the chase, and one hundred and fifty birds of prey.

Of course this Gonzaga was a soldier, and indeed he loved war better even than hunting, and delighted so much in personal feats of arms that, concealing his name and quality, in order that the combat should be in all things equal, he was wont to challenge renowned champions wherever he heard of them, and to meet them in the lists. Great part of his life was spent in the field; and he fought in turn on nearly all sides of the political questions then agitating Italy. In 1495 he was at the head of the Venetian and other Italian troops when they beat the French under Charles VIII. at Taro, and made so little use of their victory as to let their vanquished invaders escape from them after all. Nevertheless if the Gonzaga did not here show himself a great general, he did great feats of personal valor, penetrating to the midst of the French forces, wounding the king, and with his own hand taking prisoner the great Bastard of Bourbon. Venice paid him ten thousand ducats for gaining the victory, such as it was, and when peace was made he went to visit the French king at Vercelli; and there Charles gave his guest a present of two magnificent horses, which the Gonzaga returned yet more splendidly in kind. About five years later he was again at war with the French, and helped the Aragonese drive them out of Naples. In 1506 Pope Julius II. made him leader of the armies of the Church (for he had now quitted the Venetian service), and he reduced the city of Bologna to obedience to the Holy See. In 1509 he joined the League of Cambray against Venice, and, being made Imperial Captain-General, was taken prisoner by the Venetians. They liberated him, however, the following year; and in 1513 we find him at the head of the league against the French.

A curious anecdote of this Gonzaga's hospitality is also illustrative of the anomalous life of those times when good faith had as little to do with the intercourse of nations as at present; but good fortune, when she appeared in the world, liked to put on a romantic and melodramatic guise. An ambassador from the Grand Turk on his way to Rome was taken by an enemy of the Pope, despoiled of all his money, and left planted, as the Italians expressively say, at Ancona. This ambassador had come to concert with Alexander VI. the death of Bajazet's brother, prisoner in the Pope's hands, and he bore the Pope a present of 50,000 gold ducats. It was Gian Della Rovere who seized and spoiled him, and sent the papers (letters of the Pope and Sultan) to Charles VIII. of France, to whom Alexander had been obliged to give the Grand Turk's brother. The magnificent Gonzaga hears of the Turk's embarrassing mischance, sends and fetches him to Mantua, clothes him, puts abundant money in his purse, and dispatches him on his way. The Sultan, in reward of this courtesy to his servant, gave a number of fine horses to the marquis, who, possibly being tired of presenting his own horses, returned the

Porte a shipload of excellent Mantuan cheeses. The interchange of compliments seems to have led to a kind of romantic friendship between the Gonzaga and the Grand Turk, who did occasionally interest himself in the affairs of the Christian dogs; and who, when Francesco lay prisoner at Venice, actually wrote to the Serenest Senate, and asked his release as a personal grace to him, the Grand Turk. And Francesco was, thereupon, let go; the canny republic being willing to do the Sultan any sort of cheap favor.

This Gonzaga, being so much engaged in war, seems to have had little time for the adornment of his capital. The Church of Our Lady of Victory is the only edifice which he added to it; and this was merely in glorification of his own triumph over the French at Taro. Mantegna painted an altarpiece for it, representing the marquis and his wife on their knees before the Virgin, in act of rendering her thanks for the victory. The French nation avenged itself for whatever wrong was done its pride in this picture by stealing it away from Mantua in Napoleon's time; and it now hangs in the gallery of the Louvre.

Francesco died in 1519; and after him his son, Federico II., the first Duke of Mantua, reigned some twenty-one years, and died in 1540. The marquisate in his time was made a duchy by the Emperor Charles V., to whom the Gonzaga had given efficient aid in his wars against the French. This was in the year 1530; and three years later, when the Duke of Monferrato died, and the inheritance of his opulent little state was disputed by the Duke of Savoy, by the Marquis of Saluzzo, and by the Gonzaga who had married the late duke's daughter, Charles's influence secured it to the Mantuan. The dominions of the Gonzagas had now reached their utmost extent, and these dominions were not curtailed till the deposition of Fernando Carlo in 1708, when Monferrato was adjudged to the Duke of Savoy, and afterwards confirmed to him by treaty. It was separated from the capital of the Gonzagas by a wide extent of alien territory, but they held it with a strong hand, embellished the city, and founded there the strongest citadel in Italy.

Federico, after his wars for the Emperor, appears to have

reposed in peace for the rest of his days, and to have devoted himself to the adornment of Mantua and the aggrandizing of his family. His court was the home of many artists; and Titian painted for him the Twelve Cæsars which the Germans stole when they sacked the city in 1630. But his great agent and best beloved genius was Giulio Pippi, called Romano, who was conducted to Mantua by pleasant Count Baldassare Castiglione.

Pleasant Count Baldassare Castiglione! whose incomparable book of the "Cortigiano" succeeded in teaching his countrymen every gentlemanly grace but virtue. He was born at Casatico in the Mantovano, in the year 1476, and went in his boyhood to be schooled at Milan, where he learnt the profession of arms. From Milan he went to Rome, where he exercised his profession of arms till the year 1504, when he was called to gentler uses at the court of the elegant Dukes of Urbino. He lived there as courtier and court-poet, and he returned to Rome as the ambassador from Urbino. Meantime his liege, Francesco Gonzaga, was but poorly pleased that so brilliant a Mantuan should spend his life in the service and ornament of other princes, and Castiglione came back to his native country about the year 1516. He married in Mantua, and there finished his famous book of "The Courtier," and succeeded in winning back the favor of his prince. Federico, the duke, made him ambassador to Rome in 1528; and Baldassare did his master two signal services there,—he procured him to be named head of all the Papal forces, and he found him Giulio Romano. So the duke suffered him to go as the Pope's nuncio to Spain, and Baldassare finished his courtly days at Toledo in 1529.

The poet made a detour to Mantua on his way to Spain, taking with him the painter, whom the duke received with many caresses, as Vasari says, presented him a house honorably furnished, ordered provision for him and his pupils, gave them certain brave suits of velvet and satin, and, seeing that Giulio had no horse, called for his own favorite and bestowed it on him. They knew how to receive painters, those fine princes, who had merely to put their hands into their people's pocket and take out what florins they liked. So the duke presently set the artist to work, riding out with him through the gate of San Bastiano to some stables about a bow-shot from the walls, in the midst of a flat meadow, where he told Giulio that he would be glad (if it could be done without destroying the old walls) to have such buildings added to the stables as would serve him for a kind of lodge, to come out and merrily sup in when he liked. Whereupon Giulio began to think out the famous Palazzo del T.

Castiglione had found the painter at Rome, after the death of his master Raphael, when his genius, for good or for ill, began for the first time to find original expression. At Mantua he spent all the rest of his busy life, and as in Venice all the Madonnas in the street-corner shrines have some touch of color to confess the painter's subjection to Titian or Tintoretto; as in Vicenza the edifices are all stilted upon pedestals in honor and homage to Palladio; as in Parma Correggio has never died, but lives to this day in the mouths and chiaroscuro effects of all theofigures in all the pictures painted there;—so in Mantua Giulio Romano is to be found in the lines of every painting and every palace.

Giulio Romano did a little of everything for the Dukes of Mantua,—from painting the most delicate or indelicate little fresco for a bed-chamber, to restraining the Po and the Mincio with immense dikes, restoring ancient edifices and building new ones, draining swamps and demolishing and reconstructing whole streets, painting palaces and churches, and designing the city slaughter-house. He grew old and very rich in the service of the Gonzagas; but though Mrs. Jameson says he commanded respect by a sense of his own dignity as an artist, the Bishop of Casale, who wrote the "Annali di Mantova," says that the want of nobility and purity in his style, and his "gallant inventions, were conformable to his own sensual life, and that he did not disdain to prostitute himself to the infamies of Aretino."

His great architectural work in Mantua is the Palazzo del T, or Tè, as it is now written. It was first called Palazzo del T, from the convergence of roads there in the form of that letter; and the modern Mantuans call it Del Tè, from the superstition, transmitted to us by the custode of the Ducal Palace, that the Gonzagas merely used it on pleasant afternoons to take tea in! I say nothing to control the reader's choice between T and Tè, and merely adhere to the elder style out of reverence for the past. It is certain that the air of the plain on which the palace stands is most unwholesome, and it may have been true that the dukes never passed the night there. Federico did not intend to build more than a lodge in this place; but fascinated with the design offered him by Giulio, he caused the artist to go on, and contrive him a palace instead. It stands, as Vasari says, about a good bow-shot from one of the city's gates; and going out to see the palace on our second day in Mantua, we crossed a drawbridge guarded by Austrian soldiers. Below languished a bed of sullen ooze, tangled and thickly grown with long, villainous grasses, and sending up a damp and deathly stench, which made all the faces we saw look feverish and sallow. Already at that early season the air was foul and heavy, and the sun, faintly making himself seen through the dun sky of the dull spring day, seemed sick to look upon the place, where indeed the only happy and lively things were the clouds of gnats that danced before us, and welcomed us to the Palazzo del T. Damp ditches surround the palace, in which these gnats seemed to have peculiar pleasure; and they took possession of the portico of the stately entrance of the edifice as we went in, and held it faithfully till we returned.

In one of the first large rooms are the life-size portraits of the six finest horses of the Gonzaga stud, painted by the pupils of Giulio Romano, after the master's designs. The paintings attest the beauty of the Mantuan horses, and the pride and fondness of their ducal owners; and trustworthy critics have praised their eminent truth. But we presently left them for other chambers, in which the invention of Giulio had been used to please himself rather than his master. I scarcely mean to name the wonders of the palace, having, indeed, general associations with them, rather than particular recollections of them.

One of the most famous rooms is the Chamber of Psyche (the apartments are not of great size), of which the ceiling is by Giulio and the walls are by his pupils. The whole illustrates, with every variety of fantastic invention, the story of Psyche, as told by Apuleius, and deserves to be curiously studied as a part of the fair outside of a superb and corrupt age, the inside of which was full of rottenness. The civilization of Italy, as a growth from the earliest Pagan times, and only modified by Christianity and the admixture of Northern blood and thought, is yet to be carefully analyzed; and until this analysis is made, discussion of certain features must necessarily be incomplete and unsatisfactory. No one, however, can stand in this Chamber of Psyche, and not feel how great reality the old mythology must still have had, not only for the artists who painted the room, but for the people who inhabited it and enjoyed it. I do not say that they believed it as they believed in the vital articles of Christian faith, but that they accepted it with the same spirit as they accepted the martyrology of the Church; and that to the fine gentlemen and ladies of the court, those jolly satyrs and careless nymphs, those Cupids and Psyches, and Dianas and Venuses, were of the same verity as the Fathers of the Desert, the Devil, and the great body of the saints. If they did not pray to them, they swore by them, and their names were much oftener on their lips; and the art of the time was so thoroughly Pagan, that it forgot all Christian holiness, and clung only to heathen beauty. When it had not actually a mythologic subject to deal with, it paganized Christian themes. St. Sebastian was made to look like Apollo, and Mary Magdalene was merely a tearful, triste Venus. There is scarcely a ray of feeling in Italian art since Raphael's time which suggests Christianity in the artist, or teaches it to the beholder. In confessedly Pagan subjects it was happiest, as in the life of Psyche, in this room; and here it inculcated a gay and spirited license, and an elegant absence of modesty. It would be instructive to know in what spirit the common Mantuans of his day looked upon the inventions of the painter, and how far the courtly circle which frequented this room went in discussion of the unspeakable indecency of some of the scenes.[1]

Returning to the city, we visited the house of Giulio Romano, which stands in one of the fine, lonesome streets, and at the outside of which we looked. The artist designed it himself; and it is very pretty, with delicacy of feeling in the fine stucco ornamentation, but it is not otherwise interesting.

We passed it, continuing our way toward the Arsenal, near which we had seen the women at work washing the linen coats of the garrison in the twilight of the evening before; and we now saw them again from the bridge, on which we paused to look at a picturesque bit of modern life in Mantua. They washed the linen in a clear, swift-running stream, diverted from the dam of the Mincio to furnish mill-power within the city wall; and we could look down the watercourse past old arcades of masonry half submerged in it, past pleasant angles of houses and a lazy mill-wheel turning slowly, slowly, till our view ended in the gallery of a time-worn palace, through the columns of which was seen the blue sky. Under the bridge the stream ran very strong and lucid, over long, green, undulating water-grasses, which it loved to dimple over and play with. On the right were the laundresses under the eaves of a wooden shed, each kneeling, as their custom is, in a three-sided box, and leaning forward over the washboard that sloped down into the water. As they washed they held the linen in one hand, and rubbed it with the other; then heaped it into a mass upon the board and beat it with great two-handed blows of a stick. They sang, meanwhile, one of those plaintive airs of which the Italian peasants are so fond, and which rose in indescribable pathos, pulsing with their blows, and rhythmic with the graceful movement of their figures. Many of the women were young,—though they were of all ages,—and the prettiest among

---

[1] The ruin in the famous room frescoed with the Fall of the Giants commences on the very door-jambs, which are painted in broken and tumbling brick-work; and throughout there is a prodigiousness which does not surprise, and a bigness which does not impress. In Kugler's *Hand-book of Italian Painting* are two illustrations, representing parts of the fresco, which give a fair idea of the whole.

them was third from where we stood upon the bridge. She caught sight of the sketch-book which one of the travelers carried, and pointed it out to the rest, who could hardly settle to their work to be sketched. Presently an idle baker, whose shop adjoined the bridge, came out and leaned upon the parapet, and bantered the girls. "They are drawing the prettiest," he said, at which they all bridled a little; and she who knew herself to be prettiest hung her head and rubbed furiously at the linen. Long before the artist had finished the sketch, the lazy, good-humored crowd which the public practice of the fine arts always attracts in Italy had surrounded the strangers, and were applauding, commenting, comparing, and absorbing every stroke as it was made. When the book was closed and they walked away, a number of boys straggled after them some spaces, inspired by a curious longing and regret, like that which leads boys to the eager inspection of fireworks when they have gone out. We lost them at the first turning of the street, whither the melancholy chorus of the women's song had also followed us, and where it died pathetically away.

In the evening we walked to the Piazza Virgiliana, the beautiful space laid out and planted with trees by the French at the beginning of this century, in honor of the great Mantuan poet. One of its bounds is the shore of the lake which surrounds the city, and from which now rose ghostly vapors on the still twilight air. Down the slow, dull current moved one of the picturesque black boats of the Po; and beyond, the level landscape had a pleasant desolation that recalled the scenery of the Middle Mississippi. It might have been here in this very water that the first-born of our first Duke of Mantua fell from his boat while hunting water-fowl in 1550, and took a fever of which he died only a short time after his succession to the sovereignty of the duchy. At any rate, the fact of the accident brings me back from lounging up and down Mantua to my duty of chronicler. Francesco's father had left him in childhood to the care of his uncle, the Cardinal Hercules, who ruled Mantua with a firm and able hand, increasing the income of the state, spending less upon the ducal stud, and cutting down the number of mouths at the ducal table from eight hundred to three hundred and fifty-one. His justice tended to severity rather than mercy; but reformers of our own time will argue well of his heart, that he founded in that time a place of refuge and retirement for abandoned women. Good Catholics will also be pleased to know that he was very efficient in suppressing the black heresy of Calvin, which had crept into Mantua in his day,—probably from Ferrara, where the black heretic himself was then, or about then, in hiding under the protection of the ill-advised Marchioness Renée. The good cardinal received the Pope's applause for his energy in this matter, and no doubt his hand fell heavily on the Calvinists. Of the duke who died so young, the Venetian ambassador thought it worth while to write what I think it worth while to quote, as illustrating the desire of the Senate to have careful knowledge of its neighbors: "He is a boy of melancholy complexion. His eyes are full of spirit, but he does not delight in childish things, and seems secretly proud of being lord. He has an excellent memory, and shows much inclination for letters."

His brother Guglielmo, who succeeded him in 1550, seems to have had the same affection for learning; but he was willful, harsh, and cruelly ambitious, and cared, an old writer says, for nothing so much as perpetuating the race of the Gonzagas in Mantua. He was a hunchback, and some of his family (who could not have understood his character) tried to persuade him not to assume the ducal dignity; but his haughty temper soon righted him in their esteem, and it is said that all the courtiers put on humps in honor of the duke. He was not a great warrior, and there are few picturesque incidents in his reign. Indeed, nearly the last of these in Mantuan history was the coronation at Mantua of the excellent poet Lodovico Ariosto, by Charles V., in 1532, Federico II. reigning. But the Mantuans of Guglielmo's day were not without their sensations, for three Japanese ambassadors passed through their city on their way to Rome. They were also awakened to religious zeal by the reappearance of Protestantism among them. The heresy was happily suppressed by the Inquisition, acting under Pius V., though with small thanks to Duke

William, who seems to have taken no fervent part in the persecutions. The duke must have made haste after this to reconcile himself with the Church; for we read that two years later he was permitted to take a particle of the blood of Christ from the church of St. Andrea to that of Sta. Barbara, where he deposited it in a box of crystal and gold, and caused his statue to be placed before the shrine in the act of adoring the relic.

Duke William managed his finances so well as to leave his spendthrift son Vincenzo a large sum of money to make away with after his death. Part of this, indeed, he had earned by obedience to his father's wishes in the article of matrimony. The prince was in love with the niece of the Duke of Bavaria, very lovely and certainly high-born enough, but having unhappily only sixty thousand crowns to her portion. So she was not to be thought of, and Vincenzo married the sister of the Duke of Parma, of whom he grew so fond that, though two years of marriage brought them no children, he could scarce be persuaded to suffer her divorce on account of sterility. This happened, however, and the prince's affections were next engaged by the daughter of the Grand Duke of Tuscany. The lady had a portion of three hundred thousand crowns, which entirely charmed the frugal-minded Duke William, and Vincenzo married her, after certain diplomatic preliminaries demanded by the circumstances, which scarcely bear statement in English, and which the present history would blush to give even in Italian.

Indeed, he was a great beast, this splendid Vincenzo, both by his own fault and that of others; but it ought to be remembered of him, that at his solicitation the most clement lord of Ferrara liberated from durance in the hospital of St. Anna his poet Tasso, whom he had kept shut in that mad-house seven years. On his delivery, Tasso addressed his "Discorso" to Vincenzo's kinsman, the learned Cardinal Scipio Gonzaga; and to this prelate he submitted for correction the "Gerusalemme," as did Guarini his "Pastor Fido."

When Vincenzo came to power, he found a fat treasury, which he enjoyed after the fashion of the time, and which, having a princely passion for every costly pleasure, he soon emptied. He was crowned in 1587; and on his coronation day rode through the streets throwing gold to the people, after the manner of the Mantuan dukes. He kept up an army of six thousand men, among a population of eighty thousand all told; and maintained as his guard "fifty archers on horseback, who also served with the arquebuse, and fifty light-horsemen for the guard of his own person, who were all excellently mounted, the duke possessing such a noble stud of horses that he always had five hundred at his service, and kept in stable one hundred and fifty of marvelous beauty." He lent the Spanish king two hundred thousand pounds out of his father's sparings; and when the Archduchess of Austria, Margherita, passed through Mantua on her way to wed Philip II. of Spain, he gave her a diamond ring worth twelve thousand crowns. Next after women, he was madly fond of the theatre, and spent immense sums for actors. He would not, indeed, cede in splendor to the greatest monarchs, and in his reign of fifteen years he squandered fifty million crowns! No one will be surprised to learn from a contemporary writer in Mantua, that this excellent prince was adorned with all the Christian virtues; nor to be told by a later historian, that in Vincenzo's time Mantua was the most corrupt city in Europe. A satire of the year 1601, which this writer (Maffei) reduces to prose, says of that period: "Everywhere in Mantua are seen feasts, jousts, masks, banquets, plays, music, balls, delights, dancing. To these the young girls," an enormity in Italy, "as well as the matrons, go in magnificent dresses; and even the churches are scenes of love-making. Good mothers, instead of teaching their daughters the use of the needle, teach them the arts of rouging, dressing, singing, and dancing. Naples and Milan scarcely produce silk enough, or India and Peru gold and gems enough, th deck out female impudence and pride. Courtiers and warriors perfume themselves as delicately as ladies; and even the food is scented, that the mouth may exhale fragrance. The galleries and halls of the houses are painted full of the loves of Mars and Venus, Leda and the Swan, Jove and Danaë, while the devout solace themselves with such sacred subjects as Susannah and the Elders. The flower of chastity seems withered in Mantua. No longer in Lydia nor in Cyprus, but in Mantua, is fixed the realm of pleasure." The Mantuans were a different people in the old republican times, when a fine was imposed for blasphemy, and the blasphemer put into a basket and drowned in the lake, if he did not pay within fifteen days; which must have made profanity a luxury even to the rich. But in that day a man had to pay twenty soldi (seventy-five cents) if he spoke to a woman in church; and women were not allowed even the moderate diversion of going to funerals, and could not wear silk lace about the neck, nor have dresses that dragged more than a yard, nor crowns of pearls or gems, nor belts worth more than ten livres (twenty-five dollars), nor purses worth more than fifteen soldi (fifty cents).

Possibly as an antidote for the corruption brought into the world with Vincenzo, there was another Gonzaga born about the same period, who became in due time Saint Louis Gonzaga, and remains to this day one of the most powerful friends of virtue to whom a good Catholic can pray. He is particularly recommended by his biographer, the Jesuit Father Cesari, in cases of carnal temptation, and improving stories are told Italian youth of the miracles he works under such circumstances. He vowed chastity for his own part at an age when most children do not know good from evil, and he carried the fulfillment of this vow to such extreme, that, being one day at play of forfeits with other boys and girls, and being required to kiss—not one of the little maidens—but her *shadow* on the wall, he would not, preferring to lose his pawn.

San Luigi Gonzaga descended from that Ridolfo who put his wife to death, and his father was Marquis of Castiglione delle Stivere. He was born in 1568, and, being the first son, was heir to the marquisate; but from his earliest years he had a call to the Church. His family did everything possible to dissuade him—his father with harshness, and his uncle, Duke William of Mantua, with tenderness—from his vocation. The latter even sent a "bishop of rare eloquence" to labor with the boy at Castiglione; but everything was done in vain. In due time Luigi joined the Company of Jesus, renounced this world, and died at Rome in the odor of sanctity, after doing such good works as surprised every one. His brother Ridolfo succeeded to the marquisate, and fell into a quarrel with Duke William about lands, which dispute Luigi composed before his death.

From the time of the first Vincenzo's death, there are only two tragic events which lift the character of Mantuan history above the quality of *chronique scandaleuse*, namely, the Duke Ferdinand's repudiation of Camilla Faa di Casale, and the sack of Mantua in 1630. The first of these events followed close upon the demise of the splendid Vincenzo; for his son Francesco reigned but a short time, and died, leaving a little daughter of three years to the guardianship of her uncle, the Cardinal Ferdinand. The law of the Mantuan succession excluded females; and Ferdinand, dispensed from his ecclesiastical functions by the Pope, ascended the ducal throne. In 1615, not long after his accession, as the chronicles relate, in passing through a chamber of the palace he saw a young girl playing upon a cithern, and being himself young, and of the ardent temper of the Gonzagas, he fell in love with the fair minstrel. She was the daughter of a noble servant of the duke, who had once been his ambassador to the court of the Duke of Savoy, and was called Count Ardizzo Faa Monferrino di Casale. It seems that the poor girl loved her ducal wooer; and besides the ducal crown was a glittering temptation, and she consented to a marriage which, for state and family reasons, was made secret. When the fact was bruited, it raised the wrath and ridicule of Ferdinand's family, and the duke's sister Margaret, Duchess of Ferrara, had so lofty a disdain of his *mésalliance* with an inferior, that she drove him to desperation with her sarcasms. About this time Camilla's father died, with strong evidences of poisoning; and the wife being left helpless and friendless, her noble husband resorted to the artifice of feigning that there had never been any marriage, and thus sought to appease his family. Unhappily, however, he had given her a certificate of matrimony, which she refused to surrender when he put her away, so that the duke, desiring afterwards to espouse the daughter of the Grand Duke of Tuscany, was obliged to present a counterfeit certificate to his bride, who believed it the real marriage contract, and destroyed it. When the duchess discovered the imposition, she would not rest till she had wrung the real document from Camilla, under the threat of putting her son to death. The miserable mother then retired to a convent, and died of a broken heart, while Ferdinand bastardized his only legitimate son, a noble boy, whom his mother had called Jacinth. After this, a kind of retribution, amid all his political successes, seems to have pursued the guilty duke. His second wife was too fat to bear children, but not to bear malice; and she never ceased to distrust and reproach the duke, whom she could not believe in anything since the affair of the counterfeit marriage contract. She was very religious, and embittered Ferdinand's days with continued sermons and reproofs, and made him order, in the merry Mantuan court, all the devotions commanded by her confessor.

So Ferdinand died childless, and, it is said, in sore remorse, and was succeeded in 1626 by his brother Vincenzo, another hope of the faith and light of the Church. His brief reign lasted but one year, and was ignoble as it was brief, and fitly ended the direct line of the Gonzagas. Vincenzo, though an ecclesiastic, never studied anything, and was disgracefully ignorant. Lacking the hereditary love of letters, he had not the warlike boldness of his race; and resembled his ancestors only in the love he bore to horses, hunting, and women. He was enamored of the widow of one of his kinsmen, a woman no longer young, but of still agreeable person, strong will, and quick wit, and of a fascinating presence, which Vincenzo could not resist. He was wooing her, with a view to seduction, when he received the nomination of cardinal from Pope Paul V. He pressed his suit, but the lady would consent to nothing but marriage, and Vincenzo bundled up the cardinal's purple and sent it back, with a very careless and ill-mannered letter, to the ireful Pope, who swore never to make another Gonzaga cardinal. He then married the widow, but soon wearied of her, and spent the rest of his days in vain attempts to secure a divorce, in order to be restored to his ecclesiastical benefices. And one Christmas morning *he* died childless; and three years later the famous sack of Mantua took place. The events leading to this crime are part of the most complicated episodes of Italian history.

Ferdinand, as guardian of his brother's daughter Maria, claimed the Duchy of Monferrato as part of his dominion; but his claim was disputed by Maria's grandfather, the Duke of Savoy, who contended that it reverted to him, on the death of his daughter, as a fief which had been added to Mantua merely by the intermarriage of the Gonzagas with his family. He was supported in this claim by the Spaniards, then at Milan. The Venetians and the German Emperor supported Ferdinand, and the French advanced the claim of a third, the descendant of Lodovico Gonzaga, who had left Mantua a century before, and entered upon the inheritance of the Duchy of Nevers-Rethel. The Duke of Savoy was one of the boldest of his warlike race; and the Italians had great hopes of him as one great enough to drive the barbarians out of Italy. But nearly three centuries more were wanted to raise his family to the magnitude of a national purpose; and Carlo Emanuel spent his greatness in disputes with the petty princes about him. In this dispute for Monferrato he was worsted; for at the treaty of Pavia, Monferrato was assured to Duke Ferdinand of Mantua.

Ferdinand afterwards died without issue, and Vincenzo likewise died childless; and Charles Gonzaga of Nevers-Rethel, who had married Maria, Ferdinand's ward, became heir to the Duchy of Mantua, but his right was disputed by Ferrante Gonzaga of Guastalla. Charles hurriedly and half secretly introduced himself into Mantua without consultation with Venetian, Spaniard, or German. While Duke Olivares of Spain was meditating his recognition, his officer at Milan tried to seize Mantua and failed; but the German Emperor had been even more deeply offended, and claimed the remission of Charles's rights as a feudatory of the Roman Empire, until he should have regularly invested him. Charles prepared for defense. Meanwhile Spain and Savoy seized Monferrato, but they were afterwards defeated by the French, and the Spanish Milanese was overrun by the Venetians and Mantuans. The German Emperor then sent down his Landsknechts, and in 1630 besieged Mantua, while the French promised help and gave none, and the Pope exhorted Charles to submit. The Venetians, occupied with the Uskosk pirates, could do little in his defense. To the horrors of this unequal and desperate war were added those of famine; and the Jews, passing between the camp and the city, brought a pest from the army into Mantua, which raged with extraordinary violence among the hungry and miserable people. In vain they formed processions, and carried the blood of Christ about the city. So many died that there were not boats enough to bear them away to their sepulture in the lakes, and the bodies rotted in the streets. There was not wanting at this time the presence of a traitor in the devoted city, a lieutenant in the Swiss Guard of the duke; and when he had led the Germans into Mantua, and received the reward of his infamy, two German soldiers, placed over him for his protection, killed him and plundered him of his spoil.

The sack now began, and lasted three days, with unspeakable horrors. The Germans (then the most slavish and merciless of soldiers) violated Mantuan women, and buried their victims alive. The harlots of their camp cast off their rags, and robing themselves in the richest spoils they could find, rioted through the streets, and added the shame of drunken orgies to the dreadful scene of blood and tears. The Jews were driven forth almost naked from the Ghetto. The precious monuments of ages were destroyed; or such as the fury of the soldiers spared, the avarice of their generals consumed; and pictures, statues, and other works of art were stolen and carried away. The churches were plundered, the sacred houses of religion were sacked, and the nuns who did not meet a worse fate went begging through the streets.

The imperial general, Aldringher, had, immediately upon entering the city, appropriated the Ducal Palace to himself as his share of the booty. He placed a strong guard around it, and spoiled it at leisure and systematically, and gained fabulous sums from the robbery. After the sack was ended, he levied upon the population (from whom his soldiers had forced everything that terror and torture could wring from them) four contributions, amounting to a hundred thousand doubloons. This population had, during the siege and sack, been reduced from thirty to twelve thousand; and Aldringher had so thoroughly accomplished his part of the spoliation, that the Duke Charles, returning after the withdrawal of the Germans, could not find in the Ducal Palace so much as a bench to sit upon. He and his family had fled half naked from their beds on the entry of the Germans, and, after a pause in the citadel, had withdrawn to Ariano, whence the duke sent ambassadors to Vienna to expose his miserable fate to the Emperor. The conduct of Aldringher was severely rebuked at the capital; and the Emperor sent Carlo's wife ten thousand zecchini, with which they returned at length to Mantua. It is melancholy to read how his neighbors had to compassionate his destitution; how the Grand Duke of Tuscany sent him upholstery for two state chambers; how the Duke of Parma supplied his table-service; how Alfonso of Modena gave him a hundred pairs of oxen, and as many peasants to till his desolated lands. His people always looked upon him with evil eyes, as the cause of their woes; and after a reign of ten years he died of a broken heart, or, as some thought, of poison.

Carlo had appointed as his successor his nephew and namesake, who succeeded to the throne ten years after his uncle's death, the Princess Maria Gonzaga being regent during his minority. Carlo II. early manifested the amorous disposition of his blood, but his reign was not distinguished by remarkable events. He was of imperial politics during those interminable French-Austrian wars, and the French desolated his dominions more or less. In the time of this Carlo II., we read of the Jews being condemned to pay the wages of the duke's archers for the extremely improbable crime of killing some Hebrews who had been converted; and there is account of the duchess going on foot to the sanctuary of Our Lady of Grace, to render thanks for her son's recovery from a fever, and her daughter's recovery from the bite of a monkey. Mantua must also have regained something of its former gayety; for in 1652, the Austrian Archdukes and the Medici spent Carnival there. Carlo II.

died, like his father, with suspicions of poisoning, and undoubted evidences of debauchery. He was a generous and amiable prince; and, though a shameless profligate, was beloved by his subjects, with whom, no doubt, his profligacy was not a reproach.

Ferdinand Carlo, whose ignoble reign lasted from 1665 to 1708, was the last and basest of his race. The histories of his country do not attribute a single virtue to this unhappy prince, who seems to have united in himself all the vices of all the Gonzagas. He was licentious and depraved as the first Vincenzo, and he had not Vincenzo's courage; he was luxurious as the second Francesco, but had none of his generosity; he taxed his people heavily that he might meanly enjoy their substance without making them even the poor return of national glory; he was grasping as Guglielmo, but saved nothing to the state; he was as timid as the second Vincenzo, and yet made a feint of making war, and went to Hungary at one time to fight against the Turk. But he loved far better to go to Venice in his gilded barge, and to spend his Carnivals amid the variety of that city's dissoluteness. He was so ignorant as scarcely to be able to write his name; but he knew all vicious things from his cradle, as if, indeed, he had been gifted to know them by instinct through the profligacy of his parents. It is said that even the degraded Mantuans blushed to be ruled by so dull and ignorant a wretch; but in his time, nevertheless, Mantua was all rejoicings, promenades, pleasure-voyages, and merry-makings. "The duke recruited women from every country to stock his palace," says an Italian author, "where they played, sang, and made merry at his will and theirs." "In Venice," says Volta, "he surrendered himself to such diversions without shame, or stint of expense. He not only took part in all public entertainments and pleasures of that capital, but he held a most luxurious and gallant court of his own; and all night long his palace was the scene of theatrical representations by dissolute women, with music and banqueting, so that he had a worse name than Sardanapalus of old." He sneaked away to these gross delights in 1700, while the Emperor was at war with the Spaniards, and left his duchess (a brave and noble woman, the daughter of Ferrante Gonzaga, Duke of Guastalla) to take care of the duchy, then in great part occupied by Spanish and French forces. This was the War of the Spanish Succession; and it used up poor Ferdinand, who had not a shadow of interest in it. He had sold the fortress of Casale to the French in 1681, feigning that they had taken it from him by fraud; and now he declared that he was forced to admit eight thousand French and Spanish troops into Mantua. Perhaps indeed he was, but the Emperor never would believe it; and he pronounced Ferdinand guilty of felony against the Empire, and deposed him from his duchy. The duke appealed against this sentence to the Diet of Ratisbon, and, pending the Diet's decision, made a journey of pleasure to France, where the Grand Monarch named him generalissimo of the French forces in Italy, though he never commanded them. He came back to Mantua after a little, and built himself a splendid theatre,—the cheerful duke.

But his end was near. The French and Austrians made peace in 1707; and next year, Monferrato having fallen to Savoy, the Austrians entered Mantua, whence the duke promptly fled. The Austrians marched into Mantua on the 29th of February, that being leap year, and Ferdinand came back no more. Indeed, trusting in false hopes of restoration held out to him by Venice and France, he died on the 5th of July following, at Padua,—it was said by poison. So ended Ducal Mantua.

The Austrians held the city till 1797. The French Revolution took it and kept it till 1799, and then left it to the Austrians for two years. Then the Cisalpine Republic possessed it till 1802; and then it was made part of the Kingdom of Italy, and so continued twelve years; after which it fell again to Austria. In 1848, there was a revolution, and the Austrian soldiers stole the precious silver case that held the phial of the true blood. Now at last it belongs to the Kingdom of Italy, with the other forts of the Quadrilateral,—thanks to the Prussian needle-gun.

William Dean Howells was born in 1837 in an Ohio town where after hardly more than an introduction to formal studies he began, at the age of nine, to set type in his father's printing shop. When after a number of moves the family settled in Columbus Howells became a journalist. In 1860 he wrote a campaign biography of Lincoln, and Lincoln having won the election he was rewarded with the job of consul at Venice. This led to *Venetian Life* (1866), his second published book, the first having been one of verse done conjointly with another poet.

Italian Journeys appeared in 1867. In the final decades of his career — he was the editor of important reviews, he was interested in economic questions and had political involvements, he was the author of over twenty novels, six autobiographical volumes, eleven travel books, thirty-one plays for the stage — Howells came to be looked upon, in his own country and abroad, as America's foremost man of letters. He died in 1920.